GOING PUBLIC

The Entrepreneur's Guide

JOSEPH S. O'FLAHERTY

A Wiley-Interscience Publication
JOHN WILEY & SONS
New York   Chichester   Brisbane   Toronto   Singapore

Copyright © 1984 by John Wiley & Sons, Inc.

All rights reserved. Published simultaneously in Canada.

Reproduction or translation of any part of this work
beyond that permitted by Section 107 or 108 of the
1976 United States Copyright Act without the permission
of the copyright owner is unlawful. Requests for
permission or further information should be addressed to
the Permissions Department, John Wiley & Sons, Inc.

This publication is designed to provide accurate and
authoritative information in regard to the subject
matter covered. It is sold with the understanding that
the publisher is not engaged in rendering legal, accounting,
or other professional service. If legal advice or other
expert assistance is required, the services of a competent
professional person should be sought. *From a Declaration
of Principles jointly adopted by a Committee of the
American Bar Association and a Committee of Publishers.*

Library of Congress Cataloging in Publication Data

O'Flaherty, Joseph S., 1915-
   Going Public.

   "A Wiley-Interscience publication."
   Bibliography: p.
   Includes index.
   1. Going public (Securities)—Handbooks, manuals, etc.
2. Close corporations—Finance—Handbooks, manuals, etc.
I. Title.
HG4028.S7034   1984   658.1'145   83-23255
ISBN 0-471-86981-3

Printed in the United States of America

10 9 8 7 6 5 4 3 2 1

Preface

Going public is a sensible way of raising equity funds. Equally as important for many entrepreneurs, the stock market mechanism places a valuation on the shareholdings of senior management—usually enough to make those holding large blocks of stock paper-rich. Nevertheless, there is another side to the coin. The privately held business considering going public must recognize the accompanying pain and problems in such a decision.

The purpose of the book is to establish a framework of reference for entrepreneurs who head or expect to head businesses in the annual sales range of $5 million to $50 million and who will be considering going public. The primary emphasis throughout is directed toward realistic evaluations of the various financial and equity alternatives facing management, the stock market mechanism for initial public offerings, and the many aftermarket considerations.

This guide is written through the eyes of the proven entrepreneur/chief executive who is not blessed with second sight. Much has been published by securities lawyers, investment bankers, and public accountants on aspects of the privately held enterprise and the going-public process. However, the views of these staff authorities come from the expertise of their specialities, along with an inevitable amount of parochialism.

It is the entrepreneur who must sort through divergent and specialized views and make difficult financial and operating decisions on company affairs. The book offers guidance and insight in many of these decision areas. It is based on the writer's quarter century of experience as an entrepreneur/chief executive along with the lessons learned in taking public all three of his successful companies.

The guide is divided into three parts. After an opening chapter which illustrates the vagaries of the stock market and initial public offerings, Part One discusses several financial facets of typical privately held enterprises. Then, following a review of securities laws and regulations and the burgeoning roles of the public accountants and lawyers, Part One concludes with an examination of Regulation D, with its expanded exemptions from those securities laws.

Part Two is devoted to practitioners in the securities markets. The strengths and aberrations of these forces are discussed along with the evolving role of the investment banker and the so-called financial services industry.

Part Three describes in detail the going-public process. Then, various facets of the first eighteen months or so of the aftermarket are covered, including some of the unpleasant surprises encountered by the entrepreneur. The final chapter balances the ongoing costs and problems of being a public company against the undeniable benefits. In conclusion, a brief toast is offered to entrepreneurs, a hardy breed.

JOSEPH S. O'FLAHERTY

Rolling Hills, California
January 1984

*Over a long and fortunate entrepreneurial life,
I remember well —
Howard P. Hall and John L. Loeb,
Many Colleagues of Some Tumultuous Ventures,
and Louise O'Flaherty*

Acknowledgments

So long as it is understood that the text and associated conclusions and errors are the responsibility of the writer, acknowledgments are appropriate.

A number of people that the writer admires were kind enough to read substantial portions of the manuscript —

J. William Hawekotte
James P. Hynes
Thomas L. Kempner
J. Spencer Letts
Jonathan Meyers

My thanks to them, and to Sue Mullis for manuscript tabulation advice.

Contents

PART ONE THE ENVIRONMENT OF THE PRIVATELY
HELD COMPANY

1. **The Incredible Stock Market** 3

   Fickleness and Faddishness Personified 4
   The Collapse of a Game Plan 4
   A Wild Place 7
   The Deadly Market Sword 10
   "When the Cookies Are Passed . . ." 11

2. **Don't Give Up the Equity** 13

   Origin and Development of Growth Companies 13
   Financial Architecture 15
   Don't Give Up the Equity 17
   Employee Stock 19
   Summing Up 20

3. **Alternative Ways of Raising Money** 21

   The Pain Factor in Borrowed Money 21
   Unsecured and Asset-Based Loans 22

Subordinated Debt 23
Sale of Part or All of the Equity 25
A Conclusion 27

4. **A Best Foot Forward**   29

A Profit Plan for the Intermediate Term 29
Outside Presentation of Management 32
The Annual Brochure or Position Paper 35
An Aid in Any Season 39

5. **The Security Laws**   41

The Bats and Owls of the 1900s 41
America's Business Is Business—The 1920s 42
The Securities Act of 1933 43
The Securities Exchange Act of 1934 45
The Foreign Corrupt Practices Act of 1977 45
Whatever Will Be, Will Be 46

6. **The Harassed Profession**   49

Accounting Practices Through the 1920s 50
From the New Deal To Watergate 50
Current Regulatory Environment and Criticism 51
Last-Resort Litigation 52
A Need to Know the Client Company 53
Selection of a Public Accounting Firm 53
A Conclusion 54

7. **Selection of Company Counsel**   55

Importance of Company Counsel 55
Criteria for the Selection of Counsel 56
Payment of Counsel in Stock 58
The Securities Laws and the Company Counsel 60
A Full Legal Plate 61

Contents   xi

8. A New Regulation and Long Overdue   63

Offering Up to $500,000 (New Rule 504) 64
The Pros and Cons of Using Rule 504 65
Offerings from $500,000 to $5 million (New Rule 505) 67
Offerings of an Unlimited Amount (New Rule 506) 67
Accredited Investors 68
A Modest Step Away from Overregulation 69
Some Belated SEC Conclusions 69

PART TWO   PRACTITIONERS IN THE SECURITIES MARKETS

9. A Different Kind of a Game   73

Regulation of Wall Street 73
The Golden Years 74
The Blustery Winds of Change 77
A Different Kind of a Game 78
Going Public and Investment Bankers 80

10. Acceptance of Wall Street Criteria   81

Analysis of Initial Offering Patterns 81
Components of a Public Offering Package 84
Underwriting Costs 87
Price/Earnings Multiple or Ratio 87
The Over-the-Counter Market 89
The Fourth Market and the Exchanges 91
Acceptance of Wall Street Criteria 92

11. The Decision to Go   93

Institutional Investors 93
Individual Investors 95

Reserved Stock for Associates 96
The Managing Underwriter and the Selling Syndicate 97
Selling the New Issue 99
Supporting the Stock in the Aftermarket 101
The Decision to Go 104

12. Prospectus Analysis 105

Review of Other Prospectuses 105
Cover Format and Type of Paper 106
Comments on the Prospectus Text 107
Summing Up 113

PART THREE THE GOING PUBLIC PROCESS AND THE AFTERMARKET

13. Arrangements for the Offering—A Composite Example 117

Size of the Offering 118
Initial Due Diligence Request for Documents 118
Is It Material? 119
The Managing Underwriter and Its Principal 120
The Company and Its Specialists 121
Preparatory Work of the Task Force 123

14. The Registration and the Offering—A Composite Example 129

Company Attitude Toward Public Offering 130
Due Diligence Activities 131
First Sessions of Working Group 131
Intermediate Sessions and Decisions 133
The "Cold Comfort" Letter of the Auditors 134
Registration Windup 135

Contents   xiii

    Marketing the Proposed Issue 136
    SEC Review of the Registration Statement 138
    The Offering 139
    Windup of the Offering Project 140

15. Log of Official Offering Actions—A Composite Example   **143**

    Corporate Proceedings 144
    SEC Registration Proceedings 144
    Data for National Association of Securities Dealers (NASD) 146
    Documents of Selling Shareholders 147
    Underwriting Documents 147
    Blue Sky Documents 148
    Press Releases and "Tombstone" 148
    Closing Proceedings 149
    Not Mumbo Jumbo 150

16. The Board of Directors   **151**

    Corporate Accountability 151
    Notion of Board Control by Independent Directors 152
    The Entrepreneur and the Board 152
    Makeup and Role of the Board 153
    Board Oversight Committees 155
    The Audit Committee and the SEC 155
    Primary Function of the Audit Committee 156
    The Audit Committee of a Newly Public Company 157
    Legal Risks for Board Members 157
    Meetings and Compensation of Board Members 158

17. Restricted Stock Means Care and Discretion   **159**

    Definition of Rule 144 Securities 159
    Selling Rule 144 Securities 160

Section 16(b) of the 1934 Exchange Act 161
Rule 10b-5 of the SEC 162
Appropriate Timing of Stock Sale or Purchase 163
Summary Comment 164

18. "If You Can't Stand the Heat..." 167

The Privately Held Company 167
Quarterly Results and Reports 168
Form 10Q to the SEC 169
The Annual Report and the Audit 170
Form 10K 173
The 1934 Exchange Act 174
The Proxy Statement and Card 175
The First Annual Meeting 176
Shareholder Relations and the Transfer Agent 178
Master Schedule for the First Year 179
A Conclusion 181

19. The Honeymoon Is Over 183

Stock-Owning Associates 183
Safe Harbor and Inside Information 184
The Financial Community and the Company 185
The Honeymoon Is Over 187
Unwanted Attention 189
A Mushy Period 190

20. Was It All Worthwhile? 191

The Important Fixed Factor 191
A Seasoned Company 192
Continued Irritations and Costs 193
Going Private 194
A Small Toast to the Entrepreneurial Breed 195

Appendices	**197**
Bibliography	**291**
Index	**295**
Credits	**303**

Part One

The Environment of the Privately Held Company

1

The Incredible Stock Market

The entrepreneurs are back in fashion. With domestic business battered by effective foreign competition and burdened with declining productivity, the economic contributions of risk-taking chief executives of smaller companies are being recognized. The reasons usually given can be summarized by statements such as: Entrepreneurs are more bold and daring; they are the ones who make things happen; these executives run tight and lean organizations.

The cachet of success for entrepreneurs of privately held companies has been in the taking of their businesses public and, because of the going market value of their stock, becoming paper-wealthy—for a while at least. Equally important, going public represents a feasible way for raising company capital while providing a broader equity base to support future corporate borrowings.

Wall Street will take a lucky entrepreneur over one who is a good manager any day of the week, and so should anybody else for that matter. There is not a successful chief executive who will not admit the luck factor—albeit a good many only in whispers to themselves as they fall asleep at night. The best any entrepreneur can do is to reduce the inevitable mistakes to a minimum, try not to have too many of them back to back, and hope collectively that they are not too painful. If all of these things are done and there is a reasonable interleaving of luck, going public is a sensible consideration.

However, sometimes events do not move in an orderly manner, as witness some of this writer's experiences, not the least of which was gaining some appreciation of the stock market.

Fickleness and Faddishness Personified

The stock market can behave in an incredible manner. As a business, its fickleness and faddishness is comparable to that of high-style women's wear. Attracted to the stock market are bevies of alert, hyperactive people who thrive on the frenetic wheel-spinning, gossip, and rumor of their environment. Baseless, heat-lightning opinions of questionable prophets may start a sellers' or buyers' stampede.

What is prime merchandise on the market this month can be found in the bargain basement a few weeks or months later. And worse than an overbred thoroughbred, the stock market can throw itself into an overheated hysteria which feeds on rumor as the salt sweat runs into its eyes, obscuring what little vision remains. The author lived through one of those episodes.

Nobody should consider an expensive adventure into this kind of wonderland without balancing the presumed pleasures against the pain and the hazards of the unknown. Those entrepreneurs who base their financial plans on going public at some fixed point in time are very foolish, as the initial public offerings may well be delayed or not done at all. The writer made that mistake. For many months the results hurt both his company and his digestive system while he put at risk part or all of his company's equity. Some of the facts are worth emphasizing, even though they are all too familiar to an experienced entrepreneur.

The Collapse of a Game Plan

The first high-technology boom for initial public offerings after World War II had been making the entrepreneurs and their senior associates paper-rich in the late 1950s and early 1960s. With major Wall Street support, the writer's first grass-roots business was under way by late 1958. During the next several years product development, manufacture, and sales went about as planned while the enterprise became solidly profitable.

But the cash demands were becoming voracious, much beyond those projected. The business direction had shifted considerably from the original plan because a market had opened up with excellent growth possibilities. As a result, requirements for quantities of special technical equipment and facilities were going to be substantially higher than originally envisaged. Worse yet, much of the equipment required design and debugging in-house. Nevertheless, the writer was convinced that the cash requirements could be managed.

All chief executives have their financial game plans, even if they consist of scribblings on backs of used envelopes. This writer's was straightforward—simplistically so. The concern was going to live off bank money for working capital. Then the entrepreneur would slide the enterprise smoothly into an initial public offering to raise capital. Surely the same commercial bank would be understanding about the pyramiding cash requirements as time went by. So some of the key ratios of balance-sheet numbers showed deterioration quarter by quarter. The profit and loss statement was good; his kind of company was the darling of the stock market; and at the appropriate time a public issue would pay off the bank.

Then a funny thing happened in the spring of 1962. The investment community suddenly lost interest in high-technology stocks. Shortly thereafter, prices for these stocks literally collapsed. So did the writer's game plan. Going public was out of question.

Meanwhile the company continued to spend capital monies. Payoff for these expenditures was hopefully in the future, but tangible customer commitments were about as valid as a gleam in a program manager's eye. This would scarcely excite the bank's loan committee who was already licking sour loan wounds made by some other formerly glamorous high-technology concerns.

While temporizing over a decision to change the company's course in midpassage, the entrepreneur and the senior finance officer determined to stretch payables, knowing full well the problems. Since the stretch-out was only a one-shot respite, timing was all-important, as bills had to be paid regularly from then on in. They knew routine CODs were intolerable over any period of time. And old payables meant repeated vendor calls and personal follow-ups, an additional load on the finance people. On top of that, the bank holding the unsecured loans was most interested in having trade debtors paid.

All of these were praiseworthy guidelines but collecting money does not necessarily follow cash-flow plans or surveillance. It was possible to be in the position of depending upon a Saturday check in the mail to meet a Friday payroll. Any chief executive knows that this was a kind of Russian roulette and not recommended for survival.

The company was fortunate. The track record of the enterprise was good, and the financial vice president and the entrepreneur had established financial credibility with both the investment and commercial bankers. While each of these groups had a real concern that the writer and his associates might be chasing a will-o'-the-wisp into a dangerous financial swamp, both quieted their doubts. The investment bankers (who had provided the initial venture capital) gave the commercial bank a strong best-efforts letter concerning a public issue. With this, the bank loan committee agreed to an increased borrowing based on asset-pledged financing at a reasonable interest rate. The total loan was to be for a maximum of a year with the commercial bank taken out or paid down by a public offering or private placement of stock.

The writer received a telephone call in early January 1963 from the investment bankers. He was told that the senior partner sensed a coming change in market attitude toward quality initial issues. If the entrepreneur had no objections, work should be started on a Form S-1 registration statement for filing with the Securities and Exchange Commission (SEC) for a probable offering in early spring. Most assuredly, the chief executive had no objection.

Good fortune does seem to protect fools, drunks, and many entrepreneurs. Shortly before the S-1 was filed with the SEC, the "Heard on the Street" column of the *Wall Street Journal* noted that two large public companies and the writer's privately held concern had been designated as high-reliability component suppliers for the new Minuteman Missile guidance system. This program was where much of the company's capital monies had been going. For an appeal to Wall Street, which always lives on anticipation anyway, nothing could be better than the *Journal's* comment for awakening interest in a prospective public offering of the day.

The investment bankers' timing was immaculate. The new issue market was reviving, and the writer's company was "interesting." The offering went off well in early April of 1963, and it was the first national issue of a high-technology enterprise in about a year. Without doubt, several loan officers had a small "let's be thankful" celebration.

The entrepreneur did.

A Wild Place

Even the inmates of the securities community were embarrassed about the Joseph Granville episode of January 1981. So was the writer, and the short-lived Granville aberration only reinforced his conviction that the stock market was a wild place.

Again the writer-entrepreneur was in the process of preparing an initial public offering in late 1980. This company, in contrast to the one discussed in the previous section, had a plenitude of cash. A remarkable change. Further, the chief executive considered himself rather an expert on Wall Street. After all, he was now the entrepreneurial veteran of two initial public offerings, both of which were successful. And this third concern's cash position was so favorable that the bulk of the stock to be offered was from selling shareholders.

The SEC registration work and filing proceeded smoothly, and the new issue market was strong. The entrepreneur, acting for the selling shareholders and the company, was scheduled to meet with the managing underwriter in its New York offices on January 6, 1981, to agree on initial offering price the following morning and settle on the underwritng discounts or fees.

The afternoon's negotiations with the managing underwriter were settled sensibly and amiably. The executive responsible for the underwriting suggested the writer arrive at 9:30 A.M. the next morning (the effective date and time of the registration statement) to go through the formality of signing the underwriting agreement and watch the first few trades of the newly public stock. The underwriters' order book was overflowing, and the over-allotment (green shoe) of 10% of the shares being offered had been allocated among the underwriting group. An idyllic situation for the selling syndicate.

As much as it could be, all was peace and quiet in the general market. A pleasantly tired chief executive was looking forward to an early evening and a noon flight back to the Coast after the Wall Street ceremony.

That ceremony turned into a ragged affair. As an usher escorted the writer to the 9:30 A.M. conference, the underwriting manager responsible for the issue strode past with a grim look on his face. Spinning around and obviously upset, he told the entrepreneur that somebody had issued a "sell everything" advisory during the night. The result was a market stampede which had first shown up in the Paris and London exchanges because of the time differential. The pyramiding sales orders an hour before the major U.S. exchanges opened were more than worrisome. The underwriting plans were in disorder; the initial public offering was being delayed temporarily.

The group which was assembling in the conference room was quick to brief the chief executive. It seemed that telephones had begun ringing in New York around 4:00 A.M. as large quantities of sell orders piled up in the European exchanges. A man by the name of Joseph Granville who operated a special advisory service had sent a midnight message to his subscribers to sell out their shareholdings. It was already evident that a remarkable tidal bore of selling was going to occur in the national markets with no other proximate explanation than the Granville advisory. While the Granville discussion went on, the conference room telephone rang repeatedly and worried individuals excused themselves to return calls.

These Wall Street people had a range of off-the-cuff views as to how a Granville could possibly trigger an automatic knee jerk in the world stock markets. Opinions varied from "this is the way the stock market is" all the way to a technical explanation of an underlying buildup of selling sentiment. That is, like a heavy accumulation of snow on a mountainside, only a minor triggering action was needed to set off a major avalanche of selling. But whatever the reason, it was evident that sell orders from presumably sophisticated institutional investors were increasing by the minute.

After the Granville comments, the lawyers briskly laid out the underwriting agreement and associated documents. After signature by the principals, the underwriters had just acquired company stock with a value of $16 million. Payment had to be made one week later to the writer as agent for the selling shareholders and the enterprise. With the disorder and turbulence in the marketplace, an unknown number of these shares would have to be resold at unknown prices.

The meeting broke up shortly after execution of the underwriting agreement; the underwriting people had work to do. The entrepreneur, now a subdued pseudo expert on initial public offerings, left Wall Street at 10:00 A.M. for Kennedy Airport and the Coast. While sipping a Bloody Mary aloft, he kept thinking of the selling syndicate's requirement to hand him $16 million less underwriting discounts a week hence. He was glad he was not in the arena attempting to patch together a revised order book for the underwriting. Further, the writer suspected he would have a difficult time answering sensible questions about Wall Street after arriving back home at company headquarters.

The managing underwriter called the chief executive in the early evening (New York time) of the same day. The Dow Jones Industrials Index had gone down nearly 30 points, but institutional dumping was tapering off late in the session. All indexes had tumbled. The underwriting manager had let the offering go at 3:58 P.M.—two minutes before the end of the over-the-counter trading. The offering price was the agreed-upon $16 per share. This offering strategy seemed to be the best way of holding the selling syndicate together while protecting the new issue from the price battering it would have taken if released earlier in the day. The underwriting executive went on to say that he had a full evening and early next morning of continuing work in reselling a large number of shares.

The same tired underwriter called at 12:45 P.M. (New York time) the next day, January 8. His spirits had improved tremendously. Of the 1 million shares offered, 335,000 had been resold into "good hands." This could only have been done because the offering had been a reasonably hot issue. The selling syndicate had been disbanded in less than an hour into the trading session when the stock was selling at 15½. The bid price range during the morning had been in the narrow 15¼–15½ range. With the disbanding of the syndicate, the over-allotment option of 100,000 shares had died.

On January 9 at 4:45 P.M. (New York time) the underwriting executive was able to report a successful issue. The company's stock was now selling above the initial offering price of $16 at 16½ bid, 16¾ ask. The managing underwriter had been so successful in buttressing the new issue that the firm was 55,000 shares short. It could well have used the firm's portion of the over-allotment green shoe. The Granville selling spree was on its way to being forgotten except as a minor event in Wall Street history. Incidentally, by this freak occurrence, the company was not required to dilute existing shareholder equity by the 100,000-share green shoe.

The professionalism and plain hard work of the managing underwriter during a period of several trying days were impressive.

The Deadly Market Sword

Most initial public offerings do not include selling shareholders. Without acceptable reasons to the contrary, the securities community looks upon shareholder sale in such an offering as a bailout. The best justification for such sale is an outstanding performance record of a company. When this is so, the fortunate entrepreneur and senior associates can sell as much as 25% to 35% of their holdings in a warm to hot issue without dampening the initial offspring price. These people can have a large amount of cash in their hands a week later.

But for most entrepreneurs and their senior managements, going public with successful issues means that they are rich people based on the going market value of their stock. Any sensible person would say that worrying about this kind of wealth was a deliciously pleasant problem. Particularly when the stock moves ahead a point, and one's shareholdings increase as much as a hundred thousand dollars. However, that fickle and deadly market sword cuts both ways. Stock values of seasoned enterprises can and do drop dramatically over both short and long periods. Many paper millionaires find their stocks several years after initial offering selling for a fifth or less of the initial offering value.

If the vagaries and dangers of the stock market are recognized, there are SEC provisions and procedures for selling the restricted shares of the senior management, as discussed in another chapter. Too often these senior people pay no attention. They refuse to sell any of their shares.

"When the Cookies Are Passed..."

The presumption that reason and logic guide the stock market over the short-term period can be a dangerous fallacy. The essence of playing in the game of initial public offerings is timing plus always having a reasonable alternative choice for raising money. And a good investment banker can be of real assistance.

Be guided by the Wall Street aphorism: "When the cookies are passed, take one, as they may not be passed again." Paper millionaires should also mind this maxim.

2
Don't Give Up the Equity

The hope of stock appreciation is the name of the game for entrepreneurs and their immediate associates. But to participate in that game, one must first acquire the equity and then worry about keeping it.

Management equity, or at least a hunting license to acquire it, evolves from the creation or growth of privately held enterprises. The financial architecture of each company determines the equity's size and form. From then on, entrepreneurs have a running fight (oftentimes with their own immediate drives) to reduce the size or even eliminate entirely some of the recurring equity bites.

Origin and Development of Growth Companies

Privately held companies interesting to Wall Street in the $5 million to $50 million annual sales grouping attained this position in many different ways. While evolving from a number of backgrounds and combinations, most of their origins can be categorized as grass-roots/venture capital enterprises, former divisions of large corporations, and above all, Mom-and-Pop businesses.

Along with providing the excellent probability of failure, the American tradition has emphasized the growth opportunities for the small retailer, the pigeonholder and wildcatter, the manufacturer or inventor in the one-car garage, and the tiny bank and insurance operator. The smaller Mom-and-Pop concerns do have one thing in common—the intertwining of the business expenses and personal expenses of the owners as a method of tax avoidance. This comfortable expense-habit pattern is difficult to break as a business moves out of the typical Mom-and-Pop size of operation. Yet it has to be broken if a concern expects to raise capital in any quantity for the company as an independent entity or if it has any intentions of going public.

Another common characteristic of the Mom-and-Pop enterprises is the failure to provide adequate incentive to the key people of the business other than the owners and their relatives. Typically, the operation remains either a one-man show or an inside/outside partner arrangement.

Still, on occasion, new entrepreneurs appear in Mom-and-Pop businesses. They are able to demand and receive the chief executive positions and significant equity percentages of the enterprises. They insist on the separation of the business affairs from the personal affairs of the owners, and recognized regional or national auditing firms are employed. Effective management is recruited on the basis of adequate compensation packages supported by some equity ownership. These companies are now on a different growth track while already forgetting their Mom-and-Pop antecedents.

The grass-roots/venture capital category is born with a different basic philosophy than Mom-and-Pop. From the beginning the grass-roots people are thinking beyond survival and the narrow good life to major business growth, including the possibility of going public. At the start, or not long thereafter, they are seeking venture capital and are oriented toward the building of a management group in depth, as opposed to the inbred qualities of the Mom-and-Pop operators. In raising venture capital, the grass-roots entrepreneurs are fighting for a substantial block of equity which hopefully will make them and their immediate associates rich. If the grass-roots ventures do not stumble and fall (the fate of most of them), and above all else are lucky, these enterprises will emerge as public company candidates.

For any number of reasons, divisions or integrated operations of large companies are routinely being offered for sale. In many instances, these entities are bought directly by employees who are intimately familiar with the affairs of the entity being offered for sale. In the other situations the units are bought by venture capital groups who have experienced entrepreneurs available to run the enterprise. Either way, the purchases can be highly leveraged with as much as 90% term debt. In the case of the venture capital groups, they can offer veteran managements up to perhaps 50% of the purchased entities for as little as 5% of the purchase prices negotiated with the selling corporations.

The management of the purchased entities can be expected to be effective operators. Even so, the list of casualties of the highly leveraged concerns can be depressing. Illustrative of the unpleasant vagaries of circumstances, the 15% to 20% prime rates of the early 1980s made some highly leveraged enterprises almost impossible to manage.

Financial Architecture

The financial architecture of many grass-roots ventures and early-growth companies can be tilted toward the money side, tilted enough that the welfare of the enterprise can be impacted. This means that some of the structuring of the financial deal for putting the seed money in the business can turn out to be a hindrance at the very time that the success of the business may be in precarious balance. While an involved subject and beyond the scope of this chapter, several comments relating to the preservation of the equity position of management are appropriate here.

Allocation of equity increments to management based on performance over a fixed period of time may be called out in a subscription agreement at the insistence of the money side. If performance goals (to which both the entrepreneur and money sides have agreed) are not met, nothing could be more logical than penalizing management by withholding the unearned equity increment. However, logic at times does not make the best of business sense.

To begin with, writing up a performance stock section in a subscription or a similar agreement is considerably more difficult than it first appears. Technically, the stock is generally escrowed for management until pre-established formula goals are achieved. Banks are chary about accepting performance stock for escrow, as the stock certificates can breed lawsuits because of performance interpretations well after the bank has distributed the certificates in good faith. Law firms are pleased to perform the escrow task with an adequate retainer. They will also handle any litigation resulting from the escrow work, also at an adequate fee. However, it should be remembered that most law firms are partnerships which may dissolve or be subject to more business pressure than bank escrow departments.

Assuming the performance stock finds a good escrow home, the major problem still is the entrepreneur's gut reaction to the whole performance concept. Admittedly, the chief executive made the performance estimates on which the formula for escrowed stock distribution was based. Who else could do a better job of setting the goals? Nobody of course. But one thing should not be forgotten.

Above all else, the entrepreneur and the senior associates should be worrying about the business and its survival—not whether they are losing equity. And if the company survives and grows, the lost equity can be an unnecessary contaminant in the management/money relationship.

Sometimes a venture-funding package will provide for long-term debt in the form of subordinated debentures as part of the financial architecture. This means there are debentures that are subordinated to a maximum amount of superior indebtedness to lending agencies such as commercial banks. On occasion, the terms of the subordinated debentures provide for company prepayment of the notes prior to maturity. For example, seven-year debentures may require the first partial payment to be made in the fourth year. Because of the impact on operating affairs, scheduling payback of seed money before debenture maturity appears to be debatable at the best and dangerous at the worst.

Take the seven-year debenture example. If the company has established itself to the point that a partial principal payment can even be considered, management most assuredly has other driving demands for the available cash. These demands may revolve around the equity protection of what has already been accomplished or the bank borrowings for additional growth. In considering the facts in an additional loan application, a bank's enthusiasm for seed money moving out of the business and back to the investors is sure to be minimal.

Admittedly, the money side can waive prepayment of the notes, just as the debentures can be rolled over at maturity date. But the initiative on waivers and the control position rests entirely with the money side. So at the best, payback worries can be a management distraction, and at the worst can force financial decisions by management that may hurt the equity position for all concerned.

An experienced money side knows very well that it has placed a point-of-no-return bet on the entrepreneur the moment the investors make the deal. The fail-safe rationale of replacing an unsatisfactory entrepreneur downstream usually means new capital input and certainly major expense and extensive wet-nursing. Attempting to paper over these bald facts of life with a complex financial architecture at go-off may be a serious hindrance to the success of venture.

Don't Give Up the Equity

How do entrepreneurs play those key game cards of equity ownership that could make them millionaires? Oftentimes not very well in their privately held businesses. Almost always they have fought the bloody battles to gain equity positions for themselves and their key people. The sad thing for an entrepreneur in retrospect is to recall how these hard-won rights were almost casually frittered away while satisfying the expediency of a particular moment.

Always there were many more of these particular moments than any entrepreneur would have cared to visualize at go-off. Enough of them carried the sweaty fear of clear and present financial danger for the company. Those were the times that future equity value became a blurry mirage for the entrepreneur and senior associates.

Equity erosion often begins early in the venture before the real problems develop. During the euphoric period immediately after the completion of financing arrangements, the entrepreneur's lawyer and agent may both indicate that they now feel like members of the management team and would be happy to take a portion of management stock at the low buy-in cost, in lieu of a part of their fees. At about the same time an experienced executive team is being recruited, and they also are participating in the block of management stock at nominal cost. Of course, one or more of them will leave the enterprise during the next few years and will take their original stockholdings with them.

As time goes by and unpleasant surprises occur, heavy bank loans are required and then some more capital from the money side for additional equity. The business prospers and more people and money are needed. A stock option plan representing as much as 10% of the outstanding shares is approved by the stockholders, and a debenture issue with substantial conversion rights to common stock is privately placed through the company's investment banking firm. The business continues to grow; the debentures are converted; and the company has a public offering representing 25% of the outstanding stock. An evident result of the foregoing scenario is a sharply reduced percentage of valuable entrepreneurial equity; in retrospect probably a good deal more than was required.

Take for example the all-important allocation of the block of original management stock at go-off of the venture. Why turn over shares to the lawyer or agent who admittedly did yeomen work in the venture formation? Management stock should be for the people who will build the enterprise, and there never seems to be enough of this equity for them.

A principal thing to avoid in original equity allocation by the entrepreneur is the bitter remembrance of management associates who depart the company in the formative years with their stock. The resultant wasted equity can roil the bowels of an entrepreneur whose present associates are building the business but have no original shares.

In the early years a company buy-back agreement for original stock of senior associates can go a long ways in solving the departed-associate problem. The purchased stock would be reallocated to other employees by the entrepreneur. An argument can be made that a hostile board of directors could oust one group of associates under the plan and put in another. In the writer's opinion, if relations between the entrepreneur and the board of directors have deteriorated to this extent, the likelihood of the enterprise's eventual success is tenuous.

Convertible debentures can be expensive from every viewpoint for a privately held company. Even if the concern is doing reasonably well,

Summing Up

the debenture holders expect a significant return to compensate for risk—not least of which is a large equity bite if the debentures are converted into common stock. Too often the entrepreneur's decision as to the total amount of the convertible debentures to be taken down by the business is made without considering equity cost. One can be sure that conversion into common stock will not occur until the company's future looks reasonably promising—the very time the entrepreneur does not want conversion to take place.

Employee Stock

A liberal stock-option plan in a closely held enterprise should be a valuable motivator for the key employees. Other than a few of the senior associates, usually it is not. The option awards tend to be viewed as simply pieces of paper which the entrepreneur gives the recipient along with a rather boring congratulatory talk. That these scraps of paper could be worth literally hundreds of thousands of dollars is inconceivable to people. However, whether the potential values of stock options are appreciated or not, entrepreneurs rest easier if their companies have such plans.

It is a fair assumption that most employees have no concept of the potential value of their original or option stock. Thus they may sell that stock for what may turn out to be a pittance. The writer had one former employee who sold off his shareholdings to a friend for less than one-fifth of the initial public offering price two months later. The buyer simply paid the seller's asking price.

Subject only to the investment-letter kind of restrictions on a privately held concern, there are no legal prohibitions against employees selling stock. Nor should there be. Suasion and example are all that can and should be done to convince these persons that their nominal stock dollar investments can be the makings of their life estate.

Being a brother's keeper on employees' stock affairs or anything else for that matter is just another responsibility of the chief executive officer. This writer on many occasions and situations has never found the task particularly rewarding, except for the salving of his own conscience.

Summing Up

The money side can make serious mistakes in believing that venture risks can be fenced in with paper formulas or numbers. A complex financial structure can actually be a hindrance to success of the venture. Performance stock is a case in point. While accomplishing little for the investors, it is a source of distraction and irritation to the management.

The management percentage of equity in a privately held company tends to be eaten up as time passes. Yet the proximate reason for each equity bite always appears to be valid, although hindsight might show otherwise. And, finally, handling employee stock problems is simply another responsibility of the entrepreneur.

3

Alternative Ways of Raising Money

Raising money to support a growing enterprise has much in common with the frantic efforts of two adult birds attempting to feed a nest full of their hungry, squawking young. With all of the other business pressures, any entrepreneur has difficulty in retaining the visibility and judgment balance to select the appropriate method of acquiring cash at a particular time with a minimum of risk. Some of the points covered in this chapter may help to sustain this visibility.

The principal consideration and methods of raising money are touched on in the following sections, beginning with the pain factor in borrowing funds. Then there is a review of unsecured loans from commercial banks and asset-based borrowings from finance companies. Subordinated debt is next, with some emphasis on conversion rights and warrants. Finally, the sale of part or all of the equity is examined.

The Pain Factor in Borrowed Money

It is a grand idea to have your bankers loan you so much money that they become partners (albeit reluctantly) rather than lenders. Then like a defaulting nation, you can reschedule both principal and interest payments more or less at your pleasure. Unfortunately, practically all entrepreneurs must presume that they are not that skillful. Instead they must make interest and principal payments on schedule. Otherwise the loans are called; then other creditors panic; and the companies end up in bankruptcy.

Borrowed money is a fact of life for an entrepreneur, along with the hair shirt of worry that goes with it. Yet so often it seems that the chief executive stumbles into a borrowed money trap as a result of careless or optimistic assumptions that have gone awry. Working out of one of these situations takes both time and luck. Doing a better cash-planning job in the first place is much easier.

One device the writer has found helpful in his cash and borrowed-money planning is what he has come to call a Pain Table. This consists of a basic probability scale running from 1 to 10, with 10 being the certainty that borrowed money could not be paid back even with a modest time extension. At the opposite end of the spectrum is 1, which is an equal certainty that the debts would be repaid on or before the due date.

It is surprising, given a set of assumptions, how easily a probability scale number can be assigned from the Pain Table. On more than one occasion, the exercise has chilled the writer's enthusiasm for a program. He realized that the pain factor was much higher on the probability scale than he was willing to accept.

Unsecured and Asset-Based Loans

The cost of borrowed money has been a roller-coaster affair since the late 1970s. The interest on the face of an unsecured loan note could be impossibly expensive, with the real interest cost even higher because of compensating balance charges and the like. Longer-term loans during those inflationary years usually require equity sweeteners in the form of stock warrants or rights.

The bench mark in current borrowing practice is the prime rate—the fees charged by commercial banks to their most credit-worthy borrowers. The prime rate presumes a short-term loan, unsecured with a zero or token compensating balance in the company bank account. From this simplified reference point a number of money-lending decisions are made—all dependent on the size of the loan and the credit-worthiness of the borrower. Even the smaller business which has a fine record of performance and loan repayment may qualify for the prime rate.

Loans guaranteed by the Small Business Administration (SBA) can be particularly desirable because the borrowing period may be seven years or even more. If the prime rate is in the 15% area, the SBA interest rate for the long-term loan would be about two to three percentage points above the prime. The SBA charge is 1% of the government-guaranteed portion of the loan, and a fee is charged by the lender for loan preparation.

Again with the 15% prime-rate example, loans to smaller companies by commercial banks range from prime to perhaps three percentage points above the prime. The borrowings could be 90-day notes up to term loans of three to five years. While generally based on the credit of the enterprise, the commercial bank loan can carry a number of important and negotiated provisions which add to cost of the loan. These provisions include payback schedules, size of compensating balance, and maintenance of certain financial ratios or operating performance requirements. Penalty fees in the form of additional interest charges may be made if ratio or performance requirements are not met.

Still assuming a 15% prime rate, finance company borrowings are five or more percentage points above prime and almost always are asset-based. In essence it means that specific groups of assets are pledged to the lender in return for the loan. Such a loan is in the three- to six-year range and may involve substantial loan fees. It requires most careful consideration prior to borrowing negotiations as this type of debt weakens the enterprise's balance sheet. The result may make additional credit-based borrowing difficult or even impossible, and vendors can be more inflexible in their credit terms because of their unsecured position. These considerations often make long-term debt, which is junior to outstanding bank loans, a more attractive possibility than a finance company borrowing.

Subordinated Debt

Another debt alternative, particularly if maximum bank borrowing limits have been reached, is the placement of subordinated convertible debentures with private lenders, venture capital houses, or small-business investment companies. Investment banking firms are often the intermediaries with these investor groups.

Subordinated debt of smaller companies almost always carries either a conversion-into-common-stock alternative or an outright option (warrant) to purchase stock on some formula basis. The result is the same—a likely dilution of equity in the enterprise if it continues to show promise. Potential equity dilution can be substantial, and the interest rate on the borrowed funds may be one-fifth more than the prime rate at the time of borrowing. The debentures are typically for five to seven years and are not asset-based. Sinking funds may not be required, but this can be a vital trading point.

The advantage of subordinated debt which is unsecured is that it is junior to bank loans and other lendings. As a result, the senior debt holders look upon the junior borrowings as additional equity put into the business. Thus the company can work with its commercial banker in cleaning up the balance sheet while arranging for a bank term loan and still improving its working capital position.

Undertaking a subordinated company debt requires experienced advice and legal counsel. The importance of careful negotiation of conversion and option rights is evident. Not so obvious is the requirement that the enterprise have careful coordination with the senior and junior lenders prior to making the subordinated placement. This requires agreement from the lenders on a number of detailed policy points to be included in the subordinated debt agreement. An experienced company counsel can indicate specific pitfalls which the company must avoid. One example of such a pitfall is having the wording in a subordinated placement contract unsatisfactory to any one of the senior lenders. Another is allowing subordination to all creditors rather than to specific junior lenders.

Because the potential event is years away, the entrepreneur may tend to underplay or almost forget about the conversion or warrant privileges of subordinated debt. But like a ticking time device the privileges are there and will be utilized at the lender's pleasure.

Standing by themselves without allies, shareholders owning a large block of minority stock are in a lonely position in a closely held enterprise where the legal remedies are not comparable to a publicly held corporation. It is no wonder that these shareholders feel they are a creature of the majority position who control the enterprise and its purse. Understanding all of this, the subordinated debt holders exercise their conversion and warrant privileges only if such exercise is to their advantage. Some chief executives have had the painful experience of watching the exercise privilege take place, and then the new block of shareholders consumate an alliance with enough other minority stock to give the new block effective control of the business.

Sale of Part or All of the Equity

The disadvantages and problems connected with becoming a public company receive ample attention in later chapters. Of course, over and above the new money put into the business, there are many real advantages in going public. Not the least of which is that none of the other fund-raising routes is closed off.

An improved equity base as a result of the cash input of a public stock offering is a major assist in expanded borrowing capacity. As with subordinated debentures and a Regulation D offering, the company can now work with its commercial banker in arranging short-term credit or a bank term loan if required.

As for selling part or all of the business, many concerns looking for investment positions or acquisitions prefer an enterprise that is in the fishbowl world of public companies. Failure to meet the public disclosure requirements of the Securities and Exchange Commission (SEC) carries heavy penalties. Concurrently, the securities community through its analysts have usually established a network of information about the company and its competitive standing.

Sale of Regulation D securities is a viable alternative for a small business that does not want or cannot afford to have a full-fledged public offering. Discussed at length in Chapter 8, this Commission regulation expanded SEC exemptions for stock issues up to $5 million while easing certain SEC rules. Regulation D has significant drawbacks, but the importance of each of them varies with the particular company.

Taking a minority position in a privately held company, as indicated previously, is a lonely position unless other shareholder allies are available. However, in recent years there have been a fair number of instances where an outside enterprise needs to have a window into an industry or geographical area. A minority position then has a definite appeal. In some instances the purchase of a minority position is contingent on an option to acquire eventually the entire business. A number of foreign concerns during the past decade have taken minority positions as a method of phasing into U.S. markets.

Probably the most talked-about equity alternative to going public is the sale of the business to a considerably larger corporation. If the business has the performance record to make a successful equity offering, it has a definite attraction to a responsible buyer. Sophisticated purchasers do not want to be involved in business rescue operations; they want good, well-managed companies. And they will pay for them. But not as much, in most instances, as the other side believes the company is worth.

Several side comments on the business acquisition subject, while well-recognized, are worth emphasizing. The larger corporations who are acquisition-oriented have their criteria of value. These standards are based generally on some kind of an estimated pattern of earnings of the acquisition candidate during the next several years. Return on investment was a popular criterion in the early 1980s. How long the emphasis on the balance sheet standards will continue is unknown. Certainly, the price/earnings multiples are lower than what they were two decades earlier.

It is easy to forget that stock received in an acquisition is simply engraved paper. The value depends upon the performance of the surviving corporate entity. And as a rule, the financial results of the acquired business have limited impact on the future financial performance of the surviving corporation. Yet this is the performance that will determine the value of the engraved stock certificates.

So many principals of enterprises being acquired will opt for stock because capital gains taxes can be avoided with a tax-free reorganization plan. Nobody wants to pay a huge amount of federal and very often state taxes. But the stock of the acquiring company for a dozen reasons can go down as well as up. A cash sale sometimes may look very well indeed with the benefit of hindsight. Witness the decline and fall of some shaky conglomerate stocks in the 1970s. Holding or selling stock is a risk decision in which the tax consequences, at least in this writer's opinion, should play little or no part.

Selling a business for the best available terms is a difficult task and very likely one that the entrepreneur has had only limited experience. Too often an acquisition candidate needlessly becomes shopworn. Meanwhile, confidential information and proprietary know-how are given away and nothing is received in return. As a company buffer, an intermediary or an interface is highly desirable in the screening of acquisition inquiries and in the critical financial and negotiation areas.

No matter how competent the counsel and advice, the bitter-end decisions to sell the business rests with the entrepreneur. Even though an unpleasant alternative choice in many instances, the possibility of sale should be considered periodically.

A Conclusion

Proper selection of the method and timing for bringing funds into a growing business while meeting debt obligations is one of the major responsibilities of an entrepreneur. Extending as it must over a period of years, a satisfactory performance in corporate finance requires self-discipline and the maintenance of an objective visibility of the alternative choices available to the company matched against the associated risks and rewards.

4

A Best Foot Forward

In their everlasting search for money, privately held companies often make incredibly bad presentations to investment and commercial bankers as well as to venture capital houses. That is the conclusion of this writer, who served as a consultant to a large Wall Street firm for a number of years and reviewed many venture capital proposals.

A much better money proposal for most companies is not that difficult to produce. The first element is a summary planning document reflecting a forecast for the intermediate terms. This provides the foundation for a systematic presentation to an outside source for funds and reflects the management philosophy and operating controls of the enterprise.

A Profit Plan for the Intermediate Term

The basis for any financial and lending community presentation for money (or to the board of directors for that matter) is a two-year financial/operating program for the business. A product profit breakdown and quarterly financial analysis is given only for Year 1. The Year 2 summary is used to indicate the intermediate trend and overall effect of product programs launched or expanded in Year 1.

Some entrepreneurs believe that a two-year forecast is unrealistic for their type of business. They argue that nobody, including the chief executive, can be sure of what is going to happen in the forthcoming six months, let alone the next twenty-four months. Granted the unknowns. But who in the world can better assess the probabilities for the particular concern than the chief executive officer and the senior people who have demonstrated they know company affairs. Assuredly, not the security analyst or the bank loan officer. A best effort and reasonably affirmative forecast is what sophisticated outsiders should expect to receive. Other than that, all management should have (and not talk about outside) is a hip-pocket, fail-safe plan in the event of a series of unpleasant surprises.

In one form or another, most chief executives have a two-year plan, written down or not. But so often the elements of the plan are scattered in a number of analyses prepared for different purposes and at different times. As a result, there can be obvious data discrepancies apparent to an outside party reviewing the material. A typical example is the forecast for the total number of employees. Annualized sales per employee is a relevant sensor for comparison between concerns in the same industry. On the other hand, for one reason or another, the entrepreneur may have felt it necessary to emphasize how many or how few employees the business plans to have, while not giving a thought to the question of annualized sales per employee as a comparative analytical item.

The outside analyst pays little attention to a number of individual discrepancies or non sequiturs, other than developing an underlying feeling of looseness in the presentation. But beyond a certain watershed point, a sense of confusion and then lack of confidence in the company may result. This kind of a reaction can lead to an unfavorable loan decision or a back-off of the venture capital firm.

All of the key information for a two-year financial plan can be put on one page for easy comparison. The plan goes a long ways toward eliminating those contradictions and omissions in the financial and operating planning. Correlations, percentages, and ratios between numbers may readily be calculated on the face of the page. Figure 4.1 is a representative form that contains the writer's preferences. As an addi-

PRODUCT LINE ANALYSIS

OPERATING DATA		Fiscal Years 1982	Fiscal Years 1983	1st Qtr	2nd Qtr	3rd Qtr	4th Qtr	FY 1984 Plan	FY 1985 Plan
Ending Backlog									
Sales	Distributor								
	Total								
Pre-Tax Income									
Net Inc. After Taxes	Amount								
	% of Total Sales								
	Return on Invest.								
Other Income (Expense)									
Earn per Shr-	Shrs								
No. of Employees-Per. Ending									
Annualized Sales per Employee									
Floor Space-sq ft-Per. Ending									
BALANCE SHEET DATA									
Accounts Rec-Gross	Balance								
	Months of Sales								
Inventory	Ending Balance								
	Year Rate of Turn								
Accounts Payable	Total								
	Over 60 Days								
Bank Loans at End of Period									
Income Taxes Paid									
Ending Cash									
Tooling Additions									
Equipment Additions									

Product Line	Sales			Net Income					
	Fiscal Years		FY 1984	FY 1982		FY 1983		FY 1984	
	1982	1983	Plan	Amt	%	Amt	%	Amt	%
Total									

Figure 4.1 *Profit Plan Summary Form,* 1984 ($000). (From J. S. O'Flaherty, 1983.)

tional feature, the layout also provides the actual results for the previous two years in the same planning format.

The first profit plan summary is a devil to complete; the task in subsequent years is much easier. The first year's effort spawns supporting schedules which show up inadequate information or data that are patently absurd. The results do force systematic recasting of information based on thought-through assumptions.

Every organization has its advanced planning meeting of top management, which means blackboard sessions and heated discussions. But conference rhetoric is one thing, completing the profit-plan summary is another. So many pleasant assumptions capsulized in one box of the form are upset by the unpleasant results that show up on another box on the same sheet of paper. Some considerations in completing such a form are listed in Table 4.1.

For many enterprises, five-year plans are an exercise in precision forecasting that is mostly futile. Even public utilities, who always took five-year forecasts as given and considered projections a decade or so out as the intermediate term, have found that all of their forecasts required extensive modification because of energy cost and usage perturbations. Still, there is merit in the typical concern preparing a five-year plan so long as it is not taken too seriously. Also some outside lending sources feel happier with such a plan. Figure 4.2 is a one-sheet form for a five-year forecast. In the writer's opinion, an entrepreneur should have the form completed because the exercise forces new product sales analyses in the context of their financial requirements over an extended period of time.

Outside Presentation of Management

Wall Street will take a lucky management over good management any day of the week. Nevertheless, much of luck is being at the right place at the right time—and having the sense to seize the opportunity. Good management increases the success probability on the upswing of good fortune and provides protection on the downside of bad luck. The securities and lending communities know this fact very well.

Judgment, personalities, and events are the conditioning factors in building a key management group. The basic charge to each member

TABLE 4.1 Comments on Profit Plan Summary

Profit Plan Item	Comment
Ending backlog	Backlog is an important business indicator and consists of real purchase orders and no letters of intent. Wishful thinking on backlog is an endemic ailment of many entrepreneurs.
Distributor sales	Most companies have a major specialty sales category that is a key factor in total sales.
Pre-tax income minus other income (expense)	Operating income sometimes can be significantly different than pre-tax income. The writer has had "Other Income" amount to as much as 3% of annual sales.
Earnings per share	Primary and fully diluted earnings per share may have to be calculated. Primary earnings are based on shares currently outstanding. Fully diluted earnings reflect stock options, warrants, and conversion rights.
Annualized sales per employee	Total sales are divided by the average number of company employees for the period. Assuming a given level of manufacturing integration, the result is a measure of company performance.
Months of accounts receivable and cash at end of period	The accounts receivable item is a measure of the effectiveness of accounts receivable collection and also relates to cash requirements.
Inventory	The skyrocketing costs of carrying inventory affect cash planning.
Inventory rate of turn	The popular method for determining rate of turn is the cost of sales method. Given the extent of a particular inventory pipeline, the inventory-turn rate is a key sensor of inventory quality and management.
Bank loans at end of period	This item is defined as short-term bank loans. Longer-term debt, including the current portion, is footnoted to a supporting schedule.
Ending cash	Cash and short-term investments such as Treasury bills are included.
Tooling and equipment additions	Depreciation on planned capital purchases are accrued as depreciation expense throughout the year.
Product line net income	While the net income numbers will be questionable because of cost allocation problems, the exercise is worthwhile.

Source: J. S. O'Flaherty

	Past Fiscal Years		Forecast of Fiscal Years				
	1982	1983	1984	1985	1986	1987	1988
OPERATING DATA							
Ending Backlog							
Sales — Distributor							
Sales — Total							
Pre-Tax Income							
Net Inc. After Taxes — Amount							
Net Inc. After Taxes — % of Total Sales							
Net Inc. After Taxes — Return on Investmnt							
No. of Employees-Per. Ending							
Annualized Sales per Employee							
BALANCE SHEET DATA							
Accounts Rec-Gross — Balance							
Accounts Rec-Gross — Months of Sales							
Inventory — Ending Balance							
Inventory — Year Rate of Turn							
Accounts Payable — Total							
Accounts Payable — Over 60 Days							
Bank Loans							
Income Taxes							
Tooling Additions							
Equipment Additions							

PRODUCT LINE ANALYSIS

Product Line	Sales						
	1982	1983	1984	1985	1986	1987	1988
Total							

Figure 4.2 *Five-Year Forecast Form, 1984-1988.* (From J. S. O'Flaherty, 1983.)

of the team in the business environment is to provide the strong backup support for the weaknesses of the other persons in the group. The first priority of any manager is to recognize the axiom of hanging together, because otherwise both the manager and the organization may hang separately. Doing one's own job well is not enough. The requirement for supporting each other is not based on friendship but enlightened self-interest.

A direct corollary of strong backup support is at least adequate performance of all the principal tasks or functions of an enterprise. In an academic grading sense, nothing is accomplished by scoring "A's" on the bulk of the functions and "F's" on the remainder. The grade-point average idea does not apply in business survival and growth. Instead, like a holed boat when a through-hull fitting lets go, the water will gush through the "F"-graded function, and an otherwise fine business vessel can be in desperate shape.

Any written and oral presentation to the securities and lending communities should stress the management's intertwined strengths along with a demonstrated capability of least adequate performance of the concern's principal functions.

The Annual Brochure or Position Paper

While very time-consuming to prepare the first time, an annual position paper or brochure of a privately held company is worth the cost. It represents an overview of the particular business from all facets and gives a synthesis of its management philosophy, operations, and financial affairs, both in the past few years and in the two years ahead. However, a warning.

The effort can do more damage than good if it is a piece of tub-thumping exaggeration.

The annual position paper is a reasoned evaluation of the history and potentialities of the company's industry and its place in that industry. This most definitely includes a careful review of the bogies and the ghosts that may cluster around the enterprise or its industry. Then with the basic elements of the annual brochure in place, little effort is required to utilize the position paper for the particular presentation objectives of the entrepreneur.

To the extent possible, the brochure writing should have the clarity of a *Time* or *Newsweek* technical article. These magazines do a fine job of making the readers feel they not only understand the subject matter but are interested in it. This type of writing is difficult to do.

A principal advantage of the position paper to the chief executive and senior management is that the brochure provides a solid basis for verbal comments and answers to questions. The management understands that the written material has been cross-checked for presentation consistency on all of the operating facets and forecast assumptions. On this point, it is even more welcome to senior associates who know they are protected from the wrath of the entrepreneur if their comments and answers to questions are within the context of the annual brochure.

A major advantage of a closely held company in a competitive world is the fact that the concern does not have to disclose publicly, authenticated operating and financial information. In short, nothing like a Form 10K report to the Securities and Exchange Commission (SEC) is required. Yet an annual position paper has all of these data assembled in one document which may end up in the hands of a competitor. There are two answers to this legitimate concern.

Clearly, the few copies of the brochure are closely controlled from a security viewpoint. And only selected sections are given for specific purposes to the outside world. But more important than careful control is the extraordinary fact that seldom do the competitors believe or have much interest in what is considered unauthenticated data dribbling out through a third party. The competitors are not willing to accept, based on nonofficial information, that the small growth company poses any threat or is performing so well. However, there is a 180-degree change of attitude when that same growth enterprise goes public and provides authenticated operating data.

The appearance and length of the confidential annual brochure is a matter of judgment. This writer prefers the main text to be a single-spaced, typewritten document (carefully reproduced) of 30 to 40 pages with a addendum of product illustration or schematics. A table of contents is routine, and an index may be worthwhile. A printed cover that stands up to handling and a spiral binding are desirable. The end result is an underplayed, professional presentation that carries conviction. A table of contents of the type of an annual brochure developed by the writer is shown in Table 4.2 along with comments on each principal

TABLE 4.2 Comments on Brochure Table of Contents

Table of Contents	Comments
1. In general	1. This is the introduction and purpose of the position paper
2. Evolution of company's industry and its products	2. The industry's history and its present-day position are covered by a lucid but concise overview.
3. Technology of the industry	3. The evaluation of future technical weaknesses and strengths of the industry from both a domestic and international viewpoint is presented in fair detail.

4. Size, composition, and growth of the industry
  a. Market categories and company's position in those markets
  b. Company's product lines and their potential
  c. Rating of competitors and company by existing and new product lines
  d. Market sales percentages of company's products
	4. The markets for the enterprise's products are analyzed and the quality of the competition and the company's ability to compete are covered.

5. Current company sales position
  a. Type and number of customers and customer program
  b. Applications of company's products
  c. Marketing pattern and selling organization
  d. distributor or consignment sales problems and reserves
	5. The company's customers and product applications along with the extent of sales-dollar concentration and risk are examined. This is a major section of the position paper.

6. Company's history, people, and facilities
  a. History of the company
  b. Management and other key people
  c. Stock ownership of key people, stock options, and other incentives
	6. This is a reasoned, affirmative presentation with emphasis on management philosophy, strengths, and operational controls. Significant problems should be discussed briefly along with actions to cure them.

TABLE 4.2 (Continued)

Table of Contents	Comments

d. Tooling and capital equipment, and "make or buy" policy
    e. Facilities
    f. Patents, licenses, and litigation
    g. Renegotiation and other contingencies
    h. Quality of inventory and basis of valuation	

7. Principal shareholdings and potential stock dilution	7. Shareholdings of 5% or above are listed and discussed. Salient features of stock option plans, warrants, or convertible debentures are presented. Preemptive shareholder rights, if any, are indicated.

8. Audited financial history and position
    a. History of operating results (with unaudited stub period)
    b. Current audited financial statements and footnotes
	8. Five years operating results are presented in tabular form along with an unaudited stub if the brochure is prepared later on in the year. An analysis is required of past financial trends and perturbations.

9. Intermediate financial projections
    a. Profit plan for two-year period
    b. Projected changes in financial condition for three-year period
	9. As discussed in the text, a two-year Profit Plan is included along with a three-year working-capital analysis and supporting comments.

10. Five-year projection	10. The product line analysis is of particular interest in the projection.
Appendix Photographs Index	

Source: J. S. O'Flaherty

discussion subject. A final reiteration on brochure preparation. The first one requires a great deal of time. Subsequent brochures are much easier. Format then is established, and a good portion of the material is more or less boiler plate, which is easy to update.

An Aid in Any Season

All successful entrepreneurs have their own effective techniques for making outside presentations. In their dealings with the securities and lending communities, they need at hand the interrelated facts, forecasts, and evaluations for their own enterprises and their industries. Then presentation can be made with conviction and with minimal fear of surprise questions.

5

The Security Laws

The American people like to speculate in initial stock offerings. However, the speculation carries no implications that public companies are understood or well loved. And the lack of understanding goes a long ways back. Why this is so and why and how the federal securities laws have been written is a necessary consideration in the decision to go public.

The Bats and Owls of the 1900s

The government securities regulations of the 1980s had their genesis in the administration of "that damned cowboy," Theodore Roosevelt, who became president after William McKinley's assassination in 1901. Roosevelt, a shrewd politician and dedicated advocate of the strenuous life and worthy causes, was soon involved in attacks on business monopolies and trusts. Riding the Roosevelt tide was an effective assortment of writers like Lincoln Steffens and Upton Sinclair who exposed corruption and misuse of power both in business and government. They did an excellent job in laying most of these responsibilities "on the threshold of business—like a bastard on the doorstep of the father.

A tremendous disturbance resulted. There was a great fluttering and clamor among the bats and the owls . . ."

The bats and the owls had more to flutter about with the 1907 panic, which thoroughly frightened Wall Street and left a wreckage of closed banks and small-business bankruptcies around the United States. The efforts of an elderly and ailing J. P. Morgan in stemming the monetary hysteria make a memorable story. But the bitter aftertaste of the 1907 panic brought two governmental investigations of the unregulated stock market. The Pujo Committee of 1912–13 recommended much of what was to become regulatory law a score of years later. Shortly thereafter, the European War broke out and America had other things to worry about.

America's Business Is Business—The 1920s

World War I was tragically expensive for Europe not only in lives but in wealth. An untouched American economy had burgeoned with the four years of war and the Western powers had borrowed to the hilt to pay for U.S. armaments and food. America, perennially a debtor nation, now discovered that it was the world's leading creditor. Meanwhile, the Liberty Bonds in which the public had invested its heavy wartime savings had begun to mature. After a brief, sharp recession in 1921, the country was prosperous. Where was the logical place to invest again in America and its world business growth? The stock market of course. All the reformers of a decade or so earlier were forgotten. Bernard Baruch, the speculator, was the new financial hero.

For the next few years "the prosperity wagon rolled down Main Street" driven by "man—in his most vulnerable mood—the search for quick, easy money." A stock could be bought for 10% cash and a margin of 90%. Credit was cheap and stocks always went up. Holding companies with almost a labyrinth of interlocking layers of complexity were set up. If one was wary of investing in the market as an individual, investment trusts were now available to provide diversification. Even the prophets became convinced. John Moody, president of Moody's Investment Service, thought the bad old days were past when he commented in May 1925: "The lessons taught by the crude financial errors of the speculative period extending from 1898 down into the war and through the deflation days of 1920–1, had been well learned by business and financial interests all over the country."

The stock market turned a bit queasy in September and into October 1929. Beginning in the latter part of October, substantial margin selling spread to many stocks. On October 24, Black Thursday, a major market collapse was underway. The Great Depression would shortly arrive followed by the witch-hunt for the stock market scoundrels.

The Securities Act of 1933

A decade would go by before America would move forward again. And the revival would only start with Great Britain rearming and buying aircraft and materiel in the United States. But all of this were weary years ahead in the future. Franklin D. Roosevelt was elected president in November 1932, and part of his campaign platform had been financial reforms because of the excesses of the 1920s.

Nobody was quite sure what the economic plan of the new administration was going to be. A good many suspected that the President and his immediate advisors were equally vague, but it was also evident that the new administration was willing to listen to new ideas. And soon one was found that made good political sense as well. The President emphasized a new economic theme, and it was an effective one for the times ... "America was essentially a healthy society that needed democratization." However, delimiting and defining that last long word was and still is a subject of debate and frustration.

Even before Mr. Roosevelt was inaugurated, the Senate Committee on Banking and Currency began a seventeen-month investigation with Ferdinand Pecora as chief counsel. The parade of witnesses, including J. P. Morgan's son (who found a female midget on his lap as a publicity stunt during a committee session), disclosed a long list of financial sins and misdoings of the 1920s. With the temper of the times, federal securities legislation to cure these bad practices would be forthcoming shortly.

A team headed by Felix Frankfurter of the Harvard Law School and three bright attorneys in their thirties met in Washington in early

April 1933 to complete the draft of a national securities act. Benjamin Cohen was practicing corporate law in New York City. James M. Landis and Thomas G. Corcoran had served as law clerks to Supreme Court justices, and Corcoran had already been in Washington a year. These four people were to become synonymous with the landmark securities legislation of the 1930s.

Modeled generally after the British Companies Act, the Frankfurter team submitted a draft of a securities bill to a house committee on April 10. Included was the important "stop order" device whereby issuance of a security could be prohibited because of failure to disclose material matters in the registration. With only minor amendments the bill entitled "The Securities Act of 1933" moved rapidly through the House and Senate and was signed into law by President Roosevelt on May 23, 1933. While congressional passage of this bill was no more hurried than a number of other pieces of major legislation during the early hectic months of the new administration, there was considerable feeling that the securities legislative action was far too hasty.

Called the "truth in securities" bill by its advocates, the 1933 Securities Act was designed to help the potential investors in public offerings. Prior to buying stock in a public company, they would have available a disclosure of all the material facts concerning that enterprise. This disclosure was to be accomplished by a registration statement, and failure to provide required data fully and accurately could result in criminal as well as civil penalties. As with much major legislation of the time, the Act represented substantial deviations from precedent. Of prime interest to companies making initial public offerings was Section 11.

Under Section 11 of the new Securities Act, all that was required to recover from the issuer of the securities was to prove that the defendant omitted or misrepresented a material fact in the registration statement. The plaintiff did not have to show that he or she was misled by the omissions or misrepresentations. And by definition, such litigation would take place with full benefit of hindsight.

As enterprises in their SEC registrations rely on legal opinions pertaining to the sale of stock from its lawyers and opinions on financial statements from its public accountants, these groups also come under certain provisions of Section 11; hence a prime rationalization for the size of their fees for an SEC registration.

Securities Exchange Act of 1934

The 1933 legislation was implemented by the Securities Exchange Act of 1934, generally referred to as the Exchange Act. Congress established a Securities and Exchange Commission (SEC) with broad registration and reporting control powers. The struggle over the intervening years, even to the present time, has been to what extent the SEC would utilize its broad powers, particularly at the level of accounting rule-making authority. There are those who believe the SEC's failure to exercise this authority has "placed the agency in a permanently emasculated position."

These advocates feel that a United States accounting code should be established which would force comparability between individual companies and industries. As a logical extension, according to some enthusiasts, the plan could be geared to the economic system of the country and be a valuable adjunct of national economic planning.

Needless to say, the proponents of a federal accounting code have been attacked on the basis that the result would be a bureaucratic monster with attendant loss of flexibility at the individual company level. Certainly, current SEC regulations have made going public an expensive operation. What the costs would be with a federal accounting code would be difficult to visualize.

The Foreign Corrupt Practices Act of 1977

To the considerable amazement of most American publicly owned enterprises, a whole new set of federal regulations on accounting matters came into being with the passage of the Foreign Corrupt Practices Act in December 1977. The purpose of the new law was simply to make a foreign bribe by a U.S. company a federal crime. So that such payments would not be hidden, books of account were to be kept in a proper manner. The Corrupt Practices bill passed by voice vote in the Senate and unanimously in the House. Having thus neatly disposed of the foreign bribery subject, the Congress moved on to other affairs. Unfortunately, the congressional solution was neither neat nor simple.

There have been many second thoughts on the moralistic approach of the 1977 Act to foreign bribery. In addition, Section 102 of the Act turned out to be a major surprise for American business. Codified as section 13(b)(2) of the 1934 Exchange Act, it placed new federal regulations on financial records and internal accounting controls on "all business activities of U.S. companies that are either registered or file reports, or both, with the SEC under the 1934 Act."

The problem with the new section 13(b)(2) was, and still is, how management can reasonably conform to the statutory objectives when the language is simplistic and as a result open to interpretation. Fortunately, both the courts and the SEC have been sensible and cautious in their interpretation of the accounting control requirements of the section. For the entrepreneur considering going public, 13(b)(2) is merely another negative factor to be placed in the balance scale of decision.

Whatever Will Be, Will Be

The early 1980s brought a new chairman of the SEC, John Shad, and, temporarily at least, a change in emphasis in the work of the Commission. The aggressive role of the SEC's enforcement division was restricted. Stress was now on simplifying and eliminating rules and regulations. Even pressure for mandatory use of independent outside directors on company boards was eased. What all that would mean on a longer-term basis remained to be seen.

Little is accomplished by evaluating future possibilities of legislative or administrative law other than recognizing the potential for change which exists. For better or worse, the American people of this generation have a latent antipathy toward corporations, and particularly the larger ones.

Powerful lobby groups can always be mustered to support aspects of a regulatory plan. Take four of the items applying to large corporations contained in the 1980 Corporate Democracy bill introduced in the House by Rep. Benjamin S. Rosenthal:

1. "Just cause" requirements for discharge of or discrimination against employees.
2. Inclusion in the annual report of regional distribution of corporation assets, gross revenues, expenses and net income; occupational inju-

ries and illnesses, extent of pollution generated by operations; and race, sex and job classification distribution of employees.
3. Notice to and compensation of employees and municipalities for plant closings with such compensation to be determined by the Secretary of Labor.
4. Voting control of the board by independent outside directors.

This particular corporate democracy bill died in the House. But because of its basic appeal to numerous groups, like the legendary phoenix, other versions of such a bill will surely rise in youthful freshness both in the Congress and in the state legislatures.

6

The Harassed Profession

While the bulk of the attack is unwarranted, the accounting profession has been on the defensive for two generations because of its audits of publicly owned companies. Although scarcely consoling to those involved, the profession must wield considerable power to merit such sustained abuse. The latest burden is a series of pyramiding jury awards based on the notion that the independent public auditors are sort of a last-ditch insurance company. The accounting firm presumably should provide compensation when the audited enterprise has become a bankrupt and all other alternatives for recourse have failed.

An additional thorn under the accounting profession's saddle is the supercilious attitude of a good many corporation lawyers who know that they know the auditing business well. Yet these same lawyers may be admittedly vague about or have minimal interest in relevant background material that can affect an accounting decision.

The concern about outside criticism no matter how ill-founded and the real worry of litigation can affect the presentation of financial data in the SEC registration statement. These tensions and fears of the accounting profession did not happen overnight, and this background should be understood by the entrepreneur.

Accounting Practices Through the 1920s

The booming U.S. industrialization beginning in the late 1800s and then the federal legislation of the 1910s pointed up a need for systematic accounting and reporting practices and the importance of independent auditors. In contrast to European accounting codes prescribed by governments, the emerging American accounting profession did not support rigid standardization. Instead it argued for basic disclosure procedures. In a way this lack of support for a government accounting code was surprising as the Interstate Commerce Commission had established a system of uniform accounts and reporting controls for all railroads by the second decade of the 1900s. The arguments of those who believed in prescribed government accounting codes were submerged in the onrush of World War I and the massive expansion of the industrial and credit strength of the United States.

The 1920s were good days for a young accounting profession, so good that its professional bodies were busily engaged in establishing formal educational and examination criteria for admittance to the group. This formulation of admittance qualifications set into motion by enlightened self-interest was similar to what was taking place in a number of other professions, including law, medicine, and engineering.

However, there was one important difference between the accounting profession and all the others. The independent public accountants were supposedly giving financial health readings on an economic monster that was going to fall flat on its face after the 1929 debacle. To the profession's considerable amazement, the accountants discovered that their group, among others, was front-stage center in the financial postmortem theater years later. Robert Chatov's analysis was typical:

> The stock market failure of the 1920s was due partly to the failure of the accountants to provide a sorely needed moderating influence, though they were without real power to influence events at that time. Still it is fair to ask whether they sounded any warning or made efforts toward financial moderation. The answer is they did not.

From the New Deal to Watergate

Franklin Roosevelt's New Deal ignored the accounting profession in the drafting of the 1933 Securities Act. This omission probably occurred because others in the Administration shared A. A. Berle's view of the profession as a sort of a green eye-shade fraternity of "controlled, placid, practicing accountants."

The auditors may have been ignored in the drafting of the passage of the 1933 Act, but the legislation represented a fee bonanza in subsequent years for accountants as well as lawyers. Perhaps for the best, this fact was largely unrecognized at the time by the accountants. Instead, they worried about the Section 11 liabilities of the Act and the reformers' continued lobbying for a federal accounting code.

Meanwhile, the accountants continued to receive unasked-for advice during the 1930s. They were told "to be more modest—that is, to indicate more adequately the restricted function of their work, and at the same time to be more conscientious and exacting in the importance of their limited function." Yet, concurrently, they were warned that they "sometimes forget to ask themselves just what is the social function of their work." A sustained barrage of criticism of the profession, albeit somewhat muted, continued in a similar vein into the early 1970s.

Current Regulatory Environment and Criticism

The post-Watergate period of the 1970s became a political pressure cooker for a number of special causes, not the least of which was something called "corporate accounting reform." A 1976 House subcommittee report stated that "scandalous episodes of corporate illegality, unaccountability, and the use of questionable business practices raise questions about the effectiveness of our system of corporate accountability." The congressional report went on to attack the public accountants' own rule-making body (Financial Accounting Standards Board), stating that "the FASB had accomplished virtually nothing toward resolving fundamental problems plaguing the profession" and concluding that "the SEC's continued reliance on the private accounting profession is questionable."

A 1976 staff study of a Senate subcommittee echoed the principal points in the House report urging much stronger federal control. The study then expressed serious concern about the concentration of power in the profession. It pointed out that the 15 largest accounting firms serve as independent public auditors for the vast majority of publicly owned corporations in the United States. Therefore, the federal government should require that these firms report basic operational and financial data annually. The Senate study went on to urge an investigation to determine whether these 15 accounting firms had violated the federal antitrust laws.

The House and Senate study reports were symptomatic of a Congress that had become irritated with all corporations—and large ones in particular. A year later the Congress found a way to vent part of its antipathy. It passed the Foreign Corrupt Practices Act in December 1977. As indicated in Chapter 5, the purpose of the new law was to make a foreign bribe by a U.S. company a federal crime. So that such practices could not be hidden, books of account were to be kept in a proper manner. Section 102 of the Act has turned out to be a matter of concern for American business. Codified as section 13(b)(2) of the 1934 Exchange Act, it placed new federal regulations on financial records and internal accounting controls on "all business activities of all U.S. companies that are either registered or file reports or both, with the SEC under the 1934 Act."

The problem with the new section 13(b)(2), as discussed in Chapter 5, was and still is how a corporation and its public accountants can reasonably conform with its objectives when the language in the section is simplistic and therefore open to interpretation. The section invites additional litigation, something corporations and their outside auditors can do without.

While possibly a transitory attitude, under the Reagan Administration the SEC has been more conciliatory to the accounting profession. Such efforts were overdue.

Last-Resort Litigation

As a result of the volume of political rhetoric and media attention, the early 1970s showed a sharp increase in the number of lawsuits filed against publicly held corporations, their outside accountants, and even their sacrosanct lawyers. The number of these suits leveled off near the end of the decade. But in the early 1980s a series of large jury awards against accounting firms sent a chill throughout the profession. What is so disturbing is that the courts increasingly appear to be taking the view that, because the client corporation is bankrupt, the accountants represent a last-resort source of compensation. It is easy to envisage the impact on public accountants' fee structures if this last-resort idea continues or, worse yet, is expanded.

A Need to Know the Client Company

To avoid unpleasant surprises for a company considering going public, the outside auditors must not only know but also understand the enterprise and its industry segment. This means several audit engagements at least. Of prime interest are inventories, which can form an excellent basis for future lawsuits. If it were a semiconductor inventory, for example, the outside auditor must understand silicon-chip yields and valuation, a complex technical subject. Consignment sales with their implication on inventory valuation are equally dangerous, if not more so. And so on. Each company is different, and the auditors are expected to be well versed in the client's enterprise and its industry. A difficult task.

A concluding thought on the outside accountant–client relationship. The audit partner knows the agonies and the rewards of the profession—in recent years the partner may be convinced there are more of the former than the latter. If an entrepreneur believes that the accounting rules can be bent for the initial public registration statement, the company has little knowledge of its auditors.

Selection of a Public Accounting Firm

The bulk of the publicly held companies in the United States are audited by 15 accounting firms. Of that number, the "Big Eight" firms are large indeed—probably averaging well over 10,000 employees, 1000 partners, and operating in as many as 40 countries. Indicative of the extent of their operation, one of them established a training center in the early 1970s that contained 45 classrooms as well as dining and living accommodations for 600 people. The students were employees or clients who were in residence for a few days to several weeks.

In addition to the group of accounting firms who handle the auditing of the bulk of public concerns, there are a number of other firms that have stature with Wall Street on security matters. For several good reasons, the private company considering an initial public issue would be well advised to select its outside accountants only from these two groups. The managing underwriter will not mince words as to the reasons why.

In a world of variables surrounding the arrangements for an initial public issue, the underwriting manager wants as many fixed factors as possible. This means an accounting firm known and respected by the securities community and its lawyers. Not surprisingly, a fine, local firm of a half dozen certified public accountants unknown to the underwriting manager and the prospective securities marketing group will be greeted with minimal enthusiasm. And for good reason. Intimate knowledge of the applicable laws, the SEC, and post-issue procedures by experienced practitioners can be a source of comfort to the enterprise as well as the underwriter.

A Conclusion

All things considered, a private concern that is considering going public as a viable option for raising capital should engage a national or a well-known regional accounting firm years ahead of a tentative public offering date. At a minimum such a firm should be the auditors for several engagements prior to the SEC registration.

7

Selection of Company Counsel

An enterprise needs a capable company counsel. So often the management feels it is in a deadly video game with legal invaders attacking the company from all directions. An initial public offering adds substantially to the concern's legal exposure.

The selection and compensation of company counsel are discussed in this chapter, followed by a review of the lawyer's role and responsibilities in the evolving securities laws.

Importance of Company Counsel

An expanding private enterprise requires strong, competent counsel at every stage of its development. And like a growing snake which discards its skin periodically, new counsel may be required for a changed environment and the different array of problems presented for review and action.

Any lawyer may be highly competent and experienced in certain areas of the law but be unqualified to work on the particular problem at hand. Being ignorant of the accepted ways of handling a situation or taking actions on the wrong matters can be costly for the client, particularly if the attorney is overly contentious in negotiation and potential litigation. Competent company counsels recognize their limitations.

Advice from counsel is usually the principal requirement of the company client. And mastering a particular area of the law by itself is not enough to render the best client service. The better the lawyer understands the entrepreneur and the company's affairs, normally the more helpful the counsel can be. Not only does the attorney interpret legal doctrine to the chief executive, the effect on the client's affairs is reviewed as well. All of this makes a powerful argument for a long-time counsel relationship with the company. But changing conditions can vitiate the validity of counsel's knowledge and advice. At no time is this more true than when a company goes public and hence immediately becomes subject to a whole maze of legislative and administrative law.

Criteria for the Selection of Counsel

Whether it be a periodic evaluation of the present company counsel or the selection of a replacement, the evaluation criteria used reflect the entrepreneur's own requirements. A primary consideration is the current growth environment of the enterprise. Specialized knowledge of or substantial familiarity with this environment will undoubtedly be a primary criterion. However, a number of other considerations are included in the evaluation, whether they are initially recognized or not. The chief executive may really want "the laywer to be a sounding board, a neutral evaluator of client ideas, or he may merely want approval of his ideas, reassurance to bolster his morale, or perhaps respectable authority to strengthen his hand in bargaining with others."

Most companies select knowledgeable counsel by routinely utilizing a law firm that has a general practice in corporate matters. Few smaller businesses find that it makes economic sense to have in-house lawyers. However, many major corporations have built up their in-house staff because legal fees have become a significant item in administrative expense. One oil company, for example, has a department of some 150 attorneys, equal in size to many large firms.

Criteria for the Selection of Counsel

The size of the law firm as well as the competency of individual firm members is a major consideration in the selection of a company counsel. The tremendous growth during the last generation in new and expanded legislation, administrative law, and judicial decisions has generated a corresponding increase in size of many firms and a number of new specialities, such as Equal Opportunity. Not only does a very large firm employ several hundred attorneys but often it will have branch offices in other cities. Yet a relatively small firm of a dozen lawyers may be able to meet the client's needs with specialities satisfied within the firm or by other practitioners.

A major regional law firm, organized by departmental area of business or technical specialty, has status with the federal and state regulatory agencies. Also such a large professional organization has the specialists and the shock troops of associates and law clerks to throw into the breach where timing and case complexity are important. But irrespective of the size of the project, a craftsman-like job monitored by the firm's system of quality control is expected.

When the lawyers in a large firm encounter matters outside their immediate areas of competence, in-house specialist partners and associates with specific legal expertise are available to consult or handle these matters. Because of their specialization, both partners and associates can make the most efficient use of their billing hours. It requires a major firm to have the volume of work to support this kind of specialization.

However, the large law firm has its disadvantages, particularly for the smaller enterprise. The experienced partner handling the company has many tasks. Too often the smaller client finds that it is dealing with an associate who is training under the partner. These associates are capable and intelligent, but the early years out of law school with a large firm generally provide only a limited amount of the breadth of experience and learning from mistakes that the smaller client requires in legal advice.

Another argument for the use of the large firm is that specialists in a particular area are readily available to the client. This idea carries the presumption that a systematic and closed communications loop exists. Logic to the contrary and human nature being what it is, often it is quicker and easier to obtain a thoughtful opinion from an appropriate specialist in another firm.

Corporate legal costs as a percentage of general and administrative expense have increased significantly in the last two decades. While due in large part to an era of expanding legal activity, another major cost element is the compensation and hourly billing practices of the attorneys themselves.

Large law firms in the principal cities are paying first-year associates (salary and bonus) at the middle-executive level of many of their clients. These new lawyers naturally anticipate substantive yearly increases and most of them hope to be made partners seven or eight years out of law school. To support the professional salary pyramid of a large law firm requires a substantial amount of hourly billings. This can well equate to many hours of work to produce a craftsman-like job for which the law firm can be justifiably proud. Whether a particular project from the client's viewpoint requires such a detailed level of craftsmanship and resultant cost is another matter entirely.

Individual client analysis of hours billed by any law firm is a recurring task. Probably the best practice is meeting with company counsel periodically. The agenda might be the review of the scope, depth, and thoroughness-level of the assignments required by the company. An addendum would be a discussion of the lawyers working on the projects and their hourly billing rates.

The foregoing paragraphs have touched on some of the considerations involved in selecting a general counsel. Perhaps the best summary of the various criteria and the important decisions to be made is given by J. Spencer Letts, a corporation lawyer with wide experience:

> On balance, what I think most smaller companies need is not a particular kind of law firm, but a particular kind of lawyer. It is a generalist, who is capable of handling most problems primarily on his own and is willing to do so. It is also one who views his function as one of optimizing the cost/risk ratio on behalf of his client so that the money spent in further reduction of risk, never exceeds the value of the risk reduced.

Payment of Counsel in Stock

Many initial public offerings are from companies which originated as grass-roots ventures, financed almost entirely by professional money

Payment of Counsel in Stock

from investment banking house, venture capital firms, and the like. Others come from former divisions of large businesses which will be structured on a high leverage basis to provide stock to the entrepreneurial management.

Even before a preliminary agreement is reached between the money and the entrepreneurial sides of either type of a proposed venture, the entrepreneur needs a first-rate legal counsel in which there is a high level of confidence. The financial architecture of a deal, including the stock split between money and management, requires a number of negotiation meetings between the principals of both sides and their respective attorneys.

Working out a payment schedule for the lawyer by the entrepreneur is not an easy task, as no guarantee can be given by the entrepreneur that there will be agreement between the principals and that a deal will result. Counsel is usually expected to accept the engagement on a contingency basis. Probably the best time to negotiate such a payment schedule with counsel is when the money side is willing to give a loose letter of intent to engage in the venture with the entrepreneur. Under any circumstances the size of the contingency fee will vary with the likelihood of the deal being consumated and the extent of subsequent legal work with the client.

Somewhere along the line, the lawyers may propose that part of their fees be taken from management stock portions of the ventures. The attorneys' interest in stock is due to a desire for capital appreciation, something that does not exist in a professional law practice. And, after all, the logical place to take a speculative risk is with people they have come to know very well. The idea is sound. In one venture, the counsel had about a 50-times appreciation on a modest block of original stock.

As also discussed in Chapter 2, strong arguments exist for not giving stock to legal counsel as fee payment or allowing counsel to buy shares while the enterprise is private. Many law firms will not accept an ownership interest in a venture as a fee, primarily because other partners want their share in cash. But there are more powerful arguments from the ventures viewpoint. Equity should be given up by management only with the greatest reluctance.

In addition, company counsels who own stock in ventures are placed in a confusing position. In one part of their minds they are concerned as shareholders about the value of their stock, and thus their financial involvements may distort their professional and dispassionate thinking on their clients' problems.

Entrepreneurs do not need the ombudsman kind of judgment in the persons of their company counsels who own some of the company's shares.

The Securities Laws and the Company Counsel

Black Thursday, October 24, 1929, signaled a major stock market collapse. The Great Depression followed shortly. The Securities Act of 1933 was the major legislative reaction in an attempt to cure the financial excesses of the 1920s.

The 1933 Act was written by lawyers and the presumption was that it would be interpreted by lawyers, most certainly not by accountants. But the people like James M. Landis, who drafted the Act with its strong sanctions, viewed even their own profession with some reservations. Landis, who was subsequently an SEC chairman and a dean of Harvard Law School, was upset when queried by a partner of Sullivan and Cromwell, a prestigius corporation law firm, about his use of "in terrorem" in a speech. In writing to his mentor, Felix Frankfurter, Landis vented some of his ire: "For him [the partner] to pick up a phrase like that and say it manifests a sadistic desire to punish purely for punishment purposes is typical of the verbal twisting he and his ilk are always ready to indulge in . . ."

Whatever the feelings of corporation lawyers following the passage of the 1933 Securities and 1934 Exchange Acts, for many years afterward they had the best of several worlds. The lawyers could sympathize with and truly support their business clients in the scary new world of government regulation of and interference in business affairs. Meanwhile, billings and profits increased because of the burgeoning legislative and administrative laws.

The corporation lawyers could even feel a bit sorry for the slow-thinking accountants who were becoming involved in lawsuits because of audit work. Then in a litigious era, corporate counsels found that they were increasingly being named in shareholder suits. Almost as irritating, the lawyers were being told that, along with the accountants and company management, they had no social consciences and were stolid, pragmatic individuals with strong traces of anti-intellectualism. All of this was a difficult cross to carry, although increased client fees for items like registration statements were a palliative.

A Full Legal Plate

The Roosevelt New Deal of the 1930s set in place extensive new securities legislation. In the subsequent half century, the legislative and administrative laws have become a ponderous and complex mass supplemented by interpretive judicial decisions and subject to political pressures like the aftermath of Watergate and the growth of the consumerism movement.

Public companies require skilled and knowledgeable lawyers for such matters. These people are well worth their hire.

8

A New Regulation and Long Overdue

Small businesses have been complaining bitterly to their elected representatives in recent years about the federal securities laws with their deadening burden on raising capital. Almost forgotten were the state securities or "Blue Sky" laws, which had been growing like weeds during the last half century of federal legislation.

The Congress enacted the Small Business Investment Incentive Act of 1980, which among other things enabled the Securities and Exchange Commission (SEC) to issue Regulation D, effective April 15, 1982. The regulation expanded the exemption from SEC regulation and eased certain existing federal rules. This should have appeal to many smaller companies as additional individual and institutional investors presumably will be willing to invest because of the elimination of some of the restrictive rules.

However, like most things in life, the easing of the federal rules did not yield all of the hoped-for results. Only time will show the real marketing costs to smaller businesses, along with the extent of a worrisome thicket of state laws that must still be cleared away. Regulation D is examined in this chapter both as an equity fund-raising alternative as well as its interrelationships with other aspects of the securities laws.

Offering Up to $500,000 (New Rule 504)

A basic rationale for new Rule 504 of Regulation D was that the SEC would "set aside a clear and workable exemption for small offerings by small issuers to be regulated by state Blue Sky requirements and to be subject to federal anti-fraud provisions and civil liability provisions such as Section 12(2)." Some popular writing on the Rule 504 to the contrary, this kind of wording is scarcely a charter of licentious freedom for an enterprise which is now allowed to issue up to $500,000 of its securities annually without an SEC registration, particularly so when there are federal restrictions remaining on most investor stock sales.

Nevertheless, Rule 504 does give new freedom and some safe-harbor protection to the issuing business, so long as the enterprise is neither a reporting (to the SEC) business nor an investment company. The new rule permits both stock and debt issues to an unlimited number of investors with no investor qualifications required. Under old Rule 240 (now rescinded) the number of investors were limited to a hundred, and the aggregate offering to $100,000. When the rate of inflation during the last decade or so is taken into account, the aggregate amount increase between the old and new rules is not so impressive.

As to the manner of offering the 504 securities, no general solicitation is permitted except in those states that require a registration statement or a disclosure document. The old rule did not allow general solicitation under any circumstances.

Regulation D contains a major change for small business that sounds a bit better than it is—a brokerage firm is allowed to participate in the new Rule 504 offering and charge a commission which has been freely negotiated between the issuing business and the brokerage firm. The old Rule 240 prohibited commissions, which meant of course that the securities community had no interest in participating in an issue. The new rule is all to the good, but the offering still must be sold to investors.

Two-year sales restrictions for the investors apply to 504 securities unless an offering is conducted exclusively in states where the issue is registered, and where a disclosure document is delivered under applicable state law. This proviso does not offer much comfort to the ordinary small company. On the other hand, Rule 240 did not even allow the state exemption.

"Restricted" stock as used throughout Regulation D means that the purchasing shareholders must hold the restricted securities for two years even if they should desperately wish to sell. Each such stock certificate should carry a stamp or "legend" indicating that it is stock issued with SEC restrictions. A stockbroker receiving a legended certificate will ask the issuing company's transfer agent whether the stock represented by the certificate can be sold and, if so, requesting that the legend be removed. The decision to lift the automatic "stop" on a block of legended stock rests with the company secretary, and corporate general counsel may be asked for an opinion. All this means an additional potential for built-in delays, and investors do not like delay when they are ready to sell.

Regulation D has an overriding feature that applies to all its rules. As a condition of exemption from SEC registration, a Form D must be filed by the company with the Commission 15 days after the first sale, six months after the first sale, and 30 days after the last sale. This represents a significant change because the old rules required the filing as a condition of the applicable rule, not as a condition of exemption from SEC registration. In addition to the onerous chore of filing the Form D, there is the practical difficulty of determining when the final sale takes place. Nevertheless, a determination must be made in order to be safe from the punitive provisions related to selling unregistered, nonexempt stock.

The Pros and Cons of Using Rule 504

The initial reaction of small business could only be positive when first hearing about the new Rule 504. It would allow them to raise additional equity money without an SEC registration. And the new rule became effective during a year when interest rates for borrowed funds were reaching record highs.

Taking an affirmative position on financing problems of small business, the SEC emphasized that offerings up to $500,000 were of such small size that federal registration of the amounts was neither necessary nor desirable. Thus the securities regulation could be left to the individual states. With the Commission's removal of the ban on brokerage commissions, it was hoped that the selling and marketing capability of investment bankers and retail brokerage firms would become a powerful factor in merchandising the small company issues. If this were so, the result would be greatly expanded markets for the new stock issues, and selling costs that should be reasonable. Because there is no federal disclosure, the equity money-raising efforts of the small companies would move expeditiously with a minimum of red tape.

Unfortunately, there are significant drawbacks to Rule 504, the importance of which will vary with the particular enterprise. Even brokerage commissions of 15% to 20% have generated limited interest in these small offerings by the securities community, except when the proposed issue has a broader-based investment appeal. The lack of interest revolves around the built-in brokerage costs and sales management effort associated with any offering irrespective of size. This is particularly true of the medium-to-large-sized securities firms. Yet these are the very ones who have the vast bulk of the retail brokerage offices.

With Rule 504, no federal disclosures are required, but the varied state regulations (Blue Sky laws) do present timing and cost problems for the issuing business. The SEC has far to go in attaining its objective of a uniform state/federal treatment of the 504 kind of offerings. In the interim, competent company counsel must review the enterprise's proposed offering both in the home state and the other states where the offering is to be sold. This is the best way to avoid state disclosure problems and possible litigation; however, it also can be expensive.

The two-year restriction on resale of the bulk of Rule 504 securities is a serious obstacle in the original sale. Investor resistance to being locked-in for that length of time to the fortunes of a small business can hurt any offering presentation.

Listing the drawbacks of Rule 504 to some chief executives may be likened to telling a person dying of thirst that the pond of water just discovered has a thick layer of scum on the surface. However, for the rest of the small-company entrepreneurs, Rule 504 is no open-sesame for raising equity money. Considerable costs are involved, and selling the securities can be difficult.

Offerings from $500,000 to $5 Million (New Rule 505)

Annual securities offerings between $500,000 to $5 million, which are exempt from federal registration, fall under the new Rule 505 of Regulation D. Both privately and publicly held companies can sell unregistered securities, except issuers disqualified under Regulation A and investment companies. In addition, there is the problem of the "accredited investor," the definition of which is the subject of a later section in this chapter.

As with the "under $500,000" grouping, the SEC has attempted to establish a federal exemption for an intermediate-sized category of smaller business. Again the idea is to have regulation of the category provided by the State Blue Sky requirements with a residual federal overhang of anti-fraud and civil-liability provisions. New Rule 505 replaced old Rule 242 and "like its predecessor, Rule 505 permits sales to 35 purchasers that are not accredited investors and to an unlimited number of accredited investors." Brokerage commissions are permitted as in the past, and no general solicitation is allowed.

Like the other two categories of Regulation D, securities sold carry two-year resale restrictions. And, again, as a condition of exemption from SEC registration, Form D must be filed on the same time schedule as old Form 242.

New Rule 505 does not require the issuer to provide any information regarding an accredited investor. The type of data for nonaccredited investors is an involved thing and depends upon whether the issuer is a nonreporting or reporting company to the SEC. Clearly, the ideal arrangement would be sale only to accredited investors.

Offerings of an Unlimited Amount (New Rule 506)

Raising of unlimited amounts of equity money under exemptions from the federal securities laws are covered under new Rule 506 of Regulation D. Old Rule 146 is rescinded.

According to the SEC, Rule 506 is available to all issuers for offerings sold to not more than 35 purchasers. Accredited investors, however, do not count toward that limit. The SEC overview goes on to say that "Rule 506 requires an issuer to make a subjective determination that each purchaser meets certain sophistication standards, a provision that narrows a similar requirement as to all offerees under Rule 146 (now rescinded)."

As with the other new rules, there are the two-year restrictions on resale. No general solicitation or advertising is permitted, but brokerage commissions are authorized. No issuer qualifications are established. Form D must be filed with the SEC 15 days after the first sale, every six months after the first sale, and 30 days after the last sale.

Accredited Investors

A good deal of the benefits of Regulation D comes from the SEC' reasonably specific definition of the term "accredited investor." Formerly the decision rested with the stockbroker and the issuing company as to whether potential investors met a vague SEC requirement that accredited investors be wealthy or sophisticated.

Accredited persons under the Regulation D definition are individuals who have an income of at least $200,000 annually for at least two years along with the expectation of at least that much in the third year, those who have a net worth of more than $1 million, or director and officers of the enterprise raising the equity capital. Accredited investors also can be banks, insurance companies, investment companies, pension plans, and certain tax-exempt organizations.

Other than a maximum of 35 persons, all of a SEC-exempt issue over $500,000 must be sold to accredited investors, and no disclosure data such as registration statement material need be provided them. However, if even one investor fails the accredited test, full disclosure must be made to all investors.

There is one escape route if the entire offering is sold and the issuing company and its underwriter then discover an investor who does not meet the accredited test. If both of them "reasonably believed" that all of the investors were accredited persons, there was no liability because of the failure to provide disclosure documents. One would suspect that delimiting "reasonably believe" will be an interesting area of judicial interpretation.

A Modest Step Away from Overregulation

Regulation D is more than a bone thrown to smaller enterprises who need to raise equity capital. Instead it is a fair but modest attempt to reduce the costly red tape, expert advice, and delays connected with federal laws and regulations. Despite extensive SEC coordination work with the security agencies of all fifty states plus Canada and Mexico, the individual state Blue Sky laws can pose formidable legal problems for any standard securities treatment. In the interim, offering of privately held company securities across state lines can have legal peril even though all the Regulation D requirements are met.

Setting up an objective standard definition of an accredited investor is an important and positive contribution of Regulation D and much appreciated by the securities community. It is to be hoped that the state agencies will pick up this new standard definition. However, probably years will elapse before the bulk of the states conform to many of the new federal practices.

The continued "restricted" stock provision in Regulation D remains a dead hand on smaller companies having federally exempt offerings. Why should outside investors (sophisticated or not) permit themselves to be tied up for two years before being allowed to sell? Frankly, if the deal were really that good or impressive, the issuing company could easily utilize other financing routes, not least of which would be filing a registration statement for a public offering with the SEC. A public issue cuts through the heavy thickets of Blue Sky laws and draws in retail-brokerage-firm participation on a national or regional basis.

Some Belated SEC Conclusions

While Regulation D does not accomplish that much for smaller business, it is an important and overdue set of new rules. The SEC has recognized belatedly that "the registration requirements and the exemption schemes of the Securities Act impose disproportionate restraints on small issues (of securities)." Further, there now is full recognition that the Blue Sky laws of the states have grown mightily in the past half century. These must be topped or thinned out to accomplish "a basic framework of limited offering exemptions that can apply uniformly at the federal and state levels."

Part Two

Practitioners in the Securities Markets

9

A Different Kind of a Game

Investment banking firms and their securities markets (Wall Street) have been an integral part of American development and expansion since the Civil War. Like the large oil companies, these banking firms have been pilloried by events and the media since the turn of the century. Still, they and their securities underwriting activities have expanded and prospered.

An understanding of the evolution and current status of the securities community should help to explain its importance on the financial scene and specifically in public offerings.

Regulation of Wall Street

The American people have been deeply suspicious of investment banking firms for a long time. This feeling was epitomized by a standard cartoon of the heavily jowled, portly fellow in a morning coat and top hat emblazoned with dollar signs. The symbol of Wall Street, this scoundrel was often cartooned as standing with one expensive boot resting on the neck of a prostrate workingman. To many, the robber barons at the turn of the century were one and the same as these iniquitous banking firms.

The exposure of the misfeasance and malfeasance of the principal Wall Street firms during the 1920s made headlines during the 1930s. This was explicit confirmation of the public's established suspicions and dislikes. Reflecting the popular feeling that there had been gross abuse of investors, the Congress enacted a series of farreaching pieces of legislation beginning with the Securities Act of 1933 and the Exchange Act of 1934 (see Chapter 5). The latter established the Securities and Exchange Commission (SEC), which placed the investment banking industry under the scrutiny of the Commission.

In quick succession came supplementary legislation affecting Wall Street. There was the Banking Act, which forced the separation of commercial and investment banking, followed by the Chandler Act, limiting the activities of investment bankers in reorganizing publicly held corporations. Then came the 1938 Mahoney Act, which provided for SEC regulation of over-the-counter brokers and dealers through the National Association of Security Dealers (NASD). Finally, near the end of the 1930s came the Trust Indenture Act, the Investment Company Act, and the Investment Advisers Act. By the start of World War II, investment banking activities were well circumscribed by federal legislation.

With all of the trauma of the Great Depression and disenchantment with Wall Street, share trading dropped precipitously during the 1930s and into the war years of the 1940s. From an annual high of 1.1 billion shares in 1929 on the New York Stock Exchange, the yearly total bottomed out at 126 million shares in 1942. By 1983, the trading of 100 million shares per day was simply considered a particularly heavy day.

The Golden Years

The end of World War II brought a long period of major expansion to the United States. This carried in its train striking increases of income at all levels, with worker productivity nearly doubling in 25 years. On an actual dollar basis, plant and equipment expenditures increased about four times. Raising the capital required for this kind of growth in securities markets that were very nearly moribund a decade or so before was not an easy task.

While moving through the brambles of expanding federal regulation, the securities community, and the investment banking firms in particular, had to mount an appeal to the individual investor who was beginning to think in terms of securities again. The institutional investor had yet to become the dominant factor in the stock market as it is today.

Raising the amount of funds required meant building or revitalizing national networks of regional securities firms. Such a network would have confidence in and depend upon the managing underwriter for a substantive part of a new securities issue. The valued regional relationships were not built overnight by the investment banking firms.

For the public corporations requiring equity or debt monies, an orderly market for the sale of securities was a necessity during the years of expansion. The chief executives expected their senior finance people to be up-to-speed in regard to the intricacies of the financial marketplace. But many chief executives believed that such officers' time could be spent to better advantage than becoming occasional investment bankers who could make expensive mistakes. And so the quarter century or so after World War II were the golden years for securities underwriting by investment bankers. The client lists grew apace, and the established firms' positions seemed impregnable.

Meanwhile, the investing public had seized on a vehicle which, in theory at least, would spread the investors' risk. Mutual funds had been around a long time and were only moderately tainted in the market collapse of 1929. During the 1950s, mutual fund assets quintupled. And in the following decade, these assets nearly doubled again.

Similar to the investment trust boom of the 1920s, the number of mutual shareholders burgeoned. There were some three million of them in 1965. Investment and brokerage firms fattened on the commissions generated by selling mutual fund shares to eager investors while collecting brokerage fees from the buying and selling actions of the numerous funds.

The stock activities of the mutual funds represented a principal reason for price/earnings (P/E) multiples that still bring a nostalgic feeling to any longtime underwriter. The composite Dow Jones Stock Index appeared to be locked in forever at a minimal 15 to 18 times.

And a "go-go" performance fund did not choke on a 60 times earnings multiple for a popular, unseasoned company. After all, look at IBM's price/earnings ratio, the keystone of many institutional investments of the time.

With fine earnings multiples, exciting technology companies, and a reawakening of a long dormant merger fever, the 1960s became a memorable period for acquisitions with the number of mergers three times that of the previous decade. A new term, "conglomerate," was added to the financial vocabulary. A diverse array of companies entered the merger derby, and these concerns acquired a varied assortment of enterprises in all types of businesses.

During the 1960s the conglomerates and their investment bankers recognized a happy combination of circumstances which could be profitably exploited. If the stock of an acquisition-oriented conglomerate was consistently popular with the securities community, the enterprise was able to acquire smaller and less popular companies for stock rather than cash, utilizing the "pooling of interests" accounting method.

In the go-go atmosphere of the 1960s, the acquiring company's shares of stock *plus* the additional shares issued for the acquisition would retain or very possibly improve the value of each outstanding share. Or as Wall Street would say, the high price/earnings ratio or multiple of the conglomerate would remain the same or even improve after the acquisition.

The prospering investment bankers were dealing with a mixed group of leading conglomerates during the merger decade. On the one hand there were youthful ventures, like Litton Industries which intended to be the industrial giant of high-technology companies. And there was an emerging and a remarkably successful enterprise called Teledyne that would go on to equal or exceed any of its conglomerate peers in the rugged years of the 1970s.

On the other hand, well-established companies changed their articles of incorporation so that they could acquire businesses in any field. International Telephone and Telegraph was the most famous, while Textron was illustrative of an enterprise that went the conglomerate route because of the financial unattractiveness of its own industry.

The high price/earnings ratios extending from the late 1950s through the 1960s, combined with the acquisition bidding of the conglomerates, made entrepreneurs of newly acquired companies paper-rich. Then there were other entrepreneurs who began to refer to their enterprises as "mini-conglomerates" in news releases so that they too could climb on the high-multiple gravy train. They were not alone. Privately held companies by the score knew what to do—they went public when the immediate market was favorable.

Those were the days when the "going-public industry" composed of specialists from investment banking, law, and accounting firms along with financial printing houses reached a pleasurable and prosperous young maturity.

The Blustery Winds of Change

Beginning in the early 1970s, the blustery and cold winds of change raked the verdant valuations and associated price/earning ratios. The performance mutual funds shriveled in the blast with values dropping by three-quarters or more, and the go-go people were fired. Conglomerate managers had to demonstrate their ability to manage their often ungainly assortment of companies or divisions. As a tremendous personal shock, many former entrepreneurs discovered their paper fortunes in large part had vanished.

The writer continues to be astonished as to how normally astute principals of an acquired company will hold on to all of their stock. These shrewd people calmly violate the fundamental rule of cashing out part of their holdings while letting the remainder ride with the action.

The rebuttal arguments put forward against sale of principals' stock usually revolve around the SEC regulations regarding restricted stock sale (see Chapter 17) or the sale of shares which demonstrates a lack of confidence in the enterprise. Yet so often company principals have not made any effort to sell stock within the restrictive SEC provisions, nor have they made any effort to go against the conventional lack-of-confidence argument of Wall Street. Perhaps a prime rationalization for not selling a significant part of their holdings is a basic reluctance to pay the large amount of federal and state taxes. But whatever the reason, failure to sell can be disastrous because of an across-the-board drop in price/earnings multiples with whole categories of stocks becoming unattractive to investors.

The writer was through the heady, hectic days of the high-multiple rationalization by Wall Street and then the change in attitude in the last decade or so. He found it amusing to hear the same investment bankers now talk soberly about the necessity of solid balance sheets and return on investments. The recent bad old days of single-minded emphasis on earnings per share no longer existed. At least not for awhile.

A Different Kind of a Game

Wall Street had thoroughly enjoyed the golden years and their emphasis on high price/earnings multiples, but it readily adjusted to the new emphasis on balance-sheet criteria. However, the securities firms were not enjoying the increasing presence of a tremendous force in the financial markets. The institutional investors were making more and more volume trades and were complaining bitterly about the Street's fixed schedule of brokerage commissions.

These complaints were being heard loud and clear by the SEC as the institutional investors moved into a dominant trading position in the stock market. The Commission eliminated fixed commission rates in 1975, triggered in good part by these complaints. While many dire predictions because of the unfixing of rates did not come to pass, the dislocations affecting securities concerns lasted a long time. Wall Street firms reluctantly adapted to the new environment by a substantial number of mergers, and the consolidated firms continueud to compete for the business of the institutional investors.

More painful from the underwriting viewpoint were an accelerated effective date for certain types of securities wherein the normal underwriting system was bypassed and then, in 1982, Rule 415 of Regulation C.

Rule 415 was issued by the SEC in early 1982, on a trial basis for 1300 of the largest public companies. The Commission will decide in late 1983 whether to extend and/or expand the coverage of the rule. The consensus appears to be that the rule, in one form or another, will be continued and probably expanded to include additional companies. The new rule has been very popular with the large issuing companies. Wall Street has not shared this enthusiasm.

The essence of Rule 415 is contained in the part of the regulation which states that "securities may be registered for an offering to be made on a continuous or delayed basis . . . and sold within two years from the initial effective date of the registration statement. . . ." All this means is that a kind of shelf registration is filed. At the filing company's pleasure, it dips into the market for a part or all of these registered securities at any time during the two-year period with no further SEC filings other than updated financial statements. The company can choose an opportune time to make the offering and auction-bid it to eager underwriters.

Whatever the pros and cons of Rule 415 in general, several factors should be recognized by entrepreneurs considering going public. One aspect is a little-recognized fact of financial life. Unbundling of services (whether it be telephone systems, computer companies, or whatever) means that some services in the unbundling will carry more cost burden than they did before. If underwritings continue to be unbundled as a result of Rule 415, initial public offerings could be more costly.

Much more important, the changes in the rules of the game since the mid-1970s have seriously weakened the smaller national and the regional investment bankers, both from underwriting participation and fee viewpoints. These are the firms who traditionally have done many of the initial public issues for concerns with less than $10 million sales in 1980 dollars. How permanently weakened remains to be seen. It is true that the securities community has displayed remarkable recuperative powers in the past.

New forces began showing up in Wall Street during the late 1970s and well into the 1980s. So financially powerful and varied in function were these newcomers that a 1982 study of the National Association of Security Dealers (NASD) indicated that a broad-scale and integrated industry was emerging (of which the traditional Wall Street activities would only be a part). The report suggested a new name—the financial services industry.

The NASD analysis covers the shrinking network of regional firms because of mergers and then discusses at length the impact of what it calls the new financial services conglomerates. These began with the acquisition by Prudential Insurance of Bache Halsey Stuart Shields, and the acquisition by American Express of Shearson Loeb Rhoades. The advent of the "specialty" firm, one which carves out a separate niche for itself, is also reviewed. One example is the discount concern, born because of the unfixing of commission rates by the SEC in 1975. The discount firm takes a position; it never acts as dealer. And finally there is the entry of the commercial banks and savings and loans into the securities community. For example, Security Pacific National Bank, based in Los Angeles, began offering its discount brokerage services in 1983 to financial institutions on a nationwide basis with its own stock-clearing operation in New York City.

The 1980s may be a different kind of a game, as the NASD study suggests. However, Wall Street has always displayed an ability to adjust and adapt as well as recuperate. It seems reasonable to expect that this will be so in the brave new world of this decade. Some of the outlanders may learn this fact at their own expense.

Going Public and Investment Bankers

The financial planning prior to a going-public decision requires the input of a top-flight investment banker at the national or regional level. Advice on institutional investors is an example. Over any immediate period of time, institutional buying and selling can represent 65% to 70% of the market transactions. And this market action means movement of substantial blocks of stock (see Chapter 11). Issue planning must recognize these major forces and attempt to balance them off as best it can.

Much of successful business life is made up of a few grand misses that are closely coupled with game wins by inches. Of course the current wisdom of Wall Street can be fallible and often is. Still, the investment banking firms have been in business a long time. They know the probability risks of alternative courses of fund raising. And they are the folk that live with and make the incredible stock market along with the game rules of going public.

10

Acceptance of Wall Street Criteria

If the entrepreneurs are willing to accept the basic vagaries of Wall Street, they are ready to review the timing and structure of initial public offerings and where the offerings are traded. These considerations, along with the selling and aftermarket support mechanisms of initial issues (as discussed in Chapter 11), will be the determining factors in the decisions of the entrepreneurs to take their companies public.

Analysis of Initial Offering Patterns

Investment interest in initial public offerings is cyclical and difficult to predict. Table 10.1 shows the number of issues and total share values during the 1970s. The peak was 646 in 1972—yet only three years later the annual number was at a decade low of 25. It was not until 1979 that there was a marked revival and the increased activity which continued into the early 1980s.

For many Wall Street purposes, only initial public issues above a certain size and price per share are tracked in detail. In the early 1980s

TABLE 10.1 Initial Public Offerings

Year	Number of Issues	Share Value (in millions)
1979	144	$ 592
1978	64	248
1977	49	276
1976	45	271
1975	25	236
1974	55	117
1973	177	1,872
1972	646	3,301
1971	446	1,917
1970	566	1,451

Source: Initial Public Offering Overview, © 1980, Shearson/American Express Inc.

that minimum issue size and initial offering price per share was $1 million and $5 respectively. Both of these criteria would be met by the bulk of enterprises with $5 million in annual sales, the minimum company size with which this book is concerned.

Of the 144 offerings in 1979, 45 had a share value of $1 million or more and a minimum $5 offering price as shown in Table 10.2. The same table summarizes the dramatic increase in the number of these kind of issues in the following two years and analyzes the investment value of the issues as of September 30, 1981.

The investment value analysis of Table 10.2 presumes a $1000 purchase of each new public offering over a three-year period beginning October 1, 1979. Then the value of each purchase is computed as of September 30, 1982, and summarized as a consolidated gain or loss percentage. The table shows a total of 302 new issues during the three-year period with an aggregate increase of 22.9%, not up to the inflation rate of the time interval.

As an exercise, it is interesting to make a computation excluding the 169 new issues included in the 1981 time frame in Table 10.2. The exclusion argument runs, however specious, that the large number of new issues (an average of 19 a month) included a good many of lower quality which had maximum pricing at issuance and thus could only hold down the appreciation average. At any event, the aggregate in-

TABLE 10.2 Investment Value of Shares of Selected Companies[a]**—$1000 Investment in Each New Initial Issue**

Issue Year	Initial Value	$1000 Investment in Each New Initial Issue 9/30/81 Value	Percent Change
1978 (8 issues)[b]			
Increased (6)		$ 23,316	+ 288.6%
Decreased (2)		880	− 56.0%
	$ 8,000	$ 24,196	+ 202.4%
1979 (45 issues)			
Increased (28)		$ 57,124	+ 104.0%
Decreased (17)		11,881	− 30.1%
	$ 45,000	$ 69,005	+ 53.3%
1980 (80 issues)			
Increased (35)		$ 94,929	+ 171.2%
Decreased (43)		31,134	− 27.6%
No change (2)		2,000	0%
	$ 80,000	$128,064	+ 60.1%
1981 (169 issues)[b]			
Increased (34)		$ 57,102	+ 67.9%
Decreased (131)		88,838	− 32.2%
No change (4)		4,000	0%
	$169,000	$149,940	− 11.3%
Total (302 issues)			
Increased (103)		$232,472	+ 135.7%
Decreased (193)		132,733	− 31.2%
No change (6)		6,000	0%
	$302,000	$371,205	+ 22.9%

Source: Excerpts from Vol. 5, No. 4 (p. 14), *The Initial Public Offering Market*, © 1981, Shearson/American Express Inc.

(a) Excludes companies (i) for which the issue size was less than $1,000,000, (ii) for which the initial offering price per share was less than $5.00, (iii) for which current price and/or earnings information is not readily available, (iv) which were subsequently acquired by other companies, (v) which were essentially start-up operations, or (vi) for which the offering was not underwritten.

(b) Includes only offerings made in the last calendar quarter of 1978 and the first three quarters of 1981.

crease in value of the remaining 133 issues would be 67.1%. This is much more what entrepreneurs like to hear when they are considering the intricacies of a public offering.

Components of a Public Offering Package

The three principal components of an initial issue package are the dollar size, the initial share price, and the number of shares. In the structuring of a first issue, these key elements are intimately related, too much so at times from the entrepreneur's viewpoint.

The kind and extent of stock distribution will influence the technical decision as to the dollar size of the offering. If the company and its investment banker in the early 1980s expected to attract national investment interest, syndication, and aftermarket support, the minimum initial offering size would have been around $5 million. A strong regional issue would have been in the $1 million to $5 million bracket. A first public offering much below $1 million would have made the costs of an SEC registration statement and stock distribution so high that the public offering route would not have been worthwhile. Regulation D (discussed in Chapter 8) of the SEC became effective in 1982 and provided an alternative plan for the small securities issue.

Other than the technical requirements of stock distribution, the dollar size of the offering depends upon the company's (and shareholders', if applicable) requirements. However, these must be tailored to the total amount that the managing underwriter believes can be sold at a reasonable price. The enterprise's cash needs can run the gamut from a requirement for every dollar that is sold to the unusual situation where the business has little or no operating requirements for additional cash. This writer has been at both extremes in his initial public issues. In his last offering, the company only took down 10% of the issue while the other 90% was composed of selling shareholders.

Most of the time the investment banking firm, serving as a managing underwriter, can be expected to take a strong negative position with the entrepreneur on shareholders selling stock in the proposed offering. The underwriting manager's attitude is simply that prospective investors view shareholder sale as a lack of confidence in the company's future or, as Wall Street more bluntly calls such sale, a bailout.

It follows that the idea of a bailout makes the assemblage of a successful selling syndicate difficult.

Another objection to including selling shareholders in an initial offering relates to the price negotiation between the managing underwriter and the company/selling shareholders. The people selling stock naturally want as high a price as possible. The company itself, thinking of the aftermarket, might settle for a lower price and a more salable issue. After all, if the shares of the new issue go up from a conservative pricing base, wisdom would indicate that a substantial secondary issue of selling shareholders could be done six months or a year later at a considerably higher price than the initial offering.

Admittedly, the arguments against inclusion of selling shareholders in a first offering can be powerful, but often not as much as the advocates routinely present. Take the idea of having a secondary issue of selling shareholders at a substantially higher price from the offering. It is both sensible and attractive *if* the price per share of the stock increases substantially as hoped and *if* the expense inertia can be overcome to have a secondary issue. Neither is a casual *if*.

The marketing task of placing the issue is always easier if there is no shareholder selling. But if the new-issue market is reasonably strong and the track record of the enterprise is good, why exclude the idea of selling shareholders?

Each of the worlds we live in is not very predictable. After winning the hand wrestle with the underwriting manager on participation of selling shareholders, the entrepreneur may have a surprise.

The very principals who have been most vehement in their complaints about being locked in because of SEC regulations after a public issue may decide that they do not want to be selling shareholders in the planned offering. They now have rosy dreams of the aftermarket opportunities, and the complexities and dangers ahead are ignored. Not for the last time will the entrepreneur wonder about being in some kind of a dubious battle on a number of ill-defined fronts.

Related to the dollar size of any initial issue is the prospective offering price. And again technical market factors are a major consideration, assuming that a large part of the issue will be sold to individual investors. Wall Street of the early 1980s thought in terms of an offering price of $10 to $20 per share for a nationally distributed issue. Eighteen years earlier, when the writer did his first public issue, the preinflation price range was $5 to $10, with the price skewed toward the $5 number. Again in the 1980s framework, Wall Street judgment seemed to be that any price below $10 for a nationally distributed issue weakened the quality appeal both to the securities salespeople and the individual investors. Stock priced over $20 a share also had reduced selling appeal for a different reason. Typical individual investors preferred to make round-lot (100 shares) purchases, and many of them were reluctant to spend individually more than $2000 on an initial public offering.

Still using the early 1980s as a reference, offerings in the $5 to $10 range accounted for about one-third of all initial issues of $1 million or more. The dollar size of these offerings was generally under $5 million and the selling syndicate was largely composed of regional firms.

Directly related to the offering price range per share and the total dollar size of the issue is the selection of the total number of shares in the issue. Since no public shares have been traded previously, the initial offering must provide a minimum market liquidity—that is, the basis for systematic buying and selling of a reasonable number of shares. This can be of particular moment when there are block transactions of institutional investors. If a very high percentage of the outstanding stock remains closely held after a public issue, planning for market liquidity is even of more importance.

The $10 to $20 per share requirement of a nationally distributed issue could appear to conflict with market liquidity considerations. Suppose the dollar size of the issue had been set at $5 million, the managing underwriter may have an apparent dilemma. Normally, the underwriting manager would have been pressing toward a 500,000-share issue to meet the market liquidity standards. On the other hand, the reaction to the proposed issue was very good, and the price per share could easily be substantially higher than first believed. While this was a pleasant problem the underwriting manager enjoyed solving, the final solution definitely concerned the entrepreneur.

One approach to the apparent dilemma in the foregoing example was the sale in the offering of additional shares obtained by the selling syndicate by the exercise of its over-allotment option. More familiarly known as the "green shoe," the over-allotment option is always on the checklist of the investment banking firm who manages the proposed issue. If the option is exercised, such shares are sold by the selling syndicate at the initial offering price. Usually 10% of the number of shares to be offered, the green shoe presumably allows the issue to be marketed more aggressively because the selling syndicate knows that the exercised option can be used to cover any short positions. Without much pressure, the investment banking firm will also readily admit that it is pleasant to have a 10% option on a popular offering.

Underwriting Costs

The major cost of an initial public issue, as discussed in previous sections, consists of the underwriting discounts—the management fee, the underwriting fee, and the selling concession charge. These discounts (called the "gross spread") represent anywhere from 6% to 8% or more of the dollar amount of first issues, usually at the upper end of the range. In this writer's three initial issues, extending from the 1960s to the 1980s, the gross spreads were 8.0%, 7.8%, and 7.5%, respectively.

Other than a relatively narrow negotiation range, the gross-spread percentage reflects immediate past offerings of similar size and types of business plus an estimate of the difficulty of selling the proposed issue. An agreement as to the approximate percentage is reached between the principals before the decision to go public is made. The final gross-spread percentage is not negotiated until the afternoon before the offering date.

Price/Earnings Multiple or Ratio

The common denominator of stock measurement is the price/earnings (P/E) multiple or ratio. Serving as the prime standard in stock market performance or comparison, it is utilized for both current and historical analyses. The foundation of the multiple is the fully diluted earnings per share for the selected 12-month period such as a trailing year period back from the date of the most recently published financial statements. Fully diluted earnings take into account such future events as shares awarded under a stock option plan or conversion of debentures.

The other part of the multiple is the market price (the bid side in the over-the-counter quotations). With fully diluted earnings and market price per share in hand, a price/earnings multiple computation can be made in a moment. Assume the last-published 12-month earnings of a business were $0.93 a share and the market price was $15, the price/earnings multiple would be 16.1 ($15 divided by $0.93). Thus the expression—the stock is selling at 16 times earnings.

A principal factor in determining the approximate price of an initial issue by the investment banking firm is the price/earnings multiples or ratios for similar publicly owned companies, whether based on past or perceived future earnings. This means concerns which may be in the same industry segment or otherwise comparable. The investment banking firm averages out the price/earnings multiples for perhaps a half dozen selected companies, and this average becomes a major pricing guide for the proposed offering.

In anticipation of the average price/earnings multiple approach for pricing initial issues, entrepreneurs would do well to be conversant about those enterprises with whom their own companies are going to be compared. If possible, being involved in the choices is highly desirable.

In one of the writer's initial public offerings, the company's competitors in his industry segment were divisions of very large and diversified corporations except for one family-owned concern. With no price/earnings multiples available which would be meaningful, the investment banking firm selected a number of companies engaged in completely different aspects of the broad industry grouping. When queried by the entrepreneur as to the selection, the reply was that the securities community and investors would follow exactly the same kind of logic in this arbitrary grouping. Subsequent events showed the analysis to be correct. Since the selected price/earnings ratios to be averaged were more than acceptable, the writer reacted amiably to the choice. But he also knew that this situation was only good fortune and could just as well have been the reverse.

While only a general conditioning factor in pricing the proximate issue, the investment banking firm and the entrepreneur also examine the price/earnings ratios for other offerings. Table 10.3 analyzes 282 first issues made over a three-year period (October 1978 through September 1981). It points out the revival of investor interest in first offerings, with resultant improved multiples and market activity in the securities.

TABLE 10.3 Price/Earnings Ratios at the Time of the Initial Offering[a][b]

P/E Ratios	Number of Companies
Under 7.0	16
7.0 – 9.9	20
10.0 – 15.9	69
16.0[c]	177
	282

Source: Excerpts from Vol. 5, No. 4 (p. 13), *The Initial Public Offering Market,* © 1981, Shearson/American Express Inc.

(a) Price/earnings ratios are based upon trailing 12-month, fully diluted earnings per share.

(b) Companies with unavailable earnings per share have been excluded as their price/earnings ratios are not meaningful.

(c) Includes the price/earnings ratios of companies with no or negative earnings.

The Over-the-Counter Market

First public offerings are generally traded over-the-counter (OTC), a marketplace in the early 1980s that was outpacing the two major exchanges in percentage growth. The OTC did not always have such a favorable reputation. The feeling of many corporations about that marketplace in earlier years could be summarized in a paraphrase of George Ade's wry comment about Indiana: "All smart companies come from the OTC, the smarter they are the faster they come."

The over-the-counter marketplace began to change in 1971 when the National Association of Security Dealers' Quotation Service (NASDAQ) was first placed in operation. NASDAQ was a computer-based system with terminals in brokerage houses under a subscription arrangement. Over the years NASDAQ had grown to the point in the early 1980s that it provided quotations on more than 3500 securities while the New York and American Stock Exchanges had listings of about 2200 and 1000 respectively. Beginning in 1980, NASDAQ furnished highest bids and lowest offers, and "last sale" trades were initiated on a pilot basis two years later as the start of a national market system for the OTC.

Both major exchanges utilize the auction-market approach as opposed to telecommunications of the OTC, with the trading activity taking place in one location. The important lubricating force under the auction concept is the "specialist" firm, which is responsible for a group of securities in the auction market. While performing the specialist function, the firm is under the continued surveillance of the exchange. Each of these specialists has the primary function of bringing the buyer and seller together. Only in the event of a buying and selling imbalance in a particular security does the specialist firm buy and sell for its own account. Such transactions are for the purpose of narrowing price changes between transactions and giving market depth to the particular security.

The NASDAQ system is different. Some 400 financial firms in 1981 carried inventories of OTC securities from which they sold or for which they bought. These are the market makers and, while performing this function in the system's network, are registered with NASDAQ. But the market-making function for a particular security is performed for only as long as it pleases the particular financial firm. Under a combination of circumstances an OTC company can have the unpleasant experience of having the bulk of the market makers for its stock disappear.

However, OTC advocates would point out the high average number of market makers per security. In early 1981, for example, the 400-odd financial firms that made markets in NASDAQ securities "had approximately 24,000 market-making registrations in NASDAQ securities, or an average of eight market makers per security." Like many averages, the number quoted is not that meaningful because the market makers cluster around the securities where the immediate action is. With the laissez-faire policy of NASDAQ on this important function, the bid-ask spread can be too wide on lower-volume, out-of-favor securities.

The qualification standards for first inclusion in the NASDAQ system have continued to be upgraded. Minimum requirements in the first part of the 1980s were $2 million in assets and $1 million in capital and surplus. The annual fee for membership ranged from $250 to a $2500 maximum.

During the same time period about 80 newspapers carried the NASDAQ National List of some 1800 companies either daily or weekly. The *Wall Street Journal* also carried the NASDAQ Additional List of another 1000 enterprises. Based on an important semiannual ranking, to be on the National List all securities having two or more market makers also had to meet one of the two sets of criteria as shown in Table 10.4.

The Additional List during the same period was based on those other OTC companies that had the highest dollar value of average weekly volume. Also local and regional newspapers listings were set up through a country-wide network of quotation committees.

With a good deal of fanfare, last-sale trade reporting was begun in 1982 by NASDAQ on a careful shakedown basis. Called the National Market System, its eventual impact on any grand scale remains to be seen. This would be nothing less than a master national plan that would incorporate the OTC, the two national exchanges, and the Fourth Market of institutional investors.

The Fourth Market and the Exchanges

What the financial media likes to call the Fourth Market has become a force in the securities community in recent years because of the in-

TABLE 10.4 Alternative Sets of Criteria for National List Inclusion

Alternative No. 1	Alternative No. 2
1. Publicly held shares of 350,000	1. Publicly held shares of 800,000
2. Market value of publicly held shares of $2 million	2. Market value of publicly held shares of $8 million
3. Minimum bid price of $3	3. Net worth of $8 million
4. Annual net income of $300,000 in the previous fiscal year or in two of the last three fiscal years	4. Incorporated for four years

Source: NASDAQ letter of October 7, 1981, to NASDAQ companies

creasing importance of the institutional investor. A considerable number of pension and mutual funds, bank trust operations and the like are linked together with a system where "buys" and "sells" are made by each member. Thus broker intermediaries are eliminated whether it be NASDAQ or one of the auction-market exchanges.

Both the New York and American Stock Exchanges have been concerned about the Fourth Market but, much more important, with the strength of the NASDAQ system owned by the NASD. In the early 1980s the NASD believed that there were approximately 1650 NASDAQ companies that met the qualifications for listing on the New York and/or American Stock Exchanges, and that up to one-third of those companies met the requirements of the New York Stock Exchange. These two numbers undoubtedly are considered high by the two national exchanges. But agreement on even approximate totals is not that important. For one thing is very clear. There has been no rush by eligible companies to leave the OTC.

Of more immediate interest, even the most avid protagonist of the exchanges would agree that the new OTC company will find the NASDAQ system a viable, growing thing.

Acceptance of Wall Street Criteria

The underlying rigidity in the numbers and measurement criteria of the typical packaging of an initial public offering may be difficult for some entrepreneurs to accept. If a closely held business is large enough or desirable enough, perhaps more flexibility can be obtained.

But for the vast majority of companies, it is either acceptance of these criteria, subject to sales and aftermarket requirements as discussed in the next chapter, or not going public at all.

11

The Decision to Go

Selling original issue stock to security investors is no more glamorous and just as time-consuming and expensive as in other sales fields. And the aftermarket support for the new issue has much in common with product field support problems that any manufacturer encounters. A fair understanding of both of these important mechanisms will affect the decision to go public.

Institutional Investors

Institutions (pension, trust, and investment funds, etc.) account for 60% or so of all purchases and sales of stock in the securities markets. For better or worse, with a new issue, their block holdings are far larger and their handling of these holdings are far different from those of the individual investor.

There was a time that a public company, several years after its initial offering, would point with pride to the number of institutions which held blocks of stock in the enterprise, as this was a sure sign of a successful and a newly seasoned concern. No longer. Now the institutions take a position in initial issues. An entrepreneur who has a first public offering of 600,000 to 1,200,000 shares and then discovers that a fair number of institutions have 30,000 to 50,000 blocks of shares of the corporation's stock has every reason to be disturbed.

Block buys and sells by institutions can force price action on the stock of a newly public company much like an old-time elevator in operation. The price of the stock will move jerkily up and down and, without warning, plummet to the bottom of the shaft in the subbasement where the stock bangs into the safety springs of bargain price support. This kind of performance frightens existing and potential shareholders who prefer to invest in an orderly market environment.

The institutions discovered IBM in the mid-1950s. As the big computer house prospered, the money managers climbed on that blue-chip train and had a happy hour for 15 years. Then the IBM stock price flattened out and actually declined a bit, and in 1980 the stock was selling for about 10% less than it was a decade or so earlier. With onrushing inflation, institutions clearly had to find other vehicles. One candidate, previously discarded out of hand because of risk, was initial public offerings.

Emergence of high-technology enterprises by the early 1960s educated a good part of the investment community to the growth possibilities in a whole range of new industries. IBM had been an early and easy investment choice; it was well-seasoned and demonstrably king of the hill in its chosen field. But what about all of the rest of these new companies, so many with outlandish names . . . Xerox, Polaroid, and a conglomerate named Litton, plus burgeoning newcomers like Texas Instruments, Fairchild Semiconductor, and a young corporation called Digital Equipment. The institutional investor bought the stocks of these youthful businesses and thoroughly enjoyed the rapid stock appreciation. Then it was only one additional step to buy into an initial public offering, and the freshly hatched enterprise discovered that large blocks of its new stock were owned by the most important and dangerous stockholders a fledgling public company could have.

For the first public issue, the institutional investors are important because they can easily swallow up most of an initial issue in which they are interested, and dangerous because of their large block buys and sells. Many an institutional portfolio manager feels there must be quick reaction to news of an economic downturn and change the portfolio posture accordingly. But unfortunately institutional market thinking at times resembles a line of elephants holding on to each others' tails as they play "follow the leader" and sell out whole categories of stock. This can only exacerbate share price movements for the enterprises involved.

Another cause of stock price change is the quarterly portfolio adjustments of institutions. Part of the unwritten job description of any portfolio manager is the requirement to assemble the most favorable quarterly presentation of the portfolio, both from technical appearance and performance results. Oftentimes what appears to be an institutional selling aberration is quarterly cosmetic work on the portfolio.

Heavy block selling of a new stock with its relatively low trading volume or "thin market" can ruin price stability. No wonder, then, that the individual investors are courted by the managing underwriter in the planning of an original public offering.

The Individual Investors

Those rare birds, the dedicated individual investors, have survived general stock averages that have changed only modestly during the last 15 years while the investors themselves have been swamped in the recent past with double-digit inflation. So many of their brethren have left the stock market over the years, with the last exodus triggered by the high interest rates of the early 1980s. And why not? They could buy 10% to 14% Treasury Bills with the interest exempted from state income taxes. Yet even these brethren who have deserted the general stock market still keep a peripheral eye on first public offerings and add to the individual investor potential for these issues.

Whether inside or outside the pale of involvement in the general stock market, the individual investors like to speculate on initial public offerings. They are more than willing to accept the payoff potential over the evident risks no matter how emphasized in the preliminary prospectus or covered in statistical analyses. Always gilded with rationale, specualtion has a perennial appeal to most of us.

The underwriting manager of a new issue knows that once individual investors move out of a stock they seldom go back to it. Even so, their participation in the initial offering is eagerly sought by the underwriter. Wall Street has learned that, in contrast to institutions, this type of an investor does not sell en masse on the first news of an economic turn, nor does he tailor the stock portfolio quarterly. While technical opinions vary among underwriters, there is a fair consensus that an investor share mix of about 60% individual and 40% institutional is optimum.

A private enterprise generally established its roots in a particular locale and then has expanded its sales and often the operations to a regional if not nationwide basis. When the distribution of the first stock issue to the individual investor is discussed, a high marketing priority would appear to be a sales concentration in the locality where the concern established itself. On the contrary, underwriters discourage this practice but seek instead the broadest area of distribution possible. They believe that geographical concentration tends to limit the aftermarket support to a narrow base. Also, operating problems the enterprise may encounter, such as air and water pollution, can have much more of an impact on the share price if the stock is held locally.

Reserved Stock for Associates

At the best, any policy followed on reserved stock for employees, customers, and vendors will be unsatisfactory. As the selling syndicate in a very hot to warm initial issue can easily have all of the planned stock offering spoken for, little or none would be available for the enterprise's associates at the public offering. Thus a situation would be created where the people who built and supported the business have next to nothing, while outlanders presumably profit from an immediate stock rise after go-off. Superficially, it could be said that no chief executive should allow this to happen. But the situation is more complex than that.

Reserving blocks of stock for business associates at public issue time has one overriding defect. Despite the best planning by the company and the underwriter, untoward events can seriously depress the price of the stock in the aftermarket. Management will certainly find it a headache in trying to explain the vagaries of stock prices to a valued employee who has bought reserved stock with borrowed money.

In one instance where this writer was the entrepreneur, he allowed the enthusiasm for reserved stock purchases by all employee levels as well as customers and vendors to get out of hand. Even when some kind of reason finally prevailed, 11% of the nationwide distribution was reserved stock. The reserved block size was material enough that a prospectus paragraph dealt with the subject. The associates who held on to their stock ultimately did very well indeed. However, the price of the stock declined more than 50% during what the industry at the time termed the "gold flake flap." This began only about eight months after the initial offering. The company management most emphatically did not need the burden of upset associates in addition to the pressing business problems of the period.

About the only conclusion (however unsatisfactory) is that reserved stock for associates is probably a necessity in a popular issue. But exceeding some minimum amount is very debatable.

The Managing Underwriter and the Selling Syndicate

In the majority of instances the investment banking firm of the company will serve as managing underwriter for the first offering. Often, however, it may be advantageous to have a co-manager. For example, in the early 1980s, either the San Francisco firm of Hambrecht & Quist or L. F. Rothschild, Unterberg, Towbin of New York were invited to be co-managers on a number of high-technology issues. Both had developed a following of institutional and individual investors because of their knowledge of certain fields (semiconductors, for example).

The managing underwriter expects to sell some 20% to 30% of the offering, plus its proportional share of the over-allotment stock. The remainder will be sold through a syndicate which it will organize. A nationwide distribution may have a selling syndicate composed of 40 to 60 firms similar to those shown in Figure 11.1. The elements of such a syndicate would be most of the major-bracket firms, certain of the more powerful regional houses and a selected number of smaller firms with whom the underwriting manager has had a continued relationship. The selling syndicate of a regional offering would be similar in structure but tailored to the narrower requirements of the size or type of offering.

If the individual investor is the prime sales target, the retail distribution capabilities of the underwriting manager and syndicate mem-

Initial Public Offering
Illustrative Nationwide Syndication List

The First Boston Corporation
Blyth Eastman Paine Webber Incorporated
Dillon Read & Co., Inc.
Donaldson, Lufkin & Jenrette Securities Corp.
Drexel Burnham Lambert Inc.
Goldman, Sachs & Co.
E. F. Hutton & Co. Inc.
Kidder Peabody & Co. Inc.
Lazard Freres & Co.
Lehman Brothers Kuhn Loeb Incorporated
Merrill Lynch, Pierce, Fenner & Smith Inc.
L. F. Rothschild, Unterberg, Towbin
Salomon Brothers
Shearson/American Express Inc.
Smith Barney, Harris Upham & Co. Inc.
Warburg Paribas Becker Inc.
Wertheim & Co., Inc.
Dean Witter Reynolds Inc.

Alex. Brown & Sons
F. Eberstadt & Co., Inc.
A. G. Edwards & Sons, Inc.
Moseley, Hallgarten, Estabrook & Weeden Inc.
New Court Securities Corp.
Oppenheimer & Co. Inc.
Thomson Mckinnon Securities Inc.
Tucker, Anthony & R. L. Day, Inc.
Underwood, Neuhaus & Co. Inc.

Advest, Inc.
Bacon, Whipple & Co.
Robert W. Baird & Co. Inc.
Bateman Eichler, Hill Richards Incorporated
William Blair & Co.

Blunt Ellis & Loewi Inc.
Butcher & Singer Inc.
J. C. Bradford & Co.
Bruns, Nordeman, Rea & Co.
Cazenove Incorporated
Dain, Bosworth Inc.
Eppler, Guerin & Turner, Inc.
Foster & Marshall Inc.
Gruntal & Co.
Hambrecht & Quist
J. J. B. Hilliard, W. L. Lyons Inc.
Interstate Securities Corp.
Janney Montgomery Scott Inc.
Johnson, Lane, Space, Smith & Co. Inc.
Ladenburg, Thalmann & Co. Inc.
McDonald & Company
Piper Jaffray & Hopwood Inc.
Prescott, Ball & Turben
Rauscher Pierce Refsnes, Inc.
Robertson Colman Stephens & Woodman
Robinson-Humphrey Co., Inc.
Rotan Mosle Inc.
Schroeder Wagg
Sutro & Co., Inc.
Wheat, First Securities Inc.

Anderson & Strudwick, Inc.
Cowen & Co.
First Albany Corp.
A. E. Masten & Co. Inc.
Moore & Schley, Cameron & Co.
John Muir & Co.
Neuberger & Berman
Parker/Hunter Inc.
Rodman & Renshaw, Inc.
R. Rowland & Co. Inc.
Schneider, Bernet & Hickman, Inc.
Burton J. Vincent, Chesley & Co.

Figure 11.1 *A Preliminary Syndicate List* (From Shearson/American Express Inc., 1980).

bers will be of importance to the entrepreneur. In the early 1980s, 10 Wall Street firms had some 1750 retail offices in the 50 states.

Selling the New Issue

A nationwide distribution means the alerting, if not motivating, of thousands of retail brokerage people, as well as providing systematic sales coverage with the institutions. If the timing is right and the stock market is not saturated with cynicism, the task is not too difficult. But gaining the attention of a blasé investment community when conditions are not optimal requires hard work in which the enterprise itself must be involved. Experienced underwriting managers always presume the selling task is going to be difficult—which means real effort by the concern going public.

Front-line participation by company management begins about two weeks before the preliminary prospectus or "red herring" is distributed by the syndicate members to the selling organizations. This is when the chief executive is briefed on and presumably approves the selling plans of managing underwriter. The briefing includes Wall Street's preliminary reaction to the proposed offering and the extent of sales work expected of company management in the immediate weeks ahead.

Even the most stolid entrepreneur begins to react to the underwriter's repeated samplings of the investment community's interest in the planned issue. The chief executive soon talks learnedly (the conversation carefully salted with Wall Street jargon) to the senior associates about the Street's temperature readings of the proposed offering, which may range from ice-cold to red-hot. The more the readings tend toward the colder end of the thermometer scale, the more company management understands the managing underwriter's pressure for scheduling additional "road-show" meetings—that is, the chief executive of the enterprise and the underwriting team would travel around the country after the preliminary prospectus was available and meet the securities fraternity.

The usual road-show meeting consists of a 30-minute or less presentation by the chief executive followed by a question-and-answer period. This typical format is followed at a luncheon for institutional analysts (where the seat partners will query the chief executive throughout the luncheon) and an afternoon meeting after the close of the market for the retail brokers of the selling syndicate. While the road show has a good deal in common with any coast-to-coast sales trip where the sales manager has scheduled the chief executive for every available hour, the meetings with the securities community require much more effort. Because of the total unfamiliarity with the thinking and drives of that community, many executives after the road-show procedure have a feeling that their business and its management are being trotted around in an unpleasant variation of a horse auction.

Part of the registration material filed with the SEC is the preliminary prospectus. This is the basic document for the heavy selling effort that goes on from the date of registration until the SEC declares the registration effective and the issue is offered to the public. The preliminary prospectus printing required by the underwriting manager is very large—often 25,000 and more in a nationwide distribution by the selling syndicate.

Depending upon the complexity of the registration data and the workload of the Commission, the SEC review period before the offering in the early 1980s was about a month for the typical issue. While a company is in this registration period, the SEC has specific restrictive regulations as to what the enterprise can say or have published about its affairs. The basic assumption of the Commission is that the registration data and its preliminary prospectus fairly represent the company at the time of the SEC filing. If material matters occur during the Commission review period, the registration data are expected to be modified and suitable disclosure made to the securities community.

Security lawyers when queried as to what a company may discuss or publicize during the registration review period reply about as follows: No forecasts of any kind not specifically included in the preliminary prospectus should be made, and no deviation from established past policy should be allowed in any written or verbal public statements. Presumptive registration violations are sitting ducks for the hired legal guns using 20/20 hindsight. The foregoing is of little solace to the chief executive who must spend hours talking for the record about the enterprise during the registration period. The only comment which has any value is that caution should bring the company home free; vision and expansiveness on future matters could put it in a dangerous lawsuit with little to show for the risk.

Despite the legal limitations on the company and the underwriters, the proposed issue must be sold. The preliminary prospectus as the primary sales tool is supplemented with the retail brokers by background industry data and conference sales calls by the syndicate team members. Individual followup and briefing are also underway with the selected institutional investors who are prime prospects for stock placement.

In most issues the sales reports to the underwriting manager indicate an undulating market interest that is hopefully on an upward trend line. This is the time when the chief executive will find out whether he must pack a bag and head out for yet another round of analyst and broker meetings. Somehow or other the time arrives for the registration to become effective and the public offering is made successfully. Now the fledgling public enterprise must worry about the price of its stock in the aftermarket.

Supporting the Stock in the Aftermarket

Much like a frail infant, the typical initial issue, immediately after the public offering and for the 18 months at least, needs wet-nursing and tender loving care plus regular consultations with the enterprise's investment banking firm. Most discouraging is the sight of a pristine new issue rapidly becoming just another of the several thousands of OTC stocks.

Mishandling of the first issue can show up in abrupt run ups and downs in price during the first few days after the offering. The result can cast a shadow over the issue's performance for months. Underpricing the issue significantly at go-off can cause the shares to rise rapidly from the offering price in the first few hours and days. This provides a ready-made situation for the in-and-out speculator with resultant excessive trading activity or turnover. A disorderly market can also come from placing the initial offering in "weak hands" rather than with investors who have some familiarity with the enterprise and intend to hold the stock. However, no planning can prevent aberrations either in the business of the company or the stock market itself that bring on a buy or sell spree in the new issue.

For whatever reasons, the experienced underwriting manager worries about runaway trading volumes in the first few days of the aftermarket. Human nature being what it is, one can be sure that very high volumes on the downside are considerably more burdensome than upside worries. The best defense against runaway trading volumes is the development of an underlying demand for the issue that will absorb a good bit of the pricing perturbations. But no matter how well the issue is handled, the early days after the offering can be treacherous. As shown in Table 11.1, under average circumstances share turnover in the first three-day period can be as high as 35% of the initial share offering. This tabulation covers 21 issues of at least $5 million in size at go-off with a price/earnings multiple of at least 10. All of these first offerings were traded over-the-counter (OTC), a vibrant and growing marketplace, as discussed in Chapter 10.

The securities community hates surprises and is frightened by the unknown. The first four or five months after an original offering can have both. Underwriting agreements usually contain 90-day prohibitions on stock sale by a selling shareholder or a company insider, such as a control person, director, or officer. Once the 90-day period is passed, stock sales by these shareholders, even under SEC regulations,

TABLE 11.1 Trading Activity of Initial Public Offerings During First Three Days of Trading

	Trading Volume and Volume as a Percent of Shares Offered[a]			
	Day 1	Day 2	Day 3	3 Day Total
High %	40.3%	31.3%	12.6%	66.3%
Low %	4.4%	2.6%	1.0%	9.2%
Average %	17.8%	11.0%	6.3%	35.1%
Average shares	116,500	72,400	41,500	230,400

Source: Aftermarket Support—Initial Public Offering Overview, © 1980 Shearson/American Express Inc.

(a) 1979 analysis of 21 issues of at least $5 million and with P/E multiples of at least 10.

Supporting the Stock in the Aftermarket

are watched with considerable concern. Wall Street fears a bailout or liquidation of holdings by knowledgeable people.

For the purpose of maintaining an orderly aftermarket, the SEC also has certain 90-day post-offering regulations, some of which relate to public statements by the enterprise. The fear of the unknown, to Wall Street, can equate to the possibility of unpleasant surprises that show up once the registration period blackout on company announcements and the 90-day post-offering restriction period have passed.

Unless the corporation's stock continues to be what the securities industry considers to be "interesting," the number of Street analysts' calls will drop sharply after the first few months, as new offerings or new fancies attract the analysts' attention. Around the same time the volume of daily transactions will fall off, along with the price/earnings multiples of the shares. The increasingly pessimistic entrepreneur can now envisage the company's stock eventually as Number 3402 in share turnover of the NASDAQ quotations (research has shown that the remaining stocks have practically no trading at all).

How to remain interesting to Wall Street is a puzzle to a young public company, as discussed in more detail in Chapter 19. Employing a capable financial public relations house is urged by some investment banking firms. Having a continued level of modest Wall Street exposure and being periodically discovered by a popular Wall Street analyst may be another. On this point the writer by chance picked up the Business Section of the Miami *Herald* to look up the NASDAQ quotation of his concern's stock. Just before leafing to the quotation section, a page headline caught his eye. There was his company's name and an accompanying story containing a strong buy recommendation by a popular institutional consultant. While he was delighted, this particular recommendation was news to the writer.

Of course the sure way to remain interesting to the securities community is to be lucky on two points: (1) have your business in a popular growth industry and (2) have it make a considerable amount of money on a consistent upward trend basis. For the most part, this is the stuff dreams are made of.

On a probability basis, many feel that the final evaluation of an original issue by the securities community is 18 months or so after go-off. By this time Wall Street understands how the company performs, the early round of unpleasant surprises has surfaced and been assimilated by the investors, and any industry turbulence in the period since go-off has come back to some kind of predictability. The foregoing is as good a definition as any of a newly seasoned stock seen through the eyes of the Street.

The Decision to Go

Assuming the vagaries of the stock market and the basic mechanisms of an initial stock issue are understood and accepted by the entrepreneur, an action decision depends upon cyclical timing. If that timing is right, the initial public offering of a growth company will sell at a healthy to rich price.

When the Wall Street fraternity begins to tell each other and clients that the investor attitudes toward growth enterprises in the company's general business sector are favorable and allows for aggressive pricing, the time for action has come. The entrepreneur should make the decision to go public. For now the Wall Street aphorism mentioned in Chapter 1 applies—"When the cookies are passed, take one, as they may not be passed again."

12

Prospectus Analysis

The company and the managing underwriter will have highly paid experts prepare the SEC registration statement prescribed for Form S-1 or Form S-18. Both are complex registration documents that are strewn with policy decisions which will be of concern to the entrepreneur.

In an effort to simplify somewhat the registration statement process for smaller public offerings, the SEC provides for the use of Form S-18 in the registration of securities where the aggregate offering price does not exceed $5 million. Otherwise, Form S-1 must be used. Since the more comprehensive data are required for Form S-1, this kind of registration statement will be analyzed in the next several chapters.

Either the chief executive or a principal associate must become intimately familiar with the anatomy of the prospectus, the principal element of the S-1 registration document. A company position draft (with all the numbers left out) should be prepared and reviewed with company counsel well ahead of the first drafting session of the registration task force.

Review of Other Prospectuses

The best materials for development of company working papers for the S-1 registration statement are the prospectuses of other companies which recently have had a first public issues. On request, the managing underwriter can readily provide a dozen or so of them representing public offerings during the past year or so. Preferably, the ones selected will be in the general sector of the enterprise's activities—industrial, distribution, etc.

Reading a prospectus (even one's own) should be considered as a certain cure for insomnia and careful review of a dozen or so of them on an intensive basis could be classified as cruel and unusual punishment. But not necessarily. An odd thing happens after meticulous reading of the first half dozen. A hazy albeit logical overview of the anatomy of the prospectus begins to emerge. The prospectus has evolved from regulations and judicial interpretation over many years. Buried inside the cant and cadence of the lawyers' and accountants' prose are a series of detailed and interrelated policy decisions which determine where and how data are to be shown in the prospectus.

Many detailed prospectus decisions should be made by the entrepreneur. But definitely not in the heat of discussion at task force meetings of the registration team. The best way to accomplish the job is to prepare a draft of the salient elements of a prospectus. The draft would include a preliminary decision on the cover of the booklet and the kind of illustrations, if any, that will be used.

Cover Format and Type of Paper

A representative sampling of current prospectuses shows a mix of the traditional 7½" × 9" page size as well as the newer 8½ × 11" size. Most prospectuses carry the company logo in color on both the front and back covers, along with the required SEC data, which with few exceptions are printed in black. The cover paper ranges from high gloss/medium weight to the conventional prospectus paper stock. The managing underwriter generally has definite views on the cover subject because the firm tends to follow a particular format to aid in marketing recognition of a new issue.

Product or process illustrations that may appear on the inside covers or pages of the prospectus represent a subject on which the underwriter and the entrepreneur may disagree. In recent years illustrations ranging from line or flow drawings to fold-out cover pages of photographs and artwork in full color have appeared in a number of prospectuses. The prime argument for the illustrations is their help in marketing the issue; the objection, other than additional cost, is a rather murky legal one. Prospectus language as to meaning and intent has been tested in courts during the past half century; prospectus illustrations have not. There is more legal risk in using them, and how much is any securities lawyer's guess. The decision rests with the entrepreneur.

Comments on the Prospectus Text

The table of contents of a typical prospectus is shown in Table 12.1 Comments on the principal subjects are contained in the appropriate indented side heads of this part of the chapter.

TABLE 12.1 Table of Contents of Typical Prospectus

	Page
Prospectus summary	2
Use of proceeds	4
Dividend policy	5
Capitalization	5
Dilution	5
Selected consolidated financial data	6
Management's discussion and analysis	7
Business	9
Management	15
Certain transactions	18
Principal shareholders	19
Selling shareholders	20
Description of common stock	20
Underwriting	21
Shares eligible for future sale	22
Legal opinions	23
Experts	23
Financial statements	24

Source: J. S. O'Flaherty

Prospectus Summary—the Company A brief description of the enterprise and its products is required. Generally 50 to 100 words in length, the statement will be used extensively by financial publications and stock analysts in categorizing and describing the company. Writing a satisfactory paragraph is more difficult than it first appears.

Use of Proceeds If the bulk of the funds realized from the public offering will be used to pay off existing debt, the section presents no problem in writing and raises few questions from the underwriters or the stock analysts. At the other extreme, if the bulk of the new money is simply an addition to working capital, careful prosepctus explanation will be required and questions from the securities community will be persistent.

Certain Factors This section is used only occasionally in SEC registrations. If continuing conditions of a significant or overriding nature exist, the registration task force may decide to spotlight them in a *Certain Factors* section. Thus one company's prospectus emphasized its heavy concentration of stock ownership after the public offering and the fact that the concern's sales were almost entirely to U.S. military agencies.

Consolidated Summary of Selected Financial Data Audited statements of income for at least five full operating years are prescribed by the SEC. In addition, to meet both SEC and underwriter requirements for fresh financials, an unaudited stub period covering the intervening months of financial results since the last year-end audited reports and the similar period of the preceding year, are included in the section along with the results for the full operating years.

To illustrate a typical stub requirement, a business having an April 30 fiscal year and planning an SEC registration in early October would undoubtedly have a current stub for the four months ended August 31 included in the *Consolidated Summary of Operations* section, along with the results for the comparable period a year earlier. While the stub period is technically unaudited, in fact the financial results are prepared under the close surveillance of the auditors. Their conservative posture is well known when they make their final financial examination of a company going public.

Business Drafting this long section of the registration statement is an unpleasant and time-consuming effort. Unpleasant because the entrepreneur and his associates finally realize the amount of specific information that the enterprise must disclose on a continuing basis. They know these data will be read with keen interest by their competitors, customers, and vendors. The sales manager will complain even more bitterly if the enterprise's principal competitors are divisions of large corporations that do not report division operating results and backlog separately while the company gratuitously makes these data available.

The drafting of the *Business* section is time-consuming. This is not so much due to the difficulty in assembling the material, but rather it is the individual detailed decisions that must be made regarding what facts are to be included and how they should be stated.

The basic requirement for full disclosure applies with equal force to all elements of the *Business* section. If questions of disclosure exist during the preparation of the company draft of the section, the data should be included with the amount of supplementary explanation required. Company counsel must make the decision as to the pertinence of the information for the SEC registration.

Patent matters illustrate the extent of the requirement for full disclosure. Take the routine practice of industry-wide mailings by a company holding a newly issued patent. The letter notice with a copy of the patent attached offers a license under the patent. The temptation of a company receiving such a packet is to ignore the existence of this kind of patent notice in preparing preliminary registration material. The rationalization is that there is either no active negotiation on the patent or no validity as far as the enterprise's products or processes are concerned. However, ignoring these notice letters in preparing an SEC registration without opinions of patent counsel is an unwise decision. Subsequent events may show applicability to the company's operations or products, and failure to disclose the potential risk could be painful.

Management Members of the board of directors are often classified as management, interested outside (affiliates or people doing business with the enterprise), and independent outside. As discussed in Chapter 16, the current practice is to have representation for all three categories on the board; and the managing underwriter is in favor of the practice from issue marketing considerations. For the private company preparing for a public offering this requirement can probably best be met with a seven-man board. At the same time the director membership can be restructured and the number and types of senior executive officers tailored to meet the public company image. Director selection and current practice of board compensation are also discussed in Chapter 16.

Directors and executive officers of a public company have been required by the SEC to provide an increasing amount of personal data for inclusion in the SEC registration and subsequent annual proxy statements. Indicative of the data required is a part of a director's questionaire shown in Figure 12.1. Completion of a full questionnaire may change a prospective director's decision to serve on the board.

Certain Transactions An experienced reader of prospectuses looks for the *Certain Transactions* section. Being able to omit this section from an SEC registration is considered a plus in the securities community. But if there is such a section—and most prospectuses have them—it contains past corporate financial transactions that require full and careful disclosure. Transactions that are candidates for inclusion receive the close scrutiny of the registration task force because of the SEC's and securities community's interest in these data. In writing the section, the object is to be as brief as possible. But a clear and careful presentation makes brevity difficult.

The *Certain Transactions* explanation required three prospectus pages in the writer's first public offering—far longer than a typical section. Part of the data dealt with Class A and Class B common stock shares that had recently been combined. Another short explanation was concerned with the commonality of ownership in another corporation. And the last part was an involved discussion of a partnership formed by certain shareholders that was subsequently purchased by the company. The initial public offering sold well, but the long explanation under the *Certain Transactions* section did not improve either the sale of shares or the writer's disposition as he answered questions from the securities community.

Comments on "Notes to Financial Statements" Financial footnotes represent a key aspect of the registration statement and the prospectus. Prior to note-drafting sessions between the company and its auditors

Portion of a Sample Directors' and Officers' Questionnaires
(detailed footnotes omitted)

EXAMPLE 1.
j. If you are a director or a nominee to become a director, are you now, or have you been in the two years preceding *(date)*, an officer, director, employee of, or do you now own, or have you owned in the two years preceding *(date)*, directly or indirectly, in excess of a 1% equity interest in any firm, corporation, or other business or professional entity:
   (1) Which has made payments to the Company or its subsidiaries for property or services during the Company's last full fiscal year in excess of $ *(amount)*;
   (2) Which proposes to make payments to the Company or its subsidiaries for property or services during the current fiscal year in excess of $ *(amount)*;
   (3) To which the Company or its subsidiaries was indebted at any time during the Company's last fiscal year in an aggregate amount in excess of $ *(amount)*;
   (4) To which the Company or its subsidiaries has made payments for property or services during such entity's last fiscal year in excess of 1% of such entity's gross revenues for its last full fiscal year; or
   (5) To which the Company or its subsidiaries proposes to make payments for property or services during such entity's current fiscal year in excess of 1% of such entity's consolidated gross revenues for its last full fiscal year?

EXAMPLE 7. In a series of interpretive releases beginning in August, 1977, the SEC has taken the position that certain non-monetary benefits to directors and officers (commonly referred to as "fringe benefits" or "perquisites") must be valued and included in the total remuneration disclosed in proxy statements. This question is designed to assist us in complying with that requirement.
a. During the period from *(date)* through *(date)*:
   (1) Did you or any member of your family use any property or assets of the Company, its parent or any subsidiary (e.g., Company cars or club memberships paid for by the Company) for personal (i.e., non-business-related) purposes?
   (2) Did the Company, its parent or any subsidiary pay or reimburse you or any member of your family for any personal expenses (e.g., personal purchases made with Company credit cards or included in unitemized expense accounts)?
   (3) Did employees on the professional staff of the Company, its parent or any subsidiary (e.g., legal or accounting personnel) provide you or any member of your family with personal, financial, accounting, legal, or other professional services?
   (4) Did any supplier, customer, or other party with whom the Company, its parent or any subsidiary does or intends to do business (including banks, attorneys, and accountants) provide you or any member of your family with any benefits (e.g., product discounts, free or reduced-rate services, or low-interest loans) because of any compensation or promise of compensation (whether oral or written, express or implied) by the Company, its parent or any subsidiary for doing so? The term "compensation" should be taken in its broadest sense, and would include such things as an express or implied promise by the Company to continue doing business or to do increased business with the party which provided the benefit.
   (5) Did you or any member of your family receive any other type of personal benefit directly or indirectly from the Company, its parent or any subsidiary for purposes unrelated to job performance?

EXAMPLE 11. Please describe any remuneration paid to you by a third-party under an arrangement between such third-party and the Company, its parent or any subsidiary.

Figure 12.1 A sample directors' and officers' questionnaire—1983 (From Ticor Print Newwork).

the entrepeneur and his senior representative on the registration task force should consider reviewing the pattern of these notes in a number of prospectuses, particularly the notes' relationship to related discussions in the *Business* section.

Summary of Significant Policies Perhaps the most important item in this section is the inventory statement. While the financial note is always routine, inventory valuation at the time of SEC registration, in hindsight judgment, can be susceptible to successful shareholder litigation. If the company mangement has caveats on facets of the inventory subject, they should be discussed in the *Business* section after review with the auditors and company counsel.

Auditors quite properly are interested in adequate reserves whether they be for accounts receivable or for special purposes. And auditors' interest in such matters for a privately held company tends to reach a peak during the financial review period immediately prior to SEC registration. Many an entrepreneur has discovered that the corporation's earnings per share for the stub period are lower than anticipated as a result of the establishment of expanded or additional reserves. Such unpleasant surprises can be avoided by management review of the reserve subject with the accountants well in advance of the final decision to go public.

If the company has a domestic international sales corporation ("DISC"), management in conjunction with the auditors may wish to provide for the taxes on the portion of the DISC income not currently taxable. Wall Street analysts consider that the handling of the DISC item in this manner is an indication of conservative company accounting practices.

Business Segment Data The entrepreneur should consider the advisability of including several kinds of registration material in this footnote to the financial statements rather than in the *Business* section of the registration statement. The required percentage breakdown by business segment can appear here, usually with the statement that the company is engaged in one business segment.

In addition, the analysis of foreign sales in dollars by geographical area for the last three-year period may be included in the footnote. The georgraphical areas, if any, which exceeded 10% or more of the enterprise's sales are reported in total dollars.

Under any circumstances, the company can be assured that the *Business Segment Data* note will be required reading for its competitors as well as the stock analysts.

Summing Up

The entire prospectus, and the *Business* section in particular, is strewn with detailed decisions of concern to the entrepreneur. Intimate familiarity with the anatomy of this complex registration document by the chief executive or a principal associate is strongly recommended.

Part Three

The Going Public Process and the Aftermarket

13

Arrangements for the Offering— A Composite Example

Once the determination to go public has been made, the size of the proposed offering must be settled. In addition to stock market conditions, the size is influenced by company cash requirements and the entrepreneur's decision as to shareholder participation in the offering.

Other than the public issue size, the questions are when and how will the offering take place. The "when" rests with the managing underwriter. Events usually govern the "how." One thing is certain—the company will be pleased that careful prospectus homework has been done as the registration task force begins its work.

The illustrative Ever Onward Corporation is used in this and several following chapters to show the intricate steps leading to a successful public issue. Ever Onward represents a composite of three initial public offerings in which the writer was the entrepreneur.

Size of the Offering

The chief executive officer has minimum difficulty in arriving at the size of the proposed offering. Ever Onward could pay off its bank indebtedness and still have ample cash for working capital if the offering was a minimum of $6 million.

However, the managing underwriter believes a $10 to $12 million offering could be done on a nationwide basis with a very satisfactory 14 to 16 price/earnings multiple. Assuming an initial issue price in the $15 range, the number of shares offered would be a rounded 750,000. The underwriting manager also expects to sell the 10% over-allotment (to which the entrepreneur had agreed) on the same basis. With these favorable reports, the chief executive first gives serious consideration to allowing stockholders to participate in the offering package of approximately $11.3 million with $5 million allocated to selling shareholders on a pro rata basis. If the over-allotment is exercised by the selling syndicate as expected, the offering would be $12.4 million with a company portion of $7.4 million including the over-allotment proceeds.

Initial Due Diligence Request for Documents

The first due diligence (or "exercise of reasonable care") request for documents from the underwriters counsel is the early and sure sign of the start of registration work. As a Wall Street firm is the managing underwriter, the investment banking people have employed a New York law firm that is a veteran in public offering engagements and in the protection of the client group of underwriters. Ever Onward never forgets where the loyalties and interest of underwriters counsel must lie. Depending uupon the size and complexity of the proposed offering, a partner and one or more associates is assigned to the project by the law firm.

Wall Street counsel wants a great many authenticated document copies in its first due diligence request as part of the managing underwriter's responsibility to exercise reasonable care in the regulation statement process. The principal documents required from Ever Onward are shown in Table 13.1 Item No. 14 in the table is most important to the chief executive officer—"Anything else management thinks appropriate or material."

Is It Material?

One word that the entrepreneur becomes worried about and weary of hearing is "materiality" as the registration task force work progresses. The problem does not lie with the basic definition. This is simply a substantive matter relating to the affairs of the enterprise which must

TABLE 13.1 Typical Document Request for Initial Due Diligence Work from Underwriter Counsel

<table>
<tr><td colspan="2" align="center">Ever Onward Corporation
Initial Due Diligence Document Request</td></tr>
</table>

Copies of:
1. Articles of incorporation (and all amendments) for company and its subsidiaries.
2. By-laws for company and its subsidiaries.
3. Annual reports to shareholders for five previous years.
4. Annual meeting proxy statements and proxies for five previous years.
5. Management letters from auditors for five previous years.
6. Company counsel letters to auditors for five previous years.
7. Form of distributor and sales representative agreements.
8. Listing by name, date, and duration of all distributor and sales representative agreements, including a brief statement of the manner in which any differs from the basic form.
9. Form of sales agreements, terms of sale, and similar documents.
10. All stock option plans and related documents.
11. Any relevant rulings, opinions, etc. regarding the domestic international sales corporation ("DISC").
12. Any employment contracts.
13. Listing of other contracts which are material by name, date, principal terms, etc.
14. Anything else management thinks appropriate.

Access to:
1. Minute books of company and subsidiaries.
2. Terms of short-term financing.
3. Copies of debentures and related indenture agreements if any.
4. Records of other long-term debt if any.
5. Leases.
6. All contracts which are material.
7. Patents and licenses.
8. All selling literature and promotional material used during the last five years.
9. Anything else management thinks appropriate.

Source: J. S. O'Flaherty

be disclosed in the prospectus as part of the registration statement. Regrettably, in practice, the determination of what is material is often a matter of judgment and interpretation over a period of time.

One arbitrary delineation of what constitutes a material fact or event has been made by the accounting profession with its use of the 10% rule for certain financial totals. For example, if sales to a single customer represent 10% or more of the total sales of the company during any of the past three fiscal years, this fact is disclosed in the registration statement.

However, the entrepreneur soon discovers that simplistic devices like the 10% rule have definite limitations in the determination of materiality. Too often a particular subject when related to time cannot be neatly cataloged. The evaluation of business decisions of yesterday as those decisions impact the affairs of tomorrow and the more distant future is difficult at the best. But such an assessment must be made by the chief executive in order to make current value judgments on specific matters such as a patent or a new product in the prospectus presentation. Questions of a material fact or event are raised by this evaluation. If company counsel determines a question to be material, it is covered in the prospectus with necessary explanations and caveats.

The Managing Underwriter and Its Principal

For the proposed offering of Ever Onward, an underwriting principal of the managing underwriter serves as the powerful interface with the company, prospective underwriters, and the rest of the financial community (particularly institutions). As a rule, the principal's role is not an easy one. Other than the assortment of problems connected with the company client, the principal must handle a group of active egotists in the securities fraternity while fashioning a successful offering in spite of the vagaries of the stock market.

The best principals find themselves spread very thin in a favorable market for new issues. As would be expected, this is the time that the entrepreneur has made the determination to go public. The decision still must be made as to whether the proven but overextended principal be used by the company. In the writer's opinion, the answer is definitely yes. The quality of the detailed work will be adequate or can be buttressed, while the principal's experience with the financial community in fashioning a successful offering can be critical.

With the size of the proposed issue of Ever Onward and the extent of the marketing effort, the underwriter's principal uses one or two associates from the corporation finance department of the managing underwriter. Because of the geographical spread of clients, the work of the underwriting principal requires a great deal of travel.

The Company and Its Specialists

The chief executive officer is directly involved in the work of the registration task force. But he or she has a senior associate (such as the financial vice president) who serves as a representative at all the general drafting meetings of the task force and as the company contact point for individual queries. The use of the senior associate in this manner not only has the advantage of centralizing information requests but also provides a convenient buffer for the entrepreneur.

The transition to a public company means an additional workload for the enterprise. There is an evident need for a person to handle routine shareholder relations, mailing list queries, and the scheduling and control of required outside reports. This person (who has been appointed assistant secretary) attends task force drafting sessions and works under the senior associate's direction in the establishment of the company contact point for going-public matters.

Related to the registration effort is the decision as to how the corporate secretary's function will be performed. Some concerns prefer to continue to have the office filled by the outside company counsel who will also attend the board meetings in that capacity. Under this arrangement, some of the normal secretary's work, such as routine shareholders' relations, are performed by the corporation, with the remainder handled by company counsel. However, because of the extent of additional tasks to be accomplished as a public company, Ever Onward decides not to use company counsel on these matters. Instead the office is integrated into the enterprise with outside counsel called in for advice as required.

As a key element of the registration task force, company counsel has the formal responsibility of providing legal opinions for the registration statement and the applicable section of the underwriting agreement. But equally important, company counsel serves the enterprise and the chief executive officer as the wise and experienced reference point and sounding board for legal and quasi-legal matters during the public offering process. Depending upon the size and complexity of the SEC registration, the company counsel team consists of a law firm partner and one or more associates.

The bases of the Form S-1 registration are the financial statements and associated notes. They are drafted by the public accounting firm that is serving as the auditors for the company. In addition, the managing underwriter, through underwriters counsel, may have the auditors verify additional facts in the S-1 draft. As the auditors are carrying the major load in the registration effort, they are the key factors in meeting time dates in the optimistic master schedule. The underwriting manager who senses a favorable stock market is pressing for work completion.

On the other hand, the accounting profession has been bludgeoned in recent years by shareholder lawsuits. The result is that the profession is even more cautious, and additional cross-checks of the auditors' registration working papers have been established by the accounting firm.

The underwriter manager and counsel push the audit partner and his associate for interim signoffs; the auditors resist the pressure. The result is a buildup of tension and poor jokes. Somehow the work does get done, and the final time schedule date is met.

The financial printer (who also prepares the engraved stock certificate forms) is an unsolicited member of the registration task force as far as the company is concerned. While in theory the printing house is hired by the enterprise, in fact the selection is made by company counsel with the concurrence of the underwriter principal and his lawyers. Not surprisingly, the financial printer is scarcely the neighborhood printer who provides business cards on a cut-rate basis.

In fairness, the choice of a financial printer is limited—at least by the criteria of the legal and underwriter members of the task force. For registration printed proofs after word-processor drafts they require seemingly instantaneous printer turnaround day and night along with accelerated deliveries of the printed material. The managing underwriter may want 25,000 copies or more of both the preliminary and final prospectus. These must be widely and promptly distributed to the retail offices of the underwriting syndicate. As a result, the financial printing and associated mailing costs are very high.

But heaven help the Wall Street reputation of a company counsel who does not provide this kind of printing reaction time, irrespective of expense. While denying it heatedly, the enterprise's lawyers do enjoy the casual power of having a skilled printing organization with specialized facilities at their beck and call. The entrepreneur would too if the many thousands of dollars paid the financial printer were not coming out of new capital for the company and the principal of the selling shareholders.

Present practice is to combine the transfer agent and registrar functions for a smaller public company, and this is the decision of Ever Onward. The company places the transfer agent work with the corporate trust department of its commercial banker. As discussed in Chapter 18, the bank's function is to receive and issue the enterprise's stock under appropriate controls, prepare periodic share transaction lists, and maintain a current file of shareholders. The last is a regular source of address labels for company mailings.

Because of computer programming requirements of the transfer agent, legal matters such as legending of stock, and availability of appropriate new stock certificates, company counsel keeps the transfer agent abreast of public offering developments. A delay in closing an offering involving millions of dollars, merely because of avoidable technical errors, is an event not appreciated by anyone.

Preparatory Work of the Task Force

The principal of the managing underwriter had prepared a time plan for the steps leading up to the public offering. Always a tight schedule, grudging agreement is received from task force members who must do a great deal of work in the time provided.

The first formal meeting of the registration task force for the Ever Onward Corporation is scheduled for September 5 and 6 in the concern's home city (see Table 13.2). But extensive work by some task force members has begun by mid-August. Preliminary drafting of individual sections of the prospectus portion of the registration statement is

Table 13.2 Typical Preliminary Time Schedule for Offering Prepared by Underwriter

Ever Onward Corporation—Initial Public Offering
Preliminary Time Schedule for Offering
A Composite Example

Participants

Ever Onward Corporation	EOC
Company Counsel	CC
Managing Underwriter	MU
Underwriters Counsel	UC
Auditors	A
Financial Printer and Bank Note Co.	FP
Transfer Agent/Registrar	TA

Date	Activity	Responsible Party
Aug. 15	Initial due diligence documents to underwriters counsel	EOC, UC
Sept. 5–6	(a) General organization of the task force	EOC, MU
	(b) Drafting and due diligence with underwriter, company, and lawyers	CC, UC
Sept. 13	(a) Receipt of first printed proof or word-processor draft	EOC, MU, CC, UC, A, FP
Sept. 17–18	(a) Underwriters counsel delivers draft of underwriting documents to Ever Onward counsel	UC, CC
	(b) Working sessions in California	EOC, MU, CC, UC
Sept. 25	(a) Availability of four-month stub	A
Sept. 28	(a) Receipt of second printed proof	FP
Oct. 2–3	(a) Working sessions in California on second printed proof of the registration statement, underwriting documents and completion of due diligence	ALL
Oct. 4	(a) Receipt of third printed proof with financial statements and notes	A, FP
	(b) Working session for final review of documents	ALL
	(c) Printing of SEC filing	FP
Oct. 5	(a) Company files registration statement with SEC	EOC, CC
	(b) Filing of media announcements	MU, UC

Table 13.2 (Continued)

Date	Activity	Responsible Party
	(c) Filing as required of Blue Sky	UC
	(d) Printing of preliminary prospectuses in quantity	FP
Oct. 5	(e) Formation of underwriting group by managing underwriter	MU
	(f) First distribution of prospectuses by managing underwriter	MU, FP
	(g) Distribution of questionnaires to company's officers, directors, and principal shareholders	EOC
Oct. 8	(a) Distribution of draft of cold comfort by auditors	A
	(b) Transmittal letter to prospective underwriters from managing underwriter regarding proposed financing with registration statement, preliminary prospectus, proof of preliminary Blue Sky memorandum and power of attorney	MU
	(c) Release of draft of cold comfort letter by auditors	A
	(d) Release of internal sales memorandum on proposed offering by managing underwriter	MU
Oct. 15–18	(a) Information and due diligence meetings in key cities	EOC, MU
Nov. 5	(a) Receive and review SEC deficiency letter	EOC, MU, CC, UC
	(b) Acceleration letter request to SEC	EOC, MU, CC
	(c) Revision of all necessary documents	ALL
	(d) Establishment of syndicate and share retention set by underwriter	MU
	(e) Preparation of tombstone proof	MU
	(f) Return of underwriters' questionnaires to managing underwriter	MU
	(g) Circulation of closing memorandum proof	UC
Nov. 7	(a) Negotiation of price and terms between company and managing underwriter	EOC, MU
	(b) Printing of filing packages	CC, UC, FP
	(c) Notification of terms to underwriters	MU
Nov. 8	(a) Execution of agreement among underwriters (9:00 A.M.)	MU, UC, CC

125

Table 13.2 (Continued)

Date		Activity	Responsible Party
	(b)	Execution of purchase contract by company and managing underwriter (9:30 A.M.)	EOC, MU
	(c)	SEC filing by company	CC
	(d)	Commencement of offering after being effective by SEC	
Nov. 8	(e)	Announcement of offering released to press	MU
	(f)	Sales confirmation telegrams by managing underwriter to underwriters	MU
Nov. 9	(a)	Publication of newspaper advertisement	MU
	(b)	Deadline for underwriters to notify managing underwriter of names and denominations of stock to be delivered at closing	MU
	(c)	Telegraphic notification by managing underwriter to underwriters regarding payment at closing	MU
Nov. 14	(a)	Circulation of revised proof of closing memorandum	UC
	(b)	Names and denominations of certificates for shares of common stock to be delivered furnished by managing underwriter to company and transfer agent	MU, EOC, TA
	(c)	Pre-closing meeting at offices of company counsel	EOC, MU, CC, UC
Nov. 15	(a)	Closing at offices of transfer agent (7:30 A.M.): payment for and delivery of stock	EOC, MU, CC, UC, TA
	(b)	Mailing by managing underwriter of copies of opinions, officers' certificates and accountants' letter to underwriters	MU

Source: J. S. O'Flaherty

underway by the corporation and its counsel, and the first combined draft is being sent to other task force members. The initial due diligence documents are being reviewed by the underwriters counsel. Meanwhile the principal of the managing underwriter is taking preliminary soundings as to the securities community's interest in the proposed offering, and first decisions are being made as to the states where the stock might be offered by the selling syndicate.

Since Ever Onward's fiscal year ended April 30, the managing underwriter and the auditors are in agreement that a four-month stub period of financial results is required under Regulation S-X because of the planned offering date of November 8 (see Table 13.2). Although Ever Onward's public accountants have made the decision that the August 31 stub period would be reviewed but not audited, the corporation is still told by the accountants to treat the four-month period as if an audit is going to be performed. Physical inventory is taken, and appropriate schedules are prepared for review by the auditors.

To reduce errors, the registration statement draft for initial task force review has no numbers, although space is provided for subsequent insertion. The second printed proof of September 19 is the first to contain all available numbers.

The balance sheets appearing in the SEC registration are for Ever Onward's fiscal year ended April 30, for the same period a year earlier, and the stub period of four months ended August 31. The statements of income are for the three previous fiscal years, along with the August 31 stub for the current four months and the same period a year earlier.

Concomitant with the preparation of financial statements for the stub period, the auditors are conducting a policy review of accounting matters, such as the adequacy of reserves and the need for additional write-offs. This review could have a material effect on profit, line items on the financial statements, and/or the footnotes.

The company's management accomplishes nothing during the auditors' policy review by pointing out that the annual audit had been completed only two months before. If the question is asked, the company is soon told by its auditors that the decision to go public means a critical review of the financial statements to ensure protection of an unsophisticated public investor.

However laudable the auditors' purpose, both parties recognize the concern of the managing underwriter if substantive changes are required in the financial statements; concern enough, perhaps, to realize that the investment banking house might not go ahead with the underwriting or, more likely, insist that the price range for the offering be lowered from that previously indicated.

14

The Registration and the Offering— A Composite Example

On the master schedule for the public offering of the illustrative Ever Onward Corporation (see Table 13.2), September 5 and 6 are important dates. Before this first scheduled meeting of the registration task force, a great deal of work has been done in the previous three weeks. And, most important, the key decision has been made by the managing underwriter.

Based on the facts developed, including initial due diligence analysis, and securities community soundings, the underwriting manager has decided to go ahead with the proposed offering. Up to this point the handshake deal between the lead underwriter and Ever Onward could have been disposed of with minimum pain. No longer. Now the firm decision is to do the deal, subject only to material negative facts in the enterprise's affairs or unexpected stock market deterioration.

Thus from the early September meetings to the final closing, there is a pressing feeling or urgency by the task force. The remainder of this chapter chronicles these events.

As indicated in Chapter 13, the illustrative Ever Onward Corporation is a composite of three initial public offerings in which the writer was the entrepreneur.

Company Attitude Toward Public Offering

To the chief executive, the preparatory work for the public offering already has become a symbolic pain in the neck. The problem is not the time and effort so much as the attitude of the company's senior associates.

By this time the entrepreneur has a fair idea of the amount of work to be done and the care to be exercised in dealing with the sharp people on the task force who pride themselves on asking penetrating questions as part of the due diligence work. Instilling an acute awareness in company associates of the likelihood of giving poor answers to task force and subsequent stock analyst questions has not been fruitful. The chief executive knows that the associates' view of the concentrated hours already spent on the review of other prospectuses is that there is an overreaction to a new situation.

But even the calm cockiness of the associates on the Form S-1 registration subject is a subsidiary frustration compared to the less-than-effective efforts of the entrepreneur to quiet the scuttlebutt of key operating management about the public offering. Most of the senior people who have original or option stock have convinced themselves that the public offering is just a preliminary to making them all well-to-do—but not as rich as they could have been because some of the associates who received stock have gone elsewhere over the years and carried their now-valuable stock with them. For these departed associates to profit mightily seems grossly unfair to those who have stayed with the company and labored in the vineyard during the heat of the day. Others are upset as well. There are those who did not receive the now-valuable stock options and are convinced they should have. And so on.

Motivating this ménage of people who are distraced by thoughts of stock value while the success or failure of the business rests in their hands is turning out to be a worrisome and enervating experience for key management. The forthcoming due diligence and other public offering tasks are just an additional burden.

Due Diligence Activities

Under the securities laws concerned with initial public offerings, the underwriters are charged with exercising due diligence or reasonable care in the investigation of the company and its affairs. A conventional wisdom is to deprecate the extent and validity of the investigation. And certainly there are enough valid instances of poor to indifferent due diligence efforts by underwriters to buttress a rationale that the investigation is of little concern to the enterprise. Such an attitude is both foolish and dangerous.

Talk and bravado about the superficialities and weaknesses of the due diligence efforts are one thing; the penalties for casual promiscuity with facts by the company is another.

There is always the entrepreneur who is convinced that the company need not be fettered by facts. Somehow this kind of fantasy thinking must be brought to reality by the grinding public offering process and, above all, by the good sense of the company counsel.

The files of initial due diligence documents requested from the Ever Onward Corporation in early August have been examined by underwriters counsel, and questions and answers have been flowing between the lawyers on both sides. Still a long list of queries, many developed as the early September meeting progresses, must be answered by the company representatives on the task force either on the spot or after additional investigation.

Inventory valuation is an example of a sensitive financial area for many types of enterprises. The auditors are well aware of the potentialities for litigation on this subject and investigate accordingly. However, only the company can supply any additional caveats or judgment reservations which, if not disclosed, could lead to legal exposure.

All things considered, the best procedure is to eliminate the judgment reservations or to establish reserves before the decision to go public is made. Failing this, the prudent course is adequate disclosure as determined by company counsel and the public accountants.

First Sessions of the Working Group

Full contingents of most of the elements of the registration task force gather in a conference room of the Ever Onward counsel's offices on

September 5. With a public offering having nationwide distribution, the conference room needs to be fair-sized. While the auditors will usually only put in an appearance, there can be two or three representatives of the managing underwriter, two lawyers for underwriters counsel, two lawyers for company counsel, and three representatives of the Ever Onward Corporation—the senior associate, who will attend all meetings along with the assistant secretary, and the chief executive officer. The auditors are available for questions; the financial printer, who is located in the same city, may be brought in for discussion of printed proofs; and special counsel, such as patent lawyers, may be involved.

With a minimum of jocularity, the task force settles down into its routines promptly after 8:30 A.M. on September 5. Timing and organization for the public offering effort are the first agenda items. The current SEC review process and registration workload in the agency are discussed, and the technicians reaffirm the feasibility of the proposed offering schedule. Formal drafting of the registration begins with the underwriters counsel setting the pace with a word-by-word and sentence-by-sentence review of the draft. This procedure provides the basis for wide-ranging questions on all facets of the registration material.

While at times it is overwhelmingly boring, valid reasons exist for the leisurely and peripatetic drafting procedure. Questions arise to which either the senior company representative must respond in detail after additional analysis, or else the chief executive officer will have to provide the answers. The accountants may need to be queried or such special counsel as a patent attorney may have to be brought in. The underwriters' principal is concerned with a prospectus presentation that will help the marketing of the securities; both sets of lawyers or the company representative may disagree on the principal's proposals. Finally, the selection of words, phrases, or sentences is debated at length. The company representatives soon discover that the task force consists of intelligent, verbal persons who are specialists in their field. They enjoy fencing for advantage in settling a point at issue with comments flickering around the conference table. The newcomer to one of these sessions can find them both disconcerting and difficult.

As suspected, the first group meeting goes into the third day with the expected grumbling of the visiting contingent. On one of the days, the Wall Street group and their lawyers spend an afternoon visiting

Ever Onward's facilities, talking with key people, and picking up additional documents for due diligence review. At the end of the September 5 meetings, agreement is reached among the task force elements as to job assignments for the next few days of the registration statement work, so that the first coordinated draft finally can be given to the financial printer.

Intermediate Sessions and Decisions

The September 17 sessions of the Ever Onward task force also go well into the third day. Presumably the nonfinancial aspects are about completed. The meetings are not relaxed. Hours of long-distance telephone conversations, detailed policy disagreements, and just plain jostling of personalities have upset the atmosphere of good feeling. The cabin fever of registration pressure has taken hold.

Drafts of the underwriting documents are given to the company counsel during the second task force sessions. In the writer's opinion, if the underwriting documents are standard Wall Street boiler plate, attempting to make any material changes in them is akin to fighting City Hall. The enterprise is wasting its time. The terms are markedly to the advantage of the underwriters, and the efforts of a single company is not going to change them. Setting aside other irritating provisions in the documents, there is one aspect of the underwriting agreement that is most evident to the entrepreneur; the company does not have a contractual deal with the underwriters until the morning of the offering.

On the other hand, Wall Street does not always base its operation solely on the stringent terms of its legal documents. As discussed in Chapter 1, the writer had a situation where the stock market went into a selling panic the morning of the planned offering. Nevertheless, the underwriting agreement was signed a half hour before the financial markets (loaded with sell orders) were due to open. Because of the market condition the managing underwriter temporarily delayed the offering.

Ever Onward's finance people and the auditors are attempting to meet task force deadlines. The four-month stub period ended August 31 requires extensive coordination between the two groups because of an accelerated closing procedure conducted under the close surveillance of the auditors. Meanwhile, additional and expanded notes to the financial statements are drafted by the two groups to meet SEC requirements. The chief executive is well-advised to review carefully the drafts of these financial notes because of the breadth and depth of company information they contain.

The necessary financial data (which will amount to eleven printed pages in the Ever Onward prospectus) are given to company counsel by the auditors on September 25. After a cursory review, these data are handed to the financial printer. The response time is remarkably short. The second printed proof, which now contains all elements of the SEC registration including company financials, is received by those concerned on September 28.

The second printed proof generates hours of telephone calls among task force members with the auditors now being deeply involved. No one is happy with the second proof, which reflects all the joint editing to date plus the financial statements and their accompanying footnotes. A few important points remain to be resolved, but the bulk of the questions are time-consuming minutiae interlocked with proofreading and a seemingly endless task of cross-checking numbers and statements throughout the text.

The "Cold Comfort" Letter of the Auditors

The "cold comfort" letter of the auditors to the underwriters now comes front stage center. "Cold comfort" is Wall Street jargon for the auditors' review and cross-check of certain specific numbers contained in the registration statement. The accountants carefully and specifically cover in the cold comfort letter what they did in their authentication task. Their comfort work always includes the stub period financial data. But, in addition, the underwriters can and often do ask through their counsel for maximum cold comfort—that is, as a Wall Street expression has it, a review of "every number in the registration statement except the page numbers."

While providing some additional company protection, maximum comfort adds to the cost of the offering—perhaps $5,000 to $10,000 more than minimum comfort. It means additional effort on the enterprise's part and, incidentally, considerable company embarrassment if the numbers previously submitted to the task force are not confirmed by the auditors. In the proposed Ever Onward offering, underwriters counsel asks for maximum comfort on October 2. Because of staff and timing problems, company counsel and the auditors feel strongly that the expanded comfort requirements should have been discussed and settled at an earlier date.

Registration Windup

All members of the task force gather on October 2 with the third printed proof of October 1. They assemble in the familiar conference room knowing full well the hours of coordinated work involved to meet an October 5 Washington filing. The day sessions are in the conference room or in separate meetings elsewhere, the evening gatherings are at the plant of the financial printer, where on-the-spot corrections are made. Fortunately, the printer is used to this procedure. A comfortable office is provided and anything from a thick steak to a sandwich can be ordered from a restaurant.

As is practically always the case in an initial offering, nothing is coming together just right as the final sessions progress. Meanwhile, the fourth printed proof of October 2 is run. By October 3, the entrepreneur is being asked by the underwriters counsel to put pressure on the accountants for an accelerated verbal sign-off. Having reasonably good sense, the chief executive sympathizes with the principal while making a mental note to stay out of the task force arguments. However, a peacemaker is always needed in th pressure-cooker environment of final registration windup. In the Ever Onward project the senior lawyer of company counsel performs the task well, as the flare-ups, poor humor, and plain fatigue take over during final days and nights of work.

The fifth and final printed proof is run October 3, incorporating all the changes up through the previous evening. The final printing of the SEC registration and then the thousands of preliminary prospectuses is now only hours away. The final and seemingly endless review of registration proofs begins immediately. It is imperative that all material errors be caught. Otherwise each copy of the preliminary prospectus distributed to the public must carry appropriate sticker corrections. Final sign-offs are received, and the corrected proof is given to the printer in the late afternoon of October 4.

The printed files of the required SEC registration material are handed to an underwriters counsel in time for the lawyer to be on the last "redeye" airplane for Washington, D.C., during the evening of October 4. The Ever Onward registration is filed with the SEC early in the business day of October 5.

Marketing the Proposed Issue

Wall Street being what it is, the fact that Ever Onward is seriously involved in preparing an initial registration statement is scarcely a secret. The underwriting community has a fair idea of the track record of the company and its industry's possibilities. As Ever Onward nears its planned registration date, a syndicate for the planned offering is coalescing.

With the filing of the registration statement on October 5, the lead underwriter formally initiates syndicate formation. The Street reception to the proposed offering is warm and may be better than that. And this is despite the fact that one of the largest brokerage firms has backed off from inclusion in the selling syndicate because of a negative research report on the industry. A blue-ribboned syndicate was formed with 73 firms (including several foreign houses), tiered on a share takedown basis as shown in Table 14.1.

Copies of the preliminary prospectus are being sent to the underwriters from the financial printer on October 5. Several days later the managing underwriter distributes an internal sales memorandum regarding the planned offering to the hundreds of brokers in the retail offices of that investment banking firm. Also the lead underwriter's discussions with the important institutional market are stepped up. Institutional interest is strong enough that the principal of the managing underwriter now talks about limiting institutional participation to about one-third of the issue. There is an emerging consensus that the initial offering will be well received.

With these indications that the proposed issue will be popular with investors, stock for company associates and friends at the initial offer-

**TABLE 14.1 Ever Onward Underwriting Tier Groups
A Composite Example**

Number of Firms	Number of Shares to be Purchased[b]	Size of Block of Shares Purchased[b]
1[a]	165,000	165,000
15	255,000	17,000
12	120,000	10,000
30	150,000	5,000
15	60,000	4,000
73	750,000	

Source: J. S. O'Flaherty

[a] Managing underwriter.
[b] Not including the over-allotment of 75,000 shares.

ing date becomes of real interest. Even before the filing of the registration statement, the underwriting manager has raised the question as to the amount of reserved stock to be held by the lead underwriter for special purchase. The suggestion is 5000 to 10,000 shares. The entrepreneur's reply is that if anything is done, the total would be more than 10,000 shares.

After examining the pros and cons of reserved stock the entrepreneur finally decides to follow an unsatisfactory middle course of setting aside 15,000 shares. The decision initiates the time-consuming and difficult task of allocating these shares among employees, customers, vendors, and miscellaneous deserving folk.

While marketing of the Ever Onward offering is going well, the underwriters' principal is still concerned about building up underlying support and interest in the company. The "road show" is one of these mechanisms in which the chief executive is the key performer; in reality, the entrepreneur and the underwriting team travel around the country to meet and talk with the investment community.

The likelihood of having a road show had already been discussed. As the marketing of the proposed offering is going well, the Ever Onward trip is limited to four cities—a breakfast session in Boston and a luncheon meeting in New York on a Tuesday, and a similar schedule two days later in Los Angeles and San Francisco. The chief executive is fortunate. For the time of year, the weather is excellent, and the number and length of trips are minimal.

The road show meetings are well attended by institutional representatives and members of the underwriting group. While most of the people attending them have only a general knowledge of the company's industry, there are sure to be a number who are very well informed and some who have talked with competitors about the company.

A road show session is typically no more than a twenty-minute talk by the chief executive expanding on the data in the preliminary prospectus and another thirty-minute question-and-answer period. As the company is in registration, no business forecasts are expected. However, any number of questions can be asked on future operations that will be difficult to avoid answering. All in all, the sessions are hard work.

When the entrepreneur returns from the road show, a number of things must be attended to, among them answering a half dozen calls from stock analysts. The first call presents no problems—simply a parroting of the road show responses. The second call is another matter. On the other end of the wire is the recognized Wall Street specialist in the company's industry. The questions are penetrating, in depth, and all interlocked. The answers require cohesive and coherent thought as to how much detail is to be given. Sensibly, after ten minutes of conversation, a thoughtful chief executive tells the stock analyst that he must call the analyst back because of an upcoming meeting. It is clear that decisions have to be made as to the extent of disclosure of competitive and advanced information to very knowledgeable people.

SEC Review of the Registration Statement

Copies of the registration statement are delivered by hand to the SEC on October 5. The major concern to the members of the task force group is the time interval required for processing the statement in the Commission. All know that the number of registrations in the pipeline, the intensity of review, and the extent of specific questions on the Ever Onward statement will determine the number of weeks required for approval.

Underwriters counsel is particularly familiar with the current SEC processing and timing. Counsel's advice has been the basis for establishing the master schedule after the lawyers had made a first-cut review of the company's background and operating position. In this framework, the underwriting manager is pleasantly surprised when the SEC issues a letter of comment (deficiency letter) regarding the registration statement on October 23, well ahead of the estimated November 5 date in the master schedule. This means the marketing efforts can proceed comfortably as planned.

Amendment No. 1, transmitted to the SEC on November 6, represents the final registration statement of the Ever Onward Corporation. Company counsel in the transmittal letter indicates that all changes requested in the SEC deficiency letter either have been incorporated in the amendment or explained in company counsel's transmittal. Further, counsel's letter formally requests that the registration be accelerated by one day to 9:30 A.M. on November 7. Of course, all the company's responses and the acceleration request have already received verbal approval from the SEC lawyer assigned to the registration.

The Offering

The countdown to the Ever Onward offering, as far as the company is concerned, begins in the early afternoon of November 6, preparatory to a 4:00 P.M. pricing meeting in the Wall Street offices of the managing underwriter. Based in a midtown hotel room, the entrepreneur makes or receives telephone calls from various sources in the securities community. The calls give a fair sense of the current enthusiasm for tomorrow's offering, as well as the amount of effort required to sell the issue. There is now agreement that the over-allotment option granted by the company for 75,000 shares will be exercised the next day by the underwriters.

The original estimate made by the lead underwriter of $14 to $16 per share at go-off is holding. The market tone is healthy. The $15 number looks probable; even a little higher is possible. Also, the major cost of the public issue—the underwriting discounts (the gross spread)— have been fairly well pinned down. With the reasonably warm reception being accorded the proposed offering, the underwriting discounts are going to be in the 7.5% to 7.75% range. This means a cost, including over-allotment shares, of about $950,000. When the chief executive takes a cab downtown to Wall Street, $15 and 7.6% are the numbers he wants.

The pricing meeting between the principals of the underwriting manager and the entrepreneur, representing both the company and the selling shareholders, is underway by 4:15 P.M. The various underwriters' positions and where the stock is going to be placed is discussed. After easy negotiation, the price is fixed for the offering at $15 and the underwriting discounts at 7.7%. The lead underwriter is also convinced that the over-allotment option will be exercised. The chief executive makes the necessary calls as to the various aspects of the deal, declines a dinner invitation, and takes a cab back to the hotel for solitary cocktails and dinner.

At 9:30 A.M. the next day, the entrepreneur is again at the managing underwriter's offices to sign the underwriting agreement. Nothing untoward has occurred in the securities markets or in company affairs that would affect the issue. The underwriting agreement is routinely executed, and the company and the selling shareholders have a firm money commitment for the first time. The market opens and the chief executive watches the first few over-the-counter trades. The new issue shows solid market support. Shortly thereafter, the underwriting manager reports the decision to exercise the over-allotment option and the imminent dissolution of the underwriting group. By 10:30 A.M., with a successful initial offering, the chief executive is on his way to Kennedy Airport for the flight back to the West Coast and Ever Onward's offices.

After boarding, the realization of being more than a paper millionaire generates only a modest feeling of exhilaration. Instead the entrepreneur's thinking is of problems ahead followed by a delightful tiredness which leads into a two-hour nap.

Windup of the Offering Project

"Tombstone" announcements of the Ever Onward offering appear in the November 8 *Wall Street Journal, The New York Times,* the main newspaper in Ever Onward's area, and the principal trade newspaper. The advertisement follows the traditional format and lists the underwriting group in the order of the number of shares taken down in the offering.

The managing underwriter has done a good job in pricing and placing the offering for the immediate aftermarket. The issue moves upward after the offering, but there is no run up in price which can provide a situation for the in-and-out speculator with resultant heavy trading and turnover. Further, the stock is showing an underlying demand which tends to quiet any short-term selling perturbation. The price movements during the first week of NASDAQ trading is orderly and positive as shown in Table 14.2.

The week between the offering and the closing requires considerable effort in settling accounts among the underwriters and arranging for delivery of stock certificates. Concurrent with this are the final preparations for delivery of required documents by the various specialists immediately before or at closing. The company's involvement in all of this is minimal.

The closing of the public offering takes place at the offices of Ever Onward's transfer agent on November 14 at 7:30 A.M. Arrangements have been made for simultaneous stock delivery at the offices of the underwriting manager. At the closing and after a number of signatures the entrepreneur receives official bank checks for the company and the selling shareholders. These reflect actual and estimated costs that have been distributed on a pro rata basis.

So the going-public task is done except for paying the company specialists and the financial printer. Underwriters counsel's fees are

TABLE 14.2 First Five Trading Days Bid/Ask Prices and Volume of Shares

A Composite Example

Day	Bid		Ask		Volume of Shares
---	High	Low	High	Low	
1	15½	15¼	16	15½	34,827
2	16	15½	16½	16	38,236
3	16¼	16	16½	16¼	35,407
4	16¼	16	16½	16¼	14,667
5	16½	16¼	17	16½	12,539

Source: J. S. O'Flaherty

paid by the underwriting group. The outside costs to the company and selling stockholders (shared on a pro rata basis) are paid from a $225,000 account held back on a pro rata basis for this purpose. The bills straggle in for several months after closing. The outside costs amount to $196,000, grouped by the following categories:

Category	Amount
Legal	$ 90,000
Audit	35,000
Printing	65,000
All others	6,000
	$196,000

The out-of-pocket costs of raising some $12.4 million in the Ever Onward offerings amount to about $1.15 million, an impressive figure. Particularly when these costs did not include the time of company employees and associated expenses.

15

Log of Official Offering Actions—A Composite Example

Despite the jostling of events and personalities, the successful public offering project of the illustrative Ever Onward Corporation was solidly based on a coordinated series of official and legal actions. The managing underwriter with the concurrence of the Ever Onward entrepreneur prepared a master schedule of interim target dates for work segment completion (see Table 13.1). To meet the requirement of this schedule a large number of interlocked tasks were performed.

This chapter details the principal official and legal actions that were required. They are grouped by date into a number of broad categories for easier reference. Where necessary, an explanation is included for a particular action. As indicated in Chapter 13, the illustrative Ever Onward Corporation is a composite of three initial public offerings in which the writer was the entrepreneur.

Corporate Proceedings

1 Minutes of the board of directors of Ever Onward Corporation held on September 20.

These minutes contain all of the implementation resolutions relating to an initial public offering, including an increase in the number of authorized shares of the corporation.

2 Letter dated September 20 from Ever Onward Corporation to all of its shareholders transmitting a proxy and notice of a special shareholders' meeting to be held on October 11.

The letter explains the proposed public offering including a provision for shareholders to sell a portion of their stock in the offering if they wished to do so.

3 Minutes of special shareholders' meeting of October 11.

The sole business of the meeting is amending the company's Certificate of Incorporation by increasing the number of shares authorized to be issued.

4 Certificate of Amendment of Certificate of Incorporation filed on October 11.

The action is required by the increase of the number of shares authorized to be issued.

5 Minutes of board of directors' meeting held on October 23.

Two items are approved by the Ever Onward board—a change in the form of stock certificate to reflect the securities market requirements, and a stock split calculated to provide the planned number of shares to be outstanding after the proposed offering.

6 Company letter of instruction dated November 13 (the initial public offering date was November 7) to the transfer agent/registrar regarding the handling of the stock split and public issue shares.

7 Opinion of company counsel dated November 14 to transfer agent/registrar.

The opinion states that the stock-split shares are validly issued and not subject to registration requirements of certain securities laws.

SEC Registration Proceedings

1 Transmittal on October 5 of registration statement and preliminary prospectus to the Securities and Exchange Commission (SEC).

Required copies of the registration documents are delivered along with fee payment by a certified check. An effective date for the registration statement of November 8 is requested as the public offering would be made on the effective date.

2   Form S-1 registration statement (containing preliminary prospectus) dated October 5.

3   Preliminary prospectus dated October 5.

4   Letter of comment from the SEC dated October 23.

This important letter contains the SEC comments on and requests for clarification in the October 5 registration statement. In the case of the Ever Onward registration, the SEC's comments and queries are less than a page and a half in length, and conformance or satisfactory response is not difficult.

5   Letter to the SEC from the company counsel dated November 6, transmitting Amendment No. 1 to the registration statement and responding to the SEC's letter of comment dated October 23.

All SEC comments are either incorporated in Amendment No. 1 or explained in the accompanying letter. Of course, company counsel has been in continuing verbal communication with the SEC lawyer assigned to the registration. In addition to Amendment No. 1, the letter to the SEC gives the required assurance that there are no material adverse changes in company affairs. And, finally, an acceleration request is made for the registration to become effective at 9:30 A.M. on November 7, a day earlier than planned.

6   Amendment No. 1 of the registration statement dated November 6—the final registration statement.

7   Consent letter of company counsel to the company dated November 6 agreeing to the use of counsel's name in the registration statement and associated documents.

8   A "cold comfort" letter dated November 7 from the auditors to the managing underwriter, pursuant to Section 5 (j) of the underwriting agreement.

The extent of the cold comfort is discussed in Chapter 14.

9   Acceleration letters dated November 6 to the SEC from the managing underwriter, the company, and the attorney-in-fact for the selling shareholders, requesting an acceleration of the registration to become effective at 9:30 A.M., November 7.

10   Letter dated November 6 to the SEC from the managing underwriter concerning the SEC's Release No. 5231.

The release emphasizes that the SEC staff has made only a limited or summary review of the registration statement and that such review cannot be relied upon in any degree to indicate that the statement is true, complete, or accurate. The letter also affirms the statutory responsibilities of the underwriters for such matters.

11   Verbal agreement at 5:00 P.M., November 6, as to the financial terms of the offering between the managing underwriter and representative of the company and the selling shareholders.

12   SEC notification dated November 7 that the registration statement has been declared effective at 9:30 A.M. on November 7.

13   Execution of agreement among underwriters prior to 9:30 A.M., November 7, by the managing underwriter and the attorney-in-fact for the other underwriters.

14   Execution of underwriting agreement at 9:30 A.M., November 7, by the managing underwriter and representative of the company and the selling shareholders.

15   Beginning of public offering at 10:00 A.M., November 7, by the underwriting group.

16   Final prospectus dated November 7.

17   Transmission of current registration material on November 9 to all underwriters by underwriters counsel.

18   Letter to the SEC from the company counsel dated November 12, transmitting ten copies of the final prospectus pursuant to Rule 424(b).

Data for National Association of Securities Dealers (NASD)

1   Letter to the National Association of Securities Dealers (NASD) from underwriters counsel dated October 8 transmitting registration documents of Ever Onward Corporation.

The letter and documents represent the preliminary filing for an eventual NASDAQ OTC listing, and a check for the filing fee was also included.

2   Letter to NASD from company counsel dated October 10 requesting NASDAQ listing and showing preference of ticker symbol.

The listing would become effective on the first offering day.

3   Letter to NASD from underwriters counsel dated November 9 transmitting final public-issue documents for required filing.

Documents of Selling Shareholders

1 Letter to all shareholders from Ever Onward Corporation dated September 20, transmitting notice of special shareholders' meeting and form for shareholder to express interest in the sale of stock in the proposed public offering.

2 Letter dated October 11 to the shareholders who may desire to sell shares in the proposed offering.

Attachments to the letter include the preliminary prospectus and document to be executed for the sale of stock.

3 Letter to the SEC from the attorney-in-fact for the selling shareholders dated November 6.

This letter is a statement as to the amount of stock the shareholders intend to sell and the fact that there is no material adverse information concerning the company.

4 Letter to managing underwriter from attorney-in-fact for selling shareholders dated November 7.

5 Custody agreement executed November 7 between the transfer agent as custodian of stock sold by shareholders in the public offering and the attorney-in-fact of these shareholders.

6 Letter to each selling shareholder dated November 14 from the attorney-in-fact transmitting pro rata portion of proceeds of public offering.

Underwriting Documents

1 Questionnaire completed October 1 for each officer, director, and principal shareholder.

The questionnaire is a typewritten, double-spaced document, 20 pages in length, with space for answers provided in the format. The answers are summarized in the registration statement.

2 Letter to prospective underwriters from managing underwriter dated October 5 providing information on the proposed Ever Onward public issue.

3 Form of underwriters' power-of-attorney for Ever Onward offering.

4 Due diligence meeting of November 6.

Held at the offices of the managing underwriter, the meeting consists of representatives of the managing underwriter, prospective underwriters, the chief executive officer of the company, and underwriters counsel.

5   Execution of agreement among underwriters prior to 9:30 A.M. on November 7.

6   Execution of underwriting agreement at 9:30 A.M. on November 7.

The agreement is signed by the chief executive officer of the company, attorney-in-fact for the selling shareholders, and the representative of the managing underwriter.

7   Execution of selected dealer agreements on November 7.

The underwriters offer stock to certain dealers, members of NASD, under the terms of the agreements.

8   Transmittal on November 9 of underwriting document to NASD by underwriters counsel.

Blue Sky Documents

1   Preliminary Blue Sky survey by underwriters counsel dated October 5.

The survey is concerned with the securities laws of the several states and the District of Columbia. Also the survey reports the states where the stock should not be offered and indicates that action is being taken to permit the sale of the stock in the other jurisdictions.

2   Records of Blue Sky filings and qualifying orders.

These data are available but retained by underwriters counsel.

Press Releases and "Tombstone"

1   Issuance of a press release dated October 5 regarding the filing of a registration statement with the SEC.

2   Issuance of a press release dated November 7 which announced the effectiveness of the SEC registration.

3   "Tombstone" advertisement dated November 8. A tombstone advertisement announcing the public offering and listing the under-

writers appears in the *Wall Street Journal*, a number of regional newspapers, and the principal trade press.

Closing Proceedings

1 Letter to company from managing underwriter dated November 9 establishing a November 14 closing date at the offices of the transfer agent.

2 Letter to transfer agent from managing underwriter dated November 9 specifying the shareholders' names and the denominations in which stock certificates should be registered.

Stock certificates have been sent on November 13 from the transfer agent to the managing underwriter for checking and packaging.

3 Verified Certificate of Incorporation and Good Standing of the company and its subsidiary as of November 13.

4 Company recital and certification dated November 13 of legal standing and approval of actions leading to the closing.

A file of substantiating documents is included as an attachment.

5 Company recital and certification on company affairs dated November 13.

This document reaffirms, as of November 13, that representations and warranties contained in the underwriting agreement were correct, and no material events have occurred other than those reported in the registration statement as amended.

6 Certification by selling shareholders dated November 13.

The certification includes compliance with representations and warranties to the November 13 date as satisfaction of all applicable conditions and agreements.

7 Stock disposition letter to transfer agent from company dated November 13.

The letter instructs the transfer agent on the handling of the stock split of October 11 and the disposition of public offering and residual shares.

8 Final opinion dated November 14 to managing underwriter from company counsel pursuant to closing requirements of underwriting agreement.

9 Stock-issue validity letter to transfer agent from company counsel dated November 14.

10 Final opinion dated November 14 to managing underwriter from underwriters counsel.

The opinion covers the registration statement, legal standing of the company, and the validity of the shares issued.

11 Closing memorandum dated November 14. This represents a recitation of official events to and through the closing of the stock transactions and transfer of funds.

12 Closing at offices of the transfer agent on November 14 at 7:30 A.M. PST.

Stock-certificate delivery is made simultaneously at the offices of the managing underwriter.

13 Exchange of receipts dated November 14 for stock and official bank check between managing underwriter and company.

14 Exchange of receipts dated November 14 for stock of selling shareholders in transfer agent custody and official bank check between managing underwriter and transfer agent.

Not Mumbo Jumbo

From an entrepreneur's viewpoint, the recitals and certifications listed in the foregoing sections can appear to be ritualistic mumbo jumbo. Most emphatically, they are not. Take the subject of validly issued stock with the illustrative Ever Onward Corporation.

The convolutions of Ever Onward in its early days required careful review by experts as to stock validity. A grass-roots venture, the enterprise had run out of venture money a year after it was founded. With the decision to invest new funds and provide a new management team, *all* existing shareholders agreed to accept an arbitrary reallocation of stock. Assuredly, this series of share transactions would receive careful review years later by both company counsel and underwriters counsel prior to the closing of the initial offering.

16

The Board of Directors

The passage of the Foreign Corrupt Practices Act in December 1977 raised questions regarding the goal and practices of publicly owned companies as well as the establishment of a whole new set of regulations on accounting matters for *all* these enterprises. This act, in conjunction with a high tide of consumerism, has forced a review of the role of the board of directors.

Corporate Accountability

The board of directors of a public company now receives a great deal of advice on how to reform itself.

In addition to its traditional fiduciary responsibilities, the board is being urged to evaluate and interpret "society's expectations and standards of management." As a continuing task the board should be "monitoring the totality of corporate performance." To this end the officers and their board "should create a management environment whereby the middle- and lower-management levels understand the nature of corporate accountability" to shareholders and a range of constituencies of society at large.

Carrying out these kinds of praiseworthy objectives can be a smothering comfort blanket for the smaller company. Take the new Section 13(b)(2) of the 1934 Exchange Act derived from the Corrupt Practices legislation. What would be considered theoretically the best accounting control system is not reasonably affordable, nor is it likely that the employees would accept the cross-checks and the personal surveillance required. Trade-offs and rule-of-reason decisions must be considered by the smaller company management in attempting to conform to Section 13(b)(2), irrespective of the threat of legal exposure. Realistically, the management has no other choice.

Notion of Board Control by Independent Directors

To make a board of directors responsive to society's assortment of constituencies and interests, the control of the board by independent directors is being urged by many groups. When serving as SEC chairman, Harold M. Williams went further and proposed that all directors, other than the chief executive officer, be independent. His successor has been far less enthusiastic about this notion, but the idea will not go away.

The independent-director concept envisages a kind of watchdog review of corporate affairs along with an adversary relationship between the independent directors and management. At least for a smaller company, these ideas have serious limitations. Any relationship which "destroys the sense of common purpose between management and the board is ultimately destructive of the corporation's best interest."

Board control by independent directors has little relevance now to smaller public companies. However, for a certainty, outside pressure for this concept will continue, not only for adoption on a voluntary but eventually on a mandatory basis.

The Entrepreneur and the Board

The head of a successful company which is considering going public is sure to have a set of strong opinions about a number of things connected with the enterprise. And one of those things will be the selection of the members of the board of directors at the time of the preliminary prospectus.

The chief executive will listen closely to the comments of the managing underwriter who views the board makeup through the eyes of the investment community. Consideration may also be given (but probably not much) to the watchdog/adversary concept of a board. In the end, the entrepreneur will determine the makeup of the first public board of directors. Corporate accountability in the broad sense will probably be recognized in theory but not in practice.

Makeup and Role of the Board

One current classification of board directors is their involvement in corporate affairs—management, interested outside, and independent outside. Management, of course, would be representatives of the senior management of the enterprise. The interested outside category of board members could be principal investors, the concern's general counsel, vendors, or the like. The independent outside classification of directors would include the remainder, although some criteria exclude for a number of years former management or interested outside directors.

A seven-man board makes a great deal of sense for a newly public company. This size will accommodate an adequate mix of the several directors' classifications, while still being small enough for reasonable involvement of all board members. However, deciding the mix of personalities and backgrounds on the new board prior to going public requires careful consideration.

The easiest decision (or perhaps the most difficult) is the extent of representation on the board by principal shareholders. As interested outside directors, hopefully, by agreement or by trial and error, this has been worked out in the past. As to the composition of the rest of the board, ample advice is available to the chief executive. Whether it is taken or not is another matter.

In bulk of instances the entrepreneur who sits as the only management representative on the board must believe that he can speak on and for all aspects of the enterprise's operations. However, in a few cases when the chief executives opt for no other management directors, the decision may stem from being insecure about their own positions in the future. As the relationship between the other senior management and the board will then be at a minimum, the position of the chief executive vis-à-vis the outside directors will be enhanced.

The writer's observation is that, irrespective of the capabilities of the entrepreneur, the inclusion of one or possibly two other management directors would be worthwhile for ensuring a working board. One practical reason is that the chief executive is able to do less talking and more listening to the questions and opinions of the outside directors.

Interested outside directors can make a valuable contribution to the enterprise. Perhaps a case can be made that these kinds of board members are far too subservient to management. But this writer's experience is that they are knowledgeable on matters affecting the corporation's success, and their advice is sound. They want the enterprise to succeed for whatever their particular interest may be.

As to the role of the independent outside director, certain decisions should be reasonably clear to the entrepreneur in forming the going-public board. A smaller company has enough problems without adding a "constituency" director who presumably represents the forces of social change. The chief executive should be wary of the so-called professional director—a person whose occupation is serving on a number of boards at substantial compensation. The definition itself almost has the sound of an interested outside director who does not bring to the board any particular knowledge of company affairs. Much more of a case can be made for the use of academic people, despite their lack of relevant experience.

The board appointment of an outside senior executive, active or recently retired, has appeal. The rationale probably is that the outside executive as an independent director can understand the problems and thus be supportive during difficult times. The outside executive tends to be just as hardheaded as the chief executive, while the advice and counsel given can be good and unbiased. But for whatever the considerations, an independent outside director or two makes sense.

In summary, then, the chief executive will strongly influence the board, irrespective of composition. Yet this is all the more reason why capable directors should be selected from all three categories of interest in corporate affairs.

Board Oversight Committees

The conventional wisdom of the early 1980s is that the public and private reform efforts of the 1970s will "incline toward imposing greater managerial responsibilities on the directors, responsibilities that directors will be able to ignore only with increased liability. . . . The development of oversight committees—such as audit, compensation, and nomination—are examples of the attempt to place directors more in the mainstream of management."

The compensation and nomination committees are of minimum concern to the newly public enterprise. On the other hand, the extent of power being urged for the audit committee in every public company must be carefully evaluated. Otherwise what appears to be a sound idea can turn out to be a loose ship's gun in corporate affairs.

The Audit Committee and the SEC

As perhaps the key element in corporate accountability, the late 1970s found a militant SEC and harassed independent accountants united in advocating the concept of a powerful audit committee of the board of directors. Although the move failed, the SEC was pressuring the accounting profession to require an audit committee as a precondition to obtaining certification of the financial statements of any public enterprise.

The SEC's General Counsel expressed the regulatory commission's posture in 1978: "When the Commission calls for audit committees, the call is for effective, responsible audit committees, and not merely non-functioning, albeit decorative shells." He then reviewed an audit survey conducted by an accounting firm: "The Coopers & Lybrand study does not suggest that the effort underway in the private sector is anywhere near the quality necessary to ensure against preemptive federal action."

The aggressive SEC picture, the new section 13(b)(2) of the 1934 Securities Act, and an accounting profession harassed by shareholder litigation has generated a spate of urgent and sometimes contradictory advice on audit responsibility. This advice in the main is the butterknife variety. It applies to all companies, irrespective of size and whether the enterprise is multi-industry and/or multinational or neither.

Primary Function of the Audit Committee

The American Bar Association through its Committee on Corporate Laws recommended that the audit committee should have prime responsibility for the discharge of at least the following four functions:

1. To recommend the particular persons or firm to be employed by the corporation as its independent auditors.
2. To consult with the persons so chosen to be the independent auditors with regard to the plan of the audit.
3. To review, in consultation with the independent auditors, their report of audit, or proposed report of audit, and the accompanying management letter, if any.
4. To consult with the independent auditors (periodically, as appropriate, out of the presence of management) with the regard to the adequacy of internal controls, and, if need be, to consult with the internal auditors (since their product has a strong influence on the integrity of the resulting independent audit).

An idea of what some of the foregoing entails are indicated by the monitoring activities of the audit committee, as suggested by Louis Braiotta, Jr., in *The Audit Director's Guide*. While he emphasizes that the committee cannot participate in the accounting and auditing functions of a day-to-day basis, he believes that there is a consensus that the audit directors should monitor the following:

1. The internal auditing function.
2. The internal accounting and administrative controls.
3. The financial reporting disclosures.
4. Conflicts of interest.
5. Corporate perquisites.
6. Corporate contributions.
7. Other tasks as requested by the board.

Mr. Braiotta goes on to say that "in administering the monitoring function, it may be advisable for the (audit) committee to retain the necessary professional expertise, such as the corporation's outside legal counsel or outside data processing experts."

To the board of directors of a smaller company all of the foregoing may be worthy, but it is surely frightening and unquestionably expensive.

The Audit Committee of a Newly Public Company

The enterprise going public is generally a smaller corporation, in one kind of an industry or business segment, and dedicated in the main to domestic sales. This kind of a business is faced with limited staff resources and the typical pressing assortment of operating problems. Under these circumstances an audit committee based on the watchdog/monitoring concept just does not make sense.

A reasonable solution used by the boards of many smaller companies is to delineate the scrutiny and overview responsibilities of its audit committees. Thus, the committee, unless otherwise instructed by the board, would limit its activities to:

1. Recommending the choice of the outside public accountants.
2. Consulting with the outside accountants as to the audit plan.
3. Reviewing, in conjunction with the outside auditors and the enterprise's finance officer, the audit report and the management letter, if any.

Legal Risks for Board Members

Signing the initial registration statement as a preliminary to taking the enterprise public should be enough legal risk for board members. Then to realize that, as of the time of the first public offering, they have an unknown legal exposure to laws like Section 13(b)(2) of the 1934 Exchange Act should make them question their judgment on being public company directors. Particularly after they read the four-page checklist in *The Audit Director's Guide*. According to the *Guide*, the checklist is designed to minimize the Audit Committee's legal liability. However, the *Guide* does go on to make the recommendation that directors "discharge their responsibilities in a professional manner and not become totally preoccupied with legal rules and regulations."

There is no way of curing all the concern over legal risk. A presumption must be that the courts and the SEC will continue to be sensible and cautious in their careful handling and interpretations of the accounting control requirements of Section 13(b)(2). This is particularly true for the smaller enterprises that must make trade-off and rule-of-reason decisions as a business necessity. Of course, such companies should provide directors and officers liability insurance and the associated company reimbursement insurance.

Meetings and Compensation of Board Members

Quarterly meetings of the board of directors are expected for the newly public company. If possible, they are scheduled so that preliminary financial results of the quarter are available for review. The number of committees established and their meetings depend upon the particular enterprise. The boards of many smaller companies have only one standing body—its audit committee, which usually meets twice a year.

As would be expected, compensation for nonmanagement members of the board has a considerable range. Illustrative of the current practice of the smaller public company, the outside director may have an annual retainer of $5000 to $10,000 and receive payment of $200 to $400 for each board or committee meeting attended. Of course, all nonmanagement member expenses connected with attending a meeting are paid.

While nonmanagement directors' compensation has increased substantially in recent years, no one argues they are overpaid. Why able outside directors can still be recruited at all remains a puzzle to the writer.

17

Restricted Stock Means Care and Discretion

The moment an enterprise sells stock to the public, whole categories of its shares come under a series of unfamiliar restrictive securities regulation and law pertaining to stock sales and purchases. Not only are these federal rules complex and burdensome to key shareholders, but corporate counsel now will exercise independent judgment in evaluating their company stock transactions.

The company counsel recommends the procedures for stock sale and purchase for shares subject to restrictive regulation, and the attorney will give specific opinions on these transactions as required.

Definition of Rule 144 Securities

Securities that have *not* been carried through registration with the Securities and Exchange Commission (SEC) and purchased by the public come under the provisions of Rule 144. Generally, these non-registered, and therefore restricted securities, cannot be sold or transferred at will.

In the case of restricted securities, the shares are often called "legended" or "letter" shares because most stocks with restrictions of various kinds carry a "legend" stamp on each stock certificate. But what is not well recognized is that whether a particular stock certificate carries a legend or not, the transfer agent of the issuing enterprise has a "stop" on any certificate that has legal restrictions. The transfer agent will not initiate a transfer until the stop becomes a "go," the action showing that the shares have been cleared by the issuing corporation. This means the company for the particular transaction has assumed the responsibility for conformance with the securities laws and regulations on the basis of the facts that are known at the time.

Stock owned by any persons who directly or indirectly control the management and activities of the issuing enterprise is termed "control" or "affiliate" shares by the securities regulations. Not only do special rules apply to affiliate stock, but such stock is also included under the procedures and regulations governing the broader classification of restricted securities.

The decision as to who is an affiliate will rest with the company counsel. This attorney will tend to err on the side of a wider rather than a narrower interpretation because of the stringency of the applicable federal regulations. Directors, senior management, and large shareholders are usually considered affiliates. If a shareholder remotely has a choice, he would gladly forego the affiliate designation.

Selling Rule 144 Securities

The SEC's Rule 144 allows holders of affiliate and non-affiliate restricted securities to sell their shares to the public in recognized markets provided certain conditions are met. The rule establishes requirements as to availability of current public information about the corporate issues and provision for holding periods before sale of restricted securities. In addition, for affiliate holdings, guide rules apply as to the amount of securities that may be sold, restrictions on sellers' and brokers' activities or manner of sale, and notification of the proposed sale to the SEC by means of Form 144.

Holders of restricted non-affiliate or affiliate securities issued *prior* to the effective date of Rule 144 (April 15, 1972) have the option of selling their securities either under the rule or under the legal interpretations that existed prior to that date.

Company counsel will generally advise that it is preferable for the seller to proceed under Rule 144. In extraordinary cases in which time is of the essence, delays might be avoided by proceeding under the pre-1972 rule. However, most securities lawyers believe that each such case should be examined on its individual merit if and when it arises.

Non-registered, and therefore restricted securities, generally can be sold by utilizing some exemption of the 1933 Securities Act. As a practical matter, the only exemption likely to be available is that provided by Rule 144 itself. In the case of both categories of restricted stock (non-affiliate and affiliate shares), the rule continues to specify a minimum holding period of two years. But in the case of non-affiliate restricted stock, the February 6, 1981, amendments to the rule did eliminate volume limitation, manner of sale, and notice requirement for this category of securities. However, these requirements still apply to the narrower category of affiliate (control) shares.

All established stockbrokers are familiar with the terms of Rule 144, and many have legal advisory staffs who are the contact point with the corporate issuer's transfer agent and legal counsel. While the stock transaction is the broker's responsibility, under the rule, a selling shareholder must inform the broker at the first contact that the proposed transaction is restricted non-affiliate or affiliate stock. An entrepreneur may find it irritating if not embarrassing to have a valued associate blithely place a substantial block of restricted stock with a broker and then plead ignorance of the fact that the shares were Rule 144 stock. Somehow, when considerable sums of money are involved, comprehension of securities laws and regulations regarding stock sales and purchases can be blurred.

Section 16(b) of the 1934 Exchange Act

While Rule 144 deals essentially with the mechanics of sale of any category of securities coming under its domain, Section 16(b) of the 1934 Exchange Act addresses the sale of any securities by any "insider." The definition of an insider is an officer, director, or shareholder owning 10% or more of the outstanding corporation stock.

If the insider buys and sells the corporation's securities within a six-month period, Section 16(b) imposes a potential liability on such an insider if the corporation has a class of equity securities registered under the 1934 Act. Any combination of a purchase or a sale or sale and purchase that yields a profit is subject to the liability provisions of the section. An addendum comment—the law is clear that an exercise of a stock option constitutes a purchase for purposes of Section 16(b).

A company having an initial public issue is registered under the 1933 Securities Act. It also must register under the 1934 Exchange Act within 120 days from the close of the fiscal year after the initial offering. During the interim period any persons subject to Section 16(b) would be well advised to govern their actions as if the law were applicable.

At the time the enterprise registers under the 1934 Act, an insider will be required to file SEC Form 3, which is an initial statement of beneficial ownership (Note 1) of securities. Further, under Regulation 13D of the 1934 Act, all persons (including members of company management) who beneficially own more than 5% of the enterprise's stock must file Schedule 13G within 45 days after the end of the first calendar year following the initial public offering, and annually thereafter.

In the month following the sale, purchase, other acquisition or disposal of securities, the insider will file Form 4 with the SEC detailing the month's transactions and showing the month-ending share balance. Thus insiders who are selling securities and are also affiliates must file Form 144 under the 1933 Act and Form 4 under the 1934 Act. Affiliate/insider sale transactions are well publicized by the financial media because of the continued interest in these transactions by the investment public and some of its legal advocates.

Rule 10b-5 of the SEC

The SEC's Rule 10b-5, as interpreted by the SEC and the courts, makes it unlawful for anyone to buy or sell securities at a time when that person possesses "inside information" which is not public and when made public might have a material bearing on the price of the security. For employees and outside board members particularly, this rule poses a difficult problem for those who wish to sell stock. In a way it is a classic Catch 22. Nobody cares (except, of course, the selling shareholders) if the stock is sold low and subsequently goes up in price. On the other hand, if the stock is sold on a major upswing, the sellers are exposed to hindsight attempts to show they knew of some significant facts that were not publicly known at the time they sold the stock.

Because the questions of knowledge and the significance of known facts are tried in court considerably after the sale event, innocence may not always be enough. Such litigation is usually not only expensive but also most worrisome to those concerned. As discussed in the following section, the problems associated with Rule 10b-5 can be minimized, but they will not go away.

Appropriate Timing of Stock Sale or Purchase

To the complete dissatisfaction of the entrepreneur and his principal associates, there never is a best time to sell a reasonable quantity of their stock in the marketplace. The sticky molasses of federal regulation affecting affiliates and insiders, complicated by hindsight litigation considerations, is reason enough. Then add to that Wall Street's standard negative reaction to stock sales of any substantial quantity of affiliate stock. To the Street, management is "bailing out" of the enterprise because it has no confidence in the company's future. All of these pressures make for a built-in inertia against stock sales that is difficult to overcome.

Purchasing of the corporation's stock by affiliates or insiders generally has less hazards than stock sales, although a landmark case involved buying rather than selling stock. Rule 10b-5 regarding inside information is the primary exposure and this applies particularly to employee shareholders. Also it should be remembered that there is Section 16(b) exposure as well.

To provide reasonable legal safeguards, the sale or purchase of affiliate or insider stock is best made through a relatively narrow timing window. This means the transaction might best take place in a period beginning a week or two after the interim or annual financial statements have been released, and at a time where there is no material news about the enterprise's affairs in the immediate offing.

Selling securities on the basis of stale interim or annual financial statements is inappropriate and risky for the affiliate or insider. Equally so is the sale before an announcement, press release, or substantial trade-gossip speculation that could have a material effect on the enterprise's affairs. This last consideration also must be recognized by other employee shareholders who could be accused of having insider information. The entrepreneur and company counsel may have dfficulty in hammering home this point to associates.

Many underwriting agreements contain a 90-day prohibition on sale of restricted non-affiliate or affiliate stock after the initial public offering date. Prior to the end of the period, the chief executive should consider issuing a memorandum to the non-affiliate, affiliate, and insider shareholders. Among other things, the memorandum might contain data given in this chapter pertaining to the impact of securities rules and laws.

At the very least, a policy instruction should outline the procedures for the sale and purchase of securities having restrictions. Such an instruction can be one of the most inexpensive ways to eliminate misunderstandings, unconscious or otherwise, while reducing the possibilities of lawsuits and difficulities with the SEC.

Summary Comment

Care and discretion are the two watchwords in the handling of unregistered securities. Rule 144 is a feasible, albeit frustrating, way to sell restricted non-affiliate or affiliate stock. The only easy course into a safe harbor for large-block sales without a major discount is a secondary public offering with the attendant time and expense considerations.

Note 1   Ticor Print Networks, *A Sample Directors', and Officers' Questionnaire—1983*, p. 12.

On June 30, 1978, the SEC adopted a new definition of "beneficial ownership" for proxy statements (SEC Rel. No. 34–14190) You are the beneficial owner of a security, as defined in Rule 13d–3 under the Exchange Act, if you, directly or indirectly, through any contract, arrangement, understanding, relationship, or otherwise have or share (1) voting power which includes the power

Summary Comment

to vote, or to direct the voting of, such security, or (2) investment power which includes the power to dispose, or to direct the disposition, of such security. You are also the beneficial owner of a security if you, directly or indirectly, create or use a trust, proxy, power of attorney, pooling arrangement or any other contract, arrangement, or device with the purpose or effect of divesting yourself of beneficial ownership of a security or preventing the vesting of such beneficial ownership. Finally, you are deemed to be the beneficial owner of a security if you have the right to acquire beneficial ownership of such security at any time within 60 days including but not limited to any right to acquire (a) through the exercise of any option, warrant or right, (b) through the conversion of a security or (c) pursuant to the power to revoke a trust, discretionary account, or similar arrangement, or (d) pursuant to the automatic termination of a trust, discretionary account or similar arrangement.

The above definition is very broad and even though you may not actually have or share voting or investment power with respect to securities owned by persons in your family or living in your home, you may wish to include such shares in your beneficial ownership disclosure, out of an abundance of caution, and then disclaim beneficial ownership of such securities.

18

"If You Can't Stand the Heat..."

Reports and procedures connected with being a public company are time-consuming and expensive. There are few shortcuts or clever rationales to avoid the work.

With many of the reports and procedures interacting on each other, a great number of individual actions must be performed and coordinated. The person responsible for the program during the first hectic year can have an empathy with that fabled sorcerer's apprentice who was frantically attempting to deal with a misplaced spell.

The minimal shareholder reporting procedures and disclosure requirements before the business went public are now remembered with nostalgia.

The Privately Held Company

A privately held company only reports to its shareholders annually, with no interim auditor reviews, quarterly reports, or public reports of earnings. The typical annual report consists of a photocopy of one or two typewritten pages of comments on operations by the entrepreneur accompanied by a "brown-back" copy of the audited financial statements. If requested, 50 copies or so are reproduced by the public accountants. Paper-clipped to these data are photocopies of a typed notice of the annual meeting and a proxy sheet. There are no proxy statements. And, most pleasant of all, no reports are sent to the Securities and Exchange Commission (SEC).

A board of directors of a privately held concern meets regularly or at the call of the chair during the year. Audit committees usually exist only in books and articles on the expanded functions of the board of directors.

All of this idyllic scenario of relaxed freedom disappears as of public offering day.

Quarterly Results and Reports

The dust scarcely settles from the initial public offering before preparations are underway for reporting quarterly fiscal results five weeks after the end of the period. As part of this procedure, a one- to two-day limited review by the public accountants has become general practice because of SEC regulations initiated in the 1970s.

Designed to reduce the number of unpleasant surprises during the fiscal year and particularly the last fiscal quarter, the limited analysis does accomplish a good deal of what it is supposed to do. The public accountants carry out the review by examining their sensor points in the enterprise's accounting system and by making specific inquiries of responsible financial management.

The newly public company releases its quarterly and year-to-date information in the regular format utilized by the media. For security reasons, many concerns prefer to put the quarterly information on their TWX machines to the wire services they employ immediately after the stock market has closed for the day. While the tape service will carry the information to the securities community the next morning, daily newspapers like the *Wall Street Journal* do not carry the earnings report until the second morning. An alternative is to have a release in midmorning that may be picked up by the newspapers the following day.

The first quarterly report that is printed requires some policy decisions, even though the size and number of pages will probably follow standard practice. In common with most companies, the page size will be long and narrow (for example, an 8-inch-by-8½-inch sheet of paper or card stock folded lengthwise). The question is, What in the world is to be done with all the space that is available in this four-page report?

At least three decisions must be made as to the printed content of the four pages, and the importance of the decisions becomes more evident as succeeding reports are issued. Should there be a summary comment on the reasons for a successful or unsuccessful quarter? What about a review of elements of the company's operations and the competitive or market conditions? Is it desirable to include a statement of comparative earnings and balance sheets? The answers to these questions will determine the format and content of the quarterly report, including company logos, filler material, and blank space.

While there are any number of satisfactory approaches to laying out a quarterly report for a newly public company, several comments on a single-segment business (the usual initial issue) may be relevant. The first is that a cogent summation comment as to why the financial results are the way they are is a difficult piece to write each and every quarter. For that matter, writing an annual summation can be bad enough. The same comment applies equally to a quarterly review of the overall elements of the concern's operations. On the other hand, a statement of comparative earnings and summarized balance sheets provides important facts to the shareholders. The financial statements stand by themselves and are available anyway from the Form 10Q filing to the SEC, as discussed in the next section.

A sensible approach for the quarterly report, in this writer's opinion at least, is to have the front page cover contain the earnings synopsis for the quarter and the year-to-date. The financial statement summaries would be spread across the inside two pages, and the back page would only have company logo and financial quarter identification.

Form 10Q to the SEC

The first routine report to the SEC, Form 10Q, is the initial quarterly earnings document. While reflecting only the limited review of the public accountants, it should receive respectful consideration by the fledgling public enterprise and also be reviewed by company counsel. As with the annual Form 10K, the quarterly 10Q is not a blank form to be completed. Instead, the SEC provides a series of captions indicative of the type of information required by the agency. The 10Q must be filed with the SEC within 45 days after the end of each of the first three fiscal quarters of each fiscal year. No fourth-quarter filing is necessary.

Other than requiring comments on material business changes, Form 10Q instructions specify financial statements with associated footnotes and a management analysis of the income statement. The company provides this narrative management analysis of the results of operations for the quarter just ended as compared to the same period a year earlier. Also operations results for the quarter just ended are compared with those of the three months' period immediately preceding it.

The best approach to preparation of the first 10Q is a careful review of recent 10Q reports by other concerns (preferably ones in similar industries) and discussion with company counsel. It is well to remember that the three quarterly 10Q reports constitute a key support for the important 10K report to the SEC (discussed in a subsequent section) and that all of these reports are public documents.

The Annual Report and Audit

When told that the printing run of the first annual report to shareholders should be at least 2500 copies, with the possibility of a second run, the chief executive will find this hard to believe. These quantities do seem illusionary at first glance, particularly when the number of shareholders shown on the rolls of the company's transfer agent may be in the 500 to 1000 range. Howver, as discussed in a later section, there are many more shareholders than appear on these rolls. Furthermore, the retail outlets of the brokerage houses may want copies, and the corporate secretary has and will have many requests from analysts and prospective investors.

Once convinced of the extensive distribution of the annual report and the desirability of making at least a reasonably good presentation of the company, the entrepreneur must establish some annual report policies. A prime format decision revolves around the chief executive's own ego drives and whether the first annual report is to be a symbol of those drives. Masking this basic point with a set of rationales wastes a great deal of valuable time and ensures wheel-spinning in report preparation.

If the entrepreneur believes the annual report is the vehicle to be driven down the road to a kind of business immortality, that is fine. On the other hand, if understatement and underplay is the bent of the chief executive, that direction is equally valid. But a decision should be made before a serious effort on the report gets underway because there are many alternate format choices.

In planning the length of an annual report, the inside covers are generally counted as pages. And from printing/stapling considerations, pages are added or deleted in units of four. Because of the financial statement requirements and length of footnotes plus other minimal presentation material, 14 pages is usually not considered to be adequate even with the standard 8½-by-11-inch page size. Thus the workable minimum is automatically 18 pages, and the maximum length of an annual report can be more than twice that number. Undoubtedly, a factor in the chief executive's decision as to the total number of pages in the report will be affected by the company's industry. A snack-food concern may think differently from a financial service business and certainly from a specialized component manufacturer.

Given the posture of the chief executive as to ego drives, along with the decision as to the report's length and page size, real design effort can move ahead expeditiously. The work can be turned over to one of any number of design agencies who will provide cover/page layouts, color recommendations (if that is the decision as to photographs and illustrations), and other format aspects of the report.

Another approach may have validity, at least for the first annual report. The entrepreneur should consider reviewing a fair number of shareholder reports and selecting the type of features preferred. The company could then prepare a report layout incorporating these features. The layout then can be the basis for the design agency's work.

Balancing the legitimate need for keeping the shareholders informed, while restricting the amount of gratis information provided to competitors, is not easy, and chief executives have to make their own particular decisions on the matter. All are in agreement on one point: between the annual report and Form 10K (discussed in the next section) a great deal of information is made available to anybody who is interested. Most assuredly, under some circumstances it can be painful from a competitive viewpoint.

As mentioned in an earlier chapter, all of the principal competitors of the writer's enterprise with a single exception were divisions of very large corporations. The exception was a closely held family enterprise. None of the public corporations broke out financial and operating information for the divisions with whom the entrepreneur was competing, and naturally the family enterprise did not publish at all. One can be sure that the various reports and statements of the newly public business were required and interesting reading by these competitors. They did not molt one feather of concern over the writer's disclosure predicament.

Some efficiency-minded and reform souls argue strongly for incorporating all the Form 10K material in the annual report because of the great overlap of data. They believe that report costs would be reduced somewhat and much of the soaring optimism and rhetoric of some annual reports would be kept on the leash of 10K material. Both points are sensible, but there is a significant reason for not folding the 10K material into the annual report.

Form 10K is a document prepared for compliance with SEC rules and is prepared in careful "lawyer language." On the other hand, the purpose of the annual report to shareholders is just that—to summarize and evaluate the events of the year and the enterprise's present planning. A readable text should be set off by an attractive format and photographs as required. In addition, Form 10K is available to the shareholder (and anybody else for that matter) as a public document at the SEC or by simply writing the company secretary for a copy.

The chief executive's assessment of where the business stands and the supporting review of operations are the principal features of the annual report. An early decision should be made as to how long (number of words) this presentation should be. The length depends on the personality of the enterpreneur, the range of products, and the type of industry environment. The writer's view, which is shared by a good many, is that for the smaller company an optimum length might be about 1100 to 1600 words, irrespective of the format used. This range appears to strike a balance between providing the necessary information to shareholders but not giving extensive details, which can only interest the company's competitors.

No matter how well planned (a master schedule for the first year is discussed in a subsequent section), the first annual report absorbs an inordinate amount of man-hours and calendar time. Neither of these points becomes evident until time is running out and there is so much more work to be done. An example or two follows. Photographs and illustrations almost invariably are behind schedule—and when they finally are received, for any number of reasons, they are not satisfactory. Financial footnotes represent other burdens for the project manager. Why would the public accountants be tinkering with footnotes a few months after a registration was prepared with great effort? For whatever reasons, oftentimes they do. When agreement at last is reached on the footnotes, after repeated conversations with and follow-up by the company's financial people, there will be miscellaneous minor changes right up to the final proof deadline of the annual report.

Of course, the completion of the annual audit is a prerequisite for the annual report. As the enterprise has recently been through the Form S-1 registration process, both the public accountants and the concern's financial people are well familiar with each other. Nevertheless, the first audit of a newly public company may find the public accountants inflexible on one or more policy points.

Irrespective of management irritation or lack of understanding, the auditors may take the position that an accounting treatment which was marginally satisfactory as a privately held company is now submarginal and unsatisfactory for the publicly held enterprise. The auditors' position rests on the notion that there now is and will be a large group of shareholders who are unsophisticated investors. Whatever the justification, these kinds of changes can upset an already tight report schedule.

Starting from scratch, the first annual report is a three- to four-month effort involving much editing of the report content. Even so, what will be irritating and embarrassing for the people who worked so hard are the errors that show up in the final printed copy.

Form 10K

Form 10K is the major recurring report required by the SEC from each publicly held company. Submitted annually as the official overall review of company affairs, the 10K must be filed within 90 days after the end of the fiscal year. In a report format consisting of 13 item sideheads grouped into four parts, it contains both narrative material and the audited financial statements and associated footnotes. The annual report and the proxy statement (discussed in the following section) are included as attached documents, and portions of these reports may be incorporated by reference in answer or partial answer to any item in Form 10K. The procedural recitations aside, the 10K should be taken most seriously.

Companies filing Form 10Ks are encouraged but not required to discuss business projections and are expressly covered by the safe harbor rule of the SEC for such projections. In some instances company counsel and the chief executive may decide to give the forward-looking information under that 1979 rule. But many companies in filing their 10Ks will forego the projections.

The signatures required on Form 10K indicate the importance that the SEC attaches to this annual analysis of company affairs. All these people must sign the 10K—the chief executive officer, the chief financial officer, the controller or principal accounting officer, and at least a majority of the board of directors. Having a typed, single-spaced 10K of 25 pages ready for review and collection of signatures in the time available requires careful planning.

While Form 10K is a lawyer's document, simply excerpting the discussion material from the Form S-1 registration statement is not necessarily the best policy from the enterprise's current operating position. Prior to drafting the narrative items of the 10K, company counsel and the chief executive should decide what kind of revisions are needed in the relevant S-1 data. Once that is done, the enterprise can complete the drafting while allowing ample time for careful review and editing by counsel.

If Form 10K contains material misstatements of facts, it can be a potential bomb sitting in the SEC's file that may be detonated by 20/20 legal hindsight.

The 1934 Exchange Act

The registration procedure for an initial public issue is carried out under the provisions of the 1933 Securities Act. The newly public company must also register under the 1934 Exchange Act pursuant to Section 12(b) or (g) of the law. The Form 8-A filing requires little effort as the necessary data are incorporated by reference from the final registration statement or Form 10K, depending upon the order of filing.

Directors and officers must file statements of beneficial ownership of their company securities pursuant to Section 16(a) of the 1934 Act. The filing is made on Form 3—Initial Statement of Beneficial Ownership of Securities. As discussed in Chapter 17, management persons who beneficially own more than 5% of the company's stock must annually file Schedule 13G under the 1934 Act.

The Proxy Statement and Card

A good bit of senior management's privacy vanishes with the distribution annually of the proxy statement. As an example, the SEC has made it clear that all of these persons' remunerations should be disclosed and dissected for the investors' and the world's review. While the concept of full disclosure is laudable, there are disadvantages to the SEC policy on remuneration. And they go beyond the intense personal dislike of such disclosures by senior management and their spouses.

Not only investors but employees, vendors, customers, and competitors read the management remuneration section of the proxy statement and draw their own partisan conclusions. The conclusions, which can affect the affairs of the enterprise, may include dissatisfaction with the employees' wage and salary scale, a twisted justification for an increase in vendor pricing, or irritation with the compensation of an individual such as a sales vice president.

Using the sales position as an example, the board of directors and the chief executive may believe that the interest of the business can best be served by having a high level of compensation for the position, perhaps at times higher than that of the chief executive. Yet the purchasing manager of the enterprise's largest customer may be upset enough when the sales compensation is disclosed to divert business elsewhere.

The inevitable rebuttal to such complaints by the advocates of full disclosure is a variation of Harry S. Truman's famous remark: "If you can't stand the heat, why did you come into the kitchen in the first place?" What is more, the rebuttal has equal merit when directors and officers complain bitterly about the detailed answers required in the annual questionnaire of company counsel prior to proxy statement preparation.

As the years have gone by, the director/officer questionnaire, the basis of the proxy statement, has become a formidable thing. Other than new board members and some senior officers, the management of a newly public company is well familiar with the exhaustive nature of the questionnaire because of the S-1 registration statement (see Chapter 12). Nevertheless, each time one is filled out, any director or officer has to be impressed with the extent of the interlocking questions. Yet when completed and mailed to counsel, it is easy to forget that the questionnaire sits there in the lawyer's files. Those same dormant files will be among the first documents asked for in the discovery process of a shareholder's lawsuit which names the company management as a defendant.

Preparation of the proxy statement by company counsel generally goes in tandem with the annual report. Both are attached documents to Form 10K, and both are mailed (along with the proxy card) in the same envelope to shareholders.

In contrast to the annual report, a standard format prescribed by the SEC is used for the proxy statement. As time must be allowed for possible SEC comments on the proxy statement prior to its mailing to shareholders, a printed proof should be in the SEC's hands at least 10 days before the planned mailing date. While SEC comment on proxy material is not received on the bulk of the submissions, it is only prudent to allow the minimum 10-day time interval.

Little comment is necessary on the proxy card. Practice has generated a relatively standard format, size, and weight of card stock. The transfer agent (discussed in a later section) is the reference point on all of these matters.

The First Annual Meeting

If a majority of the outstanding shares are represented and are voted for the management slate, the annual meeting is largely ritualistic except for the chief executive's remarks and the question-and-answer period. Shareholder votes are cast either by being present at the meeting or by proxy. The vast majority of shares are voted by completing the proxy cards and mailing them to the transfer agent.

While it is true that a simple majority of outstanding shares are required, the target for the percentage of shares represented should be much higher for several reasons. Not only will the chief executive want to avoid the embarrassment of not having the necessary majority, the board of directors undoubtedly would prefer a heavy vote as a sign of shareholder interest in the company's affairs.

A high percentage of shareholder votes comes only from careful planning and continued follow-up. Without these efforts, there can be an unpleasant surprise as to the number of proxies received. The annual report/proxy package should be mailed to shareholders at least a month before the annual meeting. However, many of the shares will be in street (brokerage house) names, as the shareholders have left the shares in their trading accounts. On top of not having shareholders' names in street accounts, as much as 25% of the shares of the company's stock occasionally traded could be sitting in a clearinghouse established by several dozen banks and brokers.

The clearinghouse serves as a central agency to take custody temporarily of shares that the banks and brokers are holding for their own customers. Thus the traffic back and forth of the actual stock certificates is greatly reduced. The clearinghouse is formally called The Depository Trust Company but is usually known as Cede & Co. (pronounced "see-dee") or sometimes as DTC. On noticing Cede & Co. on the transfer agent's rolls for the first time, the writer still remembers wondering who that aggressive firm was that had so much of the enterprise's stock in its name.

Cede & Co. will cooperate with the company by providing a listing of the banks and brokerage firms holding shares as of the record date, but proxy material will not be forwarded. This means the company must approach each of them (as with shares held directly in a street name on the transfer agent rolls) to determine the number of annual report/proxy packages required for remailing to shareholders by the banks and brokerage firms. Remailing fees are billed to the company. Whether a proxy solicitor is used or the company utilizes its own forces, the task has to be done because of the increasing concentration of shares in these different kinds of agencies.

Attendance at the first annual meeting of a newly public enterprise varies sharply depending upon the interest in the business or anticipated announcements as well as the annual meeting location. In the case of this writer's first public company, there was considerable brokerage and analyst interest, and the location of the annual meeting was adjacent to the financial center of a very large city. As a result, the early afternoon meeting was reasonably well attended. In another instance, with roughly equal investor interest, the annual meeting was located miles from the same financial center, and the attendance was low. The percentage mix between individual shareholders and the securities community was about the same in both cases.

The remarks of the chief executive to the annual meeting are often read for reasons of preciseness, and they tend to be pedestrian. While they are also designed to anticipate questions from the floor, some floor questions can be expected at the first meeting. Many larger enterprises mail copies of the chief executive's remarks to shareholders and others on the mailing list. For the company that has recently gone public, it may be better to defer a decision on the practice until a seasoned shareholder policy is developed.

Shareholder Relations and the Transfer Agent

Outside requests for company reports begin to arrive shortly after an S-1 registration statement is filed, and these requests never stop coming in. Then, too, after the public issue, shareholders have questions that must be answered. Either replying to the queries or routing them to the proper person is not a casual job assignment, as the work requires precision and judgment. A logical extension of the shareholder relations work is performance monitoring of the master report schedule discussed in the next section.

While it is possible for the newly public business to perform the transfer/registrar for its stock, most concerns do not. From a quality of work and cost considerations the consensus seems to be that the corporate trust department of a regional commercial bank (often the company's banker) is the best choice. Promptness, accuracy, and conformance with regulatory standards are the criteria for the transfer agent. If the work is done well, the entrepreneur does not hear about the transfer agent. If not, the company soon learns about the deficiency.

The principal things to be done by the transfer agent are worth summarizing:

> Issuing and registering stock certificates and furnishing daily reports of certificates cancelled and issued.
>
> Maintaining shareholder records and complying with SEC regulations regarding requirements for registered transfer agents.
>
> Preparing lists of shareholders and corporate mailings.
>
> Mailing of proxy materials for annual meeting of shareholders and broker search cards to broker, nominee, and beneficial holders of depositories.
>
> Examining and tabulating returned proxies.

Master Schedule for the First Year

No matter how experienced the entrepreneur, the first year after an initial public offering presents a number of new things-to-do for the business. If these things are done correctly, a considerable coordination and follow-up effort is required the first time around. A master schedule, similar to that of the illustrative Ever Onward Corporation schedule shown in Table 18.1, has much to recommend it.

A first examination of the table may leave the impression that too much time has been allocated to some of the work. Yet unavoidable slippages must be accommodated in the master schedule. Take for example a delay in the audit sign-off by the public accountants. Tandem efforts on the annual report and Form 10K are held up. Time buffers built into the master schedule can generally absorb such delays.

However, buffering can only go so far. An undue delay in the sign-off example would mean a mailing holdup on the annual report/proxy material package, which in turn can slow up the return of proxies for the annual meeting.

TABLE 18.1 Master Report Schedule (Fiscal Year—June 30)— First Twelve Months

Ever Onward Corporation—A Composite Example

Date	Action
Nov. 7	Initial public offering of stock
Dec. 26	Notice to Board of Directors of Jan. 26 meeting.
Jan. 26	Quarterly Board meeting.
Jan. 28	Selection of wire service for distribution of earnings reports and other announcements.
Jan. 28	Completion of earnings format for wire service release and determination of date and time of release.
Jan. 28	Completion of final proof of layout of the interim earnings report and selected balance sheet items.
Feb. 3	Completion of quarterly earnings review by public accountants.
Feb. 4	Release of quarterly and six months' earnings to wire service and to printer.
Feb. 8	Mailing of quarterly and six months' report.
Feb. 10	Completion of drafting of first 10Q report and review by auditors and company counsel.
Feb. 12	Filing of 10Q report with the SEC.
March 24	Notice to Board of Directors of April 24 meeting.
April 24	Quarterly Board and Audit Committee meetings.
April 26	Release to designer of rough layout of cover and pages of annual report.
May 3–12	Quarterly and nine months' earnings procedures and reports.
May 29	Annual report review of the design, cover, and paper stock recommendations.
June 26	Notice to Board of Directors of July 26 meeting.
July 6	Mailing of proxy questionnaires to Board members.
July 15	Review of dummy annual report and selection of photographs.
July 26	Quarterly Board meeting.
Aug. 1	Analysis of incomplete draft of proxy statement.
Aug. 1	Completion of annual report draft of letter to shareholders and comments on operations along with a draft of management's discussion and analysis of financial condition.
Aug. 10	Registration of company under 1934 Exchange Act.
Aug. 10	Filing of insiders' stock reports with SEC.
Aug. 14	Agreement with public accountants on footnotes.
Aug. 15	Transmittal of annual report material (including draft of letter and comments to shareholders, management's discussion and analysis, and financial footnotes) to company counsel for review.
Aug. 17	Release of all available annual report material and all proxy material to printer.

TABLE 18.1 (Continued)

Ever Onward Corporation—A Composite Example

Aug. 19	Mailing by transfer agent of broker nominee search cards.
Aug. 26	Annual audit sign off by public accountants.
Aug. 29	Release of annual and fourth-quarter earnings to wire service (no quarterly or 10Q reports required).
Sept. 1	Release to printer of final edited proof of annual report, proxy statement, and proxy card.
Sept. 7	Mailing of final printer's proof of proxy statement and proxy card to the SEC.
Sept. 8	Shareholder-of-record date as established by the Board of Directors.
Sept. 17	Forwarding of printed copies of annual report along with proxy statement and card to transfer agent.
Sept. 18	Review by management of Form 10K draft, and circulation for Board signatures.
Sept. 21	Mailing of Form 10K to SEC.
Sept. 24	Mailing of annual report/proxy package by transfer agent.
Oct. 3	Notice to Board of Directors of annual, board, and audit committee meetings.
Oct. 28	Completion of analysis of public accountants' draft of suggestions for accounting improvements, and company answers to suggestions.
Nov. 1	Completion of annual meeting arrangements and chairman's remarks.
Nov 2–11	First-quarter earnings procedures and reports.
Nov. 3	Annual meeting, audit committee meeting with review of auditors' suggestions and answers, Board of Directors meeting.

Source: J. S. O'Flaherty

A Conclusion

If the extent of official responsibilities and disclosure of information as a result of going public are understood, this chapter has served its purpose. There will be little outside sympathy for the pain and problems connected with satisfying the responsibilities and meeting disclosure requirements. After all, the entrepreneur and the senior associates are learning the answer to the question "If you can't stand the heat, why did you come into the kitchen in the first place?"

19

The Honeymoon is Over

The public issue money is in hand. The pressing debts have been paid off and the dunning telephone calls have stopped. Key people can get back to neglected, important work. It is a blessed period of financial quiescence. But like the four stomachs of a cow, part of the enterprise's system is just beginning to react to a whole new set of different problems. And digestion of them is not going to be that easy.

There are people problems—the senior staff and their spouses are temporarily, at least, rich on paper—still the stuff of dreams. Then the camel of the securities community and federal regulations has just put its nose in the company tent and its head will follow shortly. And finally, becoming conspicuous as a public company breeds unpleasant surprises.

Hopefully, one fixed factor is still unchanged, and this is that the entrepreneur continues to be a reasonably rational person and reference point for the company's key individuals.

Stock-Owning Associates

To presume that enlightened self-interest will guide the behavior of some of the stock-owning associates of the entrepreneur after the public offering can be wishful thinking. Even the example and authority of the chief executive and responsible senior associates will only help to moderate the extent of poor personal decisions and ensure that work is not being neglected. One unexpected benefit of federal regulations on restricted stock (see Chapter 17) is that these restraints do help to retard precipitous associate stock sales during the months after a public offering.

One's personal affairs can be most complicated under any circumstances. Add the valuable stock factor in, say, a settlement discussion of a pending divorce, and the results can be months of emotional wheel-spinning, both at home and at work, by a valued associate. Systematic arrangements for key person consultation with company counsel and tax accountants may be money well spent for the enterprise in the months after a public issue. The entrepreneur will be surprised as to the dangerous lack of knowledgeability by some colleagues in the brave, albeit frightening, world of substantial stock ownership.

Safe Harbor and Inside Information

From the hour of the initial offering, the fledgling public company is under a close watch by the securities community and many other outsiders. And the chief executive is receiving pressure to make what the Securities and Exchange Commission (SEC) calls "forward-looking statements about future company affairs." Assuming that certain critical criteria are met, Rule 175 of the 1933 Securities Act provides for a litigation-free, safe harbor for earnings and operations projections in documents filed with the SEC.

The decision to make safe harbor projections is done only with the mature advice of company counsel plus a strong leavening of the chief executive's own good judgment. Providing the financial community or the media with this kind of specific information with or without safe harbor protection is risky, as counsel will surely point out.

An associated and worrisome consideration for the newly public company is the control and dissemination of operating and financial information. Interpretations of Rule 10b-5 under the 1934 Exchange Act make it unlawful for anyone to buy or sell securities when that person possesses "inside information" which is not public and which, when made public, might have a material bearing on the price of the security.

To satisfy Rule 10b-5, the company has an evident responsibility to make prompt public disclosure of material matters which can affect the affairs of the business. These are matters of significant importance to the shareholders and potential investors in the enterprise. Such items might be a large layoff of employees, the receipt or cancellation of a major sales program, an important mineral discovery, or the like. However, with no hard and fast definition of materiality of inside information, the release of data has to be a judgment call by the chief executive after consultation with company counsel, and possibly the public accountants or other experts. Similar to the dissemination of earnings reports, the material information is distributed by wire service to the same recipients (including the media).

Annoying if not serious fringe problems are leaks of information about company affairs to people who hope to profit from this intelligence. There are relations, friends, and even acquaintances of senior management who are anxious to buy the concern's stock so long as it goes up in price. Public company executives who are experienced on these subjects simply refuse to make a stock recommendation or talk about business prospects. An energetic sales representative of a local brokerage house can pose more of a problem by systematically accumulating operating data from unsophisticated key technical or sales staff who are flattered by the attention they receive. Controlling these kinds of leaks of fragmentary information is an educational job of top management. The organization must understand that both the shareholders and the company can be harmed.

The Financial Community and the Company

A prime method of gathering data on the newly public company by the financial community is telephone calls to or visitations with a senior executive. Even prior to the filling of the Form S-1 registration statement with the SEC, the entrepreneur should make a decision as to whom the executive will be. Whoever it is will have a time-consuming, thankless assignment. For the first year or two at least, the task is usually performed by the chief executive with senior associates participating as required.

While scarcely consoling, if financial relations mistakes are made and the company is placed in an embarrassing position, the chief execuutive will have nobody else to blame. That presumes of course that the general sales manager's regular remarks to and briefing of the trade newspapers are coordinated with the entrepreneur. Most chief executives will readily admit that this is easier said than done.

Depending upon the kind of industry and its popularity with Wall Street, the type of questions and the amount of homework done by the stock analyst or institutional researcher will vary markedly. While not expecting company projections (but always willing to receive them), the analysts are looking for current industry and company material to extrapolate a range of earnings for the present and next fiscal year. The chief executive of a newly public business should consult with both company counsel and the investment banking firm on the outside information subject. But the final decisions rest with the chief executive, and they are neither that clear nor obvious.

In the first year after the offering of a reasonably popular first issue, the chief executive will talk to representatives of 20 to perhaps 40 different financial organizations, and a fair number of them several times. Excluding the fringe calls or meetings, the caliber of these people will range from fair to excellent in their knowledge and their ability to ask penetrating questions. Company executives who have not anticipated some of these interlocking questions can find themselves neatly boxed in. To extricate themselves may mean giving out more information than is appropriate. Such situations can be embarrassing as well, because the essence of all of these conversations will eventually be standard Wall Street information.

The first brief reports written by the financial community on a reasonably popular issue may appear within three months after the going-public date. A bit later on, the investment banking firm that served as managing underwriter of the issue may release a research report on the company. Naturally, this is discounted by the rest of Wall Street as being partisan, even though the analysis may be knowledgeable and comprehensive. In this framework, the best Street report, from a new issue viewpoint, is a favorable preliminary brief from an industry analyst of another securities firm. This is the kind of comment that is picked up by institutional investors and their advisors on an unseasoned stock.

Failing the foregoing kind of a scenario or continued favorable news on the company, interest of the securities community in the company's stock slides downward toward a kind of a limbo.

The Honeymoon Is Over

After the feverish activity following a successful offering, the entrepreneur usually discovers the Wall Street analysts and the institutional researchers are calling less, and visitations to the company's facilities have dropped off markedly. This lack of attention awakens mixed emotions. It is a blessing not to have to spend the time with these people. Yet there is a sneaking suspicion that the diminished interest in the business may be due to the chief executive's overcautious handling of the eternal, probing questions of the analysts. The strong likelihood is that this worry is unfounded; it is more probable that the Street's attention has simply moved elsewhere.

Table 19.1 shows a typical decline of Wall street interest in the illustrative Ever Onward stock discussed in previous chapters, and then an indication of a revival upbeat. The composite example assumed a

TABLE 19.1 Monthly Share Volume and Number of Market Makers—A Composite Example

Month	Monthly Share Volume (in 000s)	Number of Market Makers	Month	Monthly Share Volume (in 000s)	Number of Market Makers
Go-off month	385	9			
1	224	8	10	117	7
2	194	6	11	88	8
3	329	8	12	170	7
4	203	6	13	124	6
5	152	6	14	82	7
6	170	6	15	80	8
7	119	6	16	74	8
8	86	6	17	62	8
9	143	5	18	47	8

Source: J. S. O'Flaherty

well-received initial offering of 750,000 shares plus the sale of 75,000 over-allotment shares with satisfactory liquidity and aftermarket support. Share volume declined in the seventh month and the erosion continued through the remaining months of the analysis. The pattern in the number of market makers (firms that maintain an inventory of the company's stock) is not the same. The low point of 5 was reached in the ninth month and then the number grew to 8 in the final months of the example. This increase often can be ascribed to a revival of interest in the stock that may show up later on as increased share volume.

Even though financial briefings and public relations have been a hairshirt, the entrepreneur still finds it difficult to admit that the Wall Street honeymoon is over. What this means is that the company's shares are in the process of dropping into the limbo of issues with little investor interest—the status of many hundreds of OTC stocks. Yet, while there are no neat answers, many concerns have had their stocks emerge from this limbo zone as seasoned companies with a considerable financial following.

The easiest and best way to have a revival of interest by the securities community is to be lucky. In the nature of things, counting on good fortune is usually not the best game plan. Given a continuation of the company's performance pattern, it may be that time and previous exposure to Wall Street can well assure an interest revival. Specifically, if an established analyst gives an opinion that the enterprise is now proven or seasoned and makes a "buy" recommendation, this can spark an interest by the institutions that may carry over to the individual investors.

Failing chance and an analyst's benediction, the chief executive may decide to work with the company's investment banker in packaging a road show similar to that undertaken before the public offering. A schedule of appearances at regional analysts' and brokers' meetings may also be recommended. And there is the use of a financial public relations firm to be considered seriously.

The writer's view is that company performance and sales promotion, combined with the chief executive's accessibility to the financial community, will make a kind of a good fortune happen over the first two years after the offering. But really, only the entrepreneur in the particular situation can select the best course of action.

Ironically, while Wall Street may be ignoring the company, other groups are not.

Unwanted Attention

Probably the most disagreeable aspect of being a public company is the number of first experiences that must be handled by an already overworked management. Some of the major personnel problems and the Wall Street considerations have been touched upon. But many other new experiences are forthcoming as a result of the distribution of earnings and operating reports after going public.

Not the least of these experiences and resultant unpleasant surprises arises because of the availability of the ubiquitous computer and software applications. Like other computer mailing lists that are sold, it is nothing to put the principal financial items contained in the SEC registration statement into the machine's memory and update the material from the recurring reports the enterprise submits to the SEC. And there is no problem in selling these data cheaply in many sequential arrays.

The availability of computer runs can surprise the newly public company. For example, being listed as a principal growth company in a geographical region may at first appear to be innocuous, and even appeal to the entrepreneur's vanity. However, for a business that has deliberately retained a low profile as a privately held concern, standing front stage center can be a nasty shock, particularly, as the company is brought strongly to the attention of any number of special-interest groups as a major new prospect which fairly reeks of prosperity.

Reading one's mail becomes more interesting if not more pleasant as a chief executive of a public company. Some of the letters from shareholders can scarcely be called billets-doux; others represent new problems because of the availability of the company's financial and operating data to competitors, customers, and governmental agencies. As a parenthetical note, amiable agency requests for company information to be provided on a voluntary basis are not always to be taken literally. Sometimes the alternative to voluntary cooperation is involuntary participation; for example, variations of agency subpoenas can be issued that would require company officials to give depositions and possibly serve as witnesses.

A Mushy Period

The 18 months or so after going public is a mushy and curiously unsatisfactory period for many chief executives. Between personnel and Wall Street problems compounded by new surprises, the entrepreneur may remember it as sort of a shapeless and spongy time of limited real accomplishment.

20

Was It All Worthwhile?

Most entrepreneurs who have taken their companies public have a mixed bag of feelings on the subject. The chief executives are now carrying an additional and unfamiliar load of responsibilities. Still it is pleasant to discover that no opportunity doors for the enterprise have been closed as a result of going public and, indeed, some have been opened.

A small minority of chief executives eventually come to the conclusion that their concerns should have remained private. Then they discover the difficulties of "going private."

The chapter and book conclude with a small toast to the entrepreneurial breed that grows companies.

The Important Fixed Factor

A major and usually unspoken assumption in a going-public decision is that the entrepreneur's business attitude and way of life will remain unchanged. Thus it is given that chief executives will not alter their personal perspectives or views despite the fact that they have become cash, or at least paper, millionaires. For the continued welfare of both the old and new shareholders, that supposition is correct in the bulk of the instances. These chief executives do not change their work or leisure habits, and they perform or delegate the additional public company responsibilities as well as can be expected.

In a minority of instances, the assumption that the entrepreneurs' business attitudes and way of life remain unchanged proves to be dangerously fallacious. The new-found wealth for any numbers of reasons diverts the attention of the chief executives from their company affairs. And they display no interest in the fresh assortment of personnel problems, demands of the securities community, and the unpleasant surprises connected with a public company.

The missing stability and firm directon of the entrepreneur soon becomes painfully evident in business matters, enough so that a caustic saying about a body politic in difficulty is remembered by some worried observers of the business and the errant chief executive: "The stink of a decaying fish begins at its head."

However, the consoling and typical scenario is that the ingrained work-habit patterns of the wayward entrepreneur sooner rather than later reassert themselves. This means a return of management direction and stability.

A Seasoned Company

No financial doors have been closed and some have been opened for the company as a result of going public. The most evident positive result is the ability to borrow additional short- and long-term money as a result of the improved equity base. Also the business is in a position to utilize a favorable price/earning multiple to make acquisitions by stock or stock/cash offers. And if all goes reasonably well, Wall Street will eventually recognize the company and its stock as a seasoned security.

The company's registration disclosures, which are widely distributed in the securities community, help to provide financial credence to the reported results of the concern's operations. Continued favorable financial reports for the next half dozen or so quarters with no financial surprises surfacing will move the enterprise into the seasoned category. Wall Street is justifiably wary of concerns going public at the high point of operations and then showing financial deterioration or unpleasant surprises during the immediate quarters following the issue date. The seasoned reputation of the company is sure to give support to the price/earnings multiple of the stock.

With the debts paid off as a result of the cash input of an initial offering and the consequent major improvement of the equity to debt ratios, the entrepreneur has a unique opportunity to reexamine the forward-looking alternatives available to the company. The financial options of bank term notes and institutional debentures are now readily available because of the financial posture of a seasoned public enterprise.

Continued Irritations and Costs

The responsibilities associated with being a public company can be irritating at the best and onerous at the worst, as discussed in previous chapters. While the militancy of the Securities and Exchange Commission (SEC) is considerably muted in the early 1980s when compared with that of the 1970s, the extensive rules and regulations with associated case law are all in place. And there is no reason to presume that there will not be a reappearance of congressional and SEC militancy in the regulation of public companies.

Accurately balancing the recurring costs against the benefits of being a public enterprise is difficult if not impossible. For example, what is the value of the irreplaceable time of senior executives compared to the availability of public issue funds that have provided the much-needed flexibility and mobility to the enterprise? However, recurring out-of-pocket costs can be accumulated, and they are substantial.

For a typical business, expenses connected with being a public company in the early 1980s probably totaled $80,000 to $120,000 for the first year after the initial offering. Succeeding annual periods would be somewhat less. The first year's budget included such items as additional legal expense and $5000 to $9000 in transfer agent/registration charges. A two-color, 20-page annual report with a 4000-print run was $15,000 to $25,000 the first year, with the cost of the next period being $9000 to $12,000 if an identical format was followed. Not that much effort was required to spend an additional

$5000 a year in long-distance calls to individuals in the securities community. And so the expenses build up.

Going Private

Often considerably after their initial public offerings, a small minority of entrepreneurs come to the reluctant conclusion that their enterprises should have remained private. While the combinations of reasons for such conclusions may be as varied as the individual enterprises involved, several key factors may be represented in the going private decision.

As a rule, the entrepreneur (either individually or through a group) benefically owns some 40% to 80% of the outstanding stock of the public enterprise. Over a period of time, the chief executive may have decided that the company's activities should be directed toward high-risk and/or very long-term payouts—neither of which policies would meet the investment criteria of the securities community. Or a principal consideration may be the desire to establish a family hierarchy with a consequent reluctance to continue providing SEC disclosure data for public perusal. Perhaps new legislation has affected the entrepreneur's thinking. For example, the early 1980s brought Regulation D (an improved set of rules to raise money privately) as well as a significant change in the federal inheritance-tax laws. But whatever the reasons for considering action, the results of the entrepreneur's investigations as to taking the enterprise private are bound to be discouraging.

Going private is a difficult task. SEC rules prescribe extensive procedures designed to protect the public shareholders, and court decisions support this protective posture. In fact, the public minority shareholders are so well protected that they can be in an enviable negotiating position when approached by the control group with a stock purchase offer. Still, with a long purse and considerable patience, the stock transaction can be carried out, usually over an extended period of time.

It is a great deal easier not to be involved in going private at all. However, the same dictum could be applied to so many situations that enmesh the chief executive.

A Small Toast to the Entrepreneurial Breed

Like an old, jerky movie, the entrepreneurs stagger through their environment, encountering all of the pratfalls, human frailties, big mistakes, and percentage of wins. And if they take their companies public, they enter a world of hindsight review by people who are prepared to tell them in court briefs how they should have done better jobs years earlier. All of these things require the psychological stomach of a goat and the strength of a horse.

To grow successful companies, entrepreneurs must be a stout breed apart. A traditional Irish toast is appropriate to our kind of people:

> Here's to us—
> Who's like us?
> Damned few,
> Thank God!

Appendix A

REGULATION D
Rules Governing the Limited Offer and Sale of Securities
Without Registration Under the Securities Act of 1933

Preliminary Notes

1. The following rules relate to transactions exempted from the registration requirements of section 5 of the Securities Act of 1933 (the "Act") [15 U. S. C. 77a et seq., as amended]. Such transactions are not exempt from the antifraud, civil liability, or other provisions of the federal securities laws. Issuers are reminded of their obligation to provide such further material information, if any, as may be necessary to make the information required under this regulation, in light of the circumstances under which it is furnished, not misleading.

2. Nothing in these rules obviates the need to comply with any applicable state law relating to the offer and sale of securities. Regulation D is intended to be a basic element in a uniform system of federal-state limited offering exemptions consistent with the provisions of sections 18 and 19(c) of the Act. In those states that have adopted Regulation D, or any version of Regulation D, special attention should be directed to the applicable state laws and regulations, including those relating to registration of persons who receive remuneration in connection with the offer and sale of securities, to disqualification of issuers and other persons associated with offerings based on state administrative orders or judgments, and to requirements for filings of notices of sales.

Source: Ticor Print Network/Jeffries Banknote Company *Securities Regulations Handbook*, updated to January 31, 1983

3. Attempted compliance with any rule in Regulation D does not act as an exclusive election; the issuer can also claim the availability of any other applicable exemption. For instance, an issuer's failure to satisfy all the terms and conditions of Rule 506 shall not raise any presumption that the exemption provided by section 4(2) of the Act is not available.

4. These rules are available only to the issuer of the securities and not to any affiliate of that issuer or to any other person for resales of the issuer's securities. The rules provide an exemption only for the transactions in which the securities are offered or sold by the issuer, not for the securities themselves.

5. These rules may be used for business combinations that involve sales by virtue of Rule 145(a) or otherwise.

6. In view of the objectives of these rules and the policies underlying the Act, Regulation D is not available to any issuer for any transaction or chain of transactions that, although in technical compliance with these rules, is part of a plan or scheme to evade the registration provisions of the Act. In such cases, registration under the Act is required.

7. Offers and sales of securities to foreign persons made outside the United States effected in a manner that will result in the securities coming to rest abroad generally need not be registered under the Act. See Release No. 33-4708 (July 9, 1964) [29 FR 828]. This interpretation may be relied on for such offers and sales even if coincident offers and sales are made under Regulation D inside the United States. Thus, for example, persons who are not citizens or residents of the United States would not be counted in the calculation of the number of purchasers. Similarly, proceeds from sales to foreign purchasers would not be included in the aggregate offering price. The provisions of this note, however, do not apply if the issuer elects to rely solely on Regulation D for offers or sales to foreign persons.

Rule 501. Definitions and Terms Used in Regulation D.

As used in Regulation D, the following terms shall have the meaning indicated:

(a) *Accredited investor.* "Accredited investor" shall mean any person who comes within any of the following categories, or who the issuer reasonably believes comes within any of the following categories, at the time of the sale of the securities to that person:

(1) Any bank as defined in section 3(a)(2) of the Act whether acting in its individual or fiduciary capacity; insurance company as defined in section 2(13) of the Act; investment company registered under the Investment Company Act of 1940 or a business development company as defined in section 2(a)(48) of that Act; Small Business Investment Company licensed by the U. S. Small Business Administration under section 301(c) or (d) of the Small Business Investment Act of 1958; employee benefit plan within the meaning of Title I of the Employee Retirement Income Security Act of 1974, if the investment decision is made by a plan fiduciary, as defined in section 3(21) of such Act, which is either a bank, insurance company, or registered investment adviser, or if the employee benefit plan has total assets in excess of $5,000,000;

(2) Any private business development company as defined in section 202(a)(22) of the Investment Advisers Act of 1940;

(3) Any organization described in Section 501(c)(3) of the Internal Revenue Code with total assets in excess of $5,000,000;

(4) Any director, executive officer, or general partner of the issuer of the securities being offered or sold, or any director, executive officer, or general partner of a general partner of that issuer;

Appendix A

(5) Any person who purchases at least $150,000 of the securities being offered, where the purchaser's total purchase price does not exceed 20 percent of the purchaser's net worth at the time of sale, or joint net worth with that person's spouse, for one or any combination of the following: (i) cash, (ii) securities for which market quotations are readily available, (iii) an unconditional obligation to pay cash or securities for which market quotations are readily available which obligation is to be discharged within five years of the sale of the securities to the purchaser, or (iv) the cancellation of any indebtedness owed by the issuer to the purchaser;

(6) Any natural person whose individual net worth, or joint net worth with that person's spouse, at the time of his purchase exceeds $1,000,000;

(7) Any natural person who had an individual income in excess of $200,000 in each of the two most recent years and who reasonably expects an income in excess of $200,000 in the current year; and

(8) Any entity in which all of the equity owners are accredited investors under paragraph (a)(1), (2), (3), (4), (6), or (7) of this Rule 501.

(b) *Affiliate.* An "affiliate" of, or person "affiliated" with, a specified person shall mean a person that directly, or indirectly through one or more intermediaries, controls or is controlled by, or is under common control with, the person specified.

(c) *Aggregate offering price.* "Aggregate offering price" shall mean the sum of all cash, services, property, notes, cancellation of debt, or other consideration received by an issuer for issuance of its securities. Where securities are being offered for both cash and non-cash consideration, the aggregate offering price shall be based on the price at which the securities are offered for cash. If securities are not offered for cash, the aggregate offering price shall be based on the value of the consideration as established by bona fide sales of that consideration made within a reasonable time, or, in the absence of sales, on the fair value as determined by an accepted standard.

(d) *Business combination.* "Business combination" shall mean any transaction of the type specified in paragraph (a) of Rule 145 under the Act and any transaction involving the acquisition by one issuer, in exchange for all or a part of its own or its parent's stock, of stock of another issuer if, immediately after the acquisition, the acquiring issuer has control of the other issuer (whether or not it had control before the acquisition).

(e) *Calculation of number of purchasers.* For purposes of calculating the number of purchasers under Rules 505(b) and 506(b) only, the following shall apply:

(1) The following purchasers shall be excluded:

(i) Any relative, spouse or relative of the spouse of a purchaser who has the same principal residence as the purchaser;

(ii) Any trust or estate in which a purchaser and any of the persons related to him as specified in paragraph (e)(1)(i) or (e)(1)(iii) of this Rule 501 collectively have more than 50 percent of the beneficial interest (excluding contingent interests);

(iii) Any corporation or other organization of which a purchaser and any of the persons related to him as specified in paragraph (e)(1)(i) or (e)(1)(ii) of this Rule 501 collectively are beneficial owners of more than 50 percent of the equity securities (excluding directors' qualifying shares) or equity interests; and

(iv) Any accredited investor.

(2) A corporation, partnership or other entity shall be counted as one purchaser. If, however, that entity is organized for the specific purpose of acquiring the securities offered and is not an accredited investor under paragraph (a)(8) of this Rule 501, then each beneficial owner of equity securities or equity interests in the entity shall count as a separate purchaser for all provisions of Regulation D.

Note: The issuer must satisfy all the other provisions of Regulation D for all purchasers whether or not they are included in calculating the number of purchasers. Clients of an investment adviser or customers of a broker or dealer shall be considered the "purchasers" under Regulation D regardless of the amount of discretion given to the investment adviser or broker or dealer to act on behalf of the client or customer.

(f) *Executive officer.* "Executive officer" shall mean the president, any vice president in charge of a principal business unit, division or function (such as sales, administration or finance), any other officer who performs a policy making function, or any other person who performs similar policy making functions for the issuer. Executive officers of subsidiaries may be deemed executive officers of the issuer if they perform such policy making functions for the issuer.

(g) *Issuer.* The definition of the term "issuer" in section 2(4) of the Act shall apply, except that in the case of a proceeding under the Federal Bankruptcy Code [11 U. S. C. 101 et seq.], the trustee or debtor in possession shall be considered the issuer in an offering under a plan or reorganization, if the securities are to be issued under the plan.

(h) *Purchaser representative.* "Purchaser representative" shall mean any person who satisfies all of the following conditions or who the issuer reasonably believes satisfies all of the following conditions:

(1) Is not an affiliate, director, officer or other employee of the issuer, or beneficial owner of 10 percent or more of any class of the equity securities or 10 percent or more of the equity interest in the issuer, except where the purchaser is:

(i) A relative of the purchaser representative by blood, marriage or adoption and not more remote than a first cousin;

(ii) A trust or estate in which the purchaser representative and any person related to him as specified in paragraph (h)(1)(i) or (h)(1)(iii) of this Rule 501 collectively have more than 50 percent of the beneficial interest (excluding contingent interest) or of which the purchaser representative serves as trustee, executor, or in any similar capacity; or

(iii) A corporation or other organization of which the purchaser representative and any persons related to him as specified in paragraph (h)(1)(i) or (h)(1)(ii) of this Rule 501 collectively are the beneficial owners of more than 50 percent of the equity securities (excluding directors' qualifying shares) or equity interests;

(2) Has such knowledge and experience in financial and business matters that he is capable of evaluating, alone, or together with other purchaser representatives of the purchaser, or together with the purchaser, the merits and risks of the prospective investment;

(3) Is acknowledged by the purchaser in writing, during the course of the transaction, to be his purchaser representative in connection with evaluating the merits and risks of the prospective investment; and

(4) Discloses to the purchaser in writing prior to the acknowledgment specified in paragraph (h)(3) of this Rule 501 any material relationship between himself or his affiliates and the issuer or its affiliates that then exists, that is mutually understood to be contemplated, or that has existed at any time during the previous two years, and any compensation received or to be received as a result of such relationship.

Note 1: A person acting as a purchaser representative should consider the applicability of the registration and antifraud provisions relating to brokers and dealers under the Securities Exchange Act of 1934 ("Exchange Act") [15 U. S. C. 78a et seq., as amended] and relating to investment advisers under the Investment Advisers Act of 1940.

Note 2: The acknowledgment required by paragraph (h)(3) and the disclosure required by paragraph (h)(4) of this Rule 501 must be made with specific reference to each prospective investment. Advance blanket acknowledgment, such as for "all securities transactions" or "all private placements," is not sufficient.

Note 3: Disclosure of any material relationships between the purchaser representative or his affiliates and the issuer or its affiliates does not relieve the purchaser representative of this obligation to act in the interest of the purchaser.

Rule 502. General Conditions to Be Met.

The following conditions shall be applicable to offers and sales made under Regulation D:

(a) *Integration.* All sales that are part of the same Regulation D offering must meet all of the terms and conditions of Regulation D. Offers and sales that are made more than six months before the start of a Regulation D offering or are made more than six months after completion of a Regulation D offering will not be considered part of that Regulation D offering, so long as during those six month periods there are no offers or sales of securities by or for the issuer that are of the same or a similar class as those offered or sold under Regulation D, other than those offers or sales of securities under an employee benefit plan as defined in Rule 405 under the Act.

Note: The term "offering" is not defined in the Act or in Regulation D. If the issuer offers or sells securities for which the safe harbor rule in paragraph (a) of this Rule 502 is unavailable, the determination as to whether separate sales of securities are part of the same offering (*i.e.* are considered "integrated") depends on the particular facts and circumstances. Generally, transactions otherwise meeting the requirements of an exemption will not be integrated with simultaneous offerings being made outside the United States effected in a manner that will result in the securities coming to rest abroad. See Release No. 33-4708 (July 9, 1964) [29 F.R. 828].

The following factors should be considered in determining whether offers and sales should be integrated for purposes of the exemptions under Regulation D:

(a) whether the sales are part of a single plan of financing;

(b) whether the sales involve issuance of the same class of securities;

(c) whether the sales have been made at or about the same time;

(d) whether the same type of consideration is received; and

(e) whether the sales are made for the same general purpose.

See Release No. 33-4552 (November 6, 1962) (27 FR 11316).

(b) *Information requirements.*

(1) *When information must be furnished.*

(i) If the issuer sells securities either under Rule 504 or only to accredited investors, paragraph (b) of this Rule 502 does not require that specific information be furnished to purchasers.

(ii) If the issuer sells securities under Rule 505 or 506 to any purchaser that is not an accredited investor, the issuer shall furnish the information specified in paragraph (b)(2) of this Rule 502 to all purchasers during the course of the offering and prior to sale.

(2) *Type of information to be furnished.*

(i) If the issuer is not subject to the reporting requirements of section 13 or 15(d) of the Exchange Act, the issuer shall furnish the following information, to the extent material to an understanding of the issuer, its business, and the securities being offered:

(A) *Offerings up to $5,000,000.* The same kind of information as would be required in Part I of Form S-18, except that only the financial statements for the issuer's most recent fiscal year must be certified by an independent public or certified accountant. If Form S-18 is not available to an issuer, then the issuer shall furnish the same kind of information as would be required in Part I of a registration statement filed under the Act on the form that the issuer would be entitled to use, except that only the financial statements for the most recent two fiscal years prepared in accordance with generally accepted accounting principles shall be furnished and only the financial statements for the issuer's most recent fiscal year shall be certified by an independent public or certified accountant. If an issuer, other than a limited partnership, cannot obtain audited financial statements without unreasonable effort or expense, then only the issuer's balance sheet, which shall be dated within 120 days of the start of the offering, must be audited. If the issuer is a limited partnership and cannot obtain the required financial statements without unreasonable effort or expense, it may furnish financial statements that have been prepared on the basis of federal income tax requirements and examined and reported on in accordance with generally accepted auditing standards by an independent public or certified accountant.

(B) *Offerings over $5,000,000.* The same kind of information as would be required in Part I of a registration statement filed under the Act on the form that the issuer would be entitled to use. If an issuer, other than a limited partnership, cannot obtain audited financial statements without unreasonable effort or expense, then only the issuer's balance sheet, which shall be dated within 120 days of the start of the offering, must be audited. If the issuer is a limited partnership and cannot obtain the required financial statements without unreasonable effort or expense, it may furnish financial statements that have been prepared on the basis of federal income tax requirements and examined and reported on in accordance with generally accepted auditing standards by an independent public or certified accountant.

(C) If the issuer is a foreign private issuer eligible to use Form 20-F the issuer shall disclose the same kind of information required to be included in a registration statement filed under the Act on the form that the issuer would be entitled to use. The financial statements need be certified only to the extent required by paragraph (b)(2)(i) (A) or (B) as appropriate.

(ii) If the issuer is subject to the reporting requirements of section 13 or 15(d) of the Exchange Act, the issuer shall furnish the information specified in paragraph (b)(2)(ii)(A) or (b)(2)(ii)(B), and in either event the information specified in paragraph (b)(2)(ii)(C) of this Rule 502:

(A) The issuer's annual report to shareholders for the most recent fiscal year, if such annual report meets the requirements of Rule 14a-3 or 14c-3 under the Exchange Act, the definitive proxy statement filed in connection with that annual report, and, if requested by the purchaser in writing, a copy of the issuer's most recent Form 10-K under the Exchange Act.

(B) The information contained in an annual report on Form 10-K under the Exchange Act or in a registration statement on Form S-1 under the Act or on Form 10 under the Exchange Act, whichever filing is the most recent required to be filed.

(C) The information contained in any reports or documents required to be filed by the issuer under sections 13(a), 14(a), 14(c), and 15(d) of the Exchange Act since the distribution or filing of the report or registration statement specified in paragraph (A) and (B), and a brief description of the securities being offered, the use of the proceeds from the offering, and any material changes in the issuer's affairs that are not disclosed in the documents furnished.

(D) If the issuer is a foreign private issuer eligible to use Form 20-F, the issuer may provide in lieu of the information specified in paragraphs (b)(2)(ii)(A) or (B) of this section, the information contained in its most recent filing on Form 20-F or Form F-1.

Appendix A

(iii) Exhibits required to be filed with the Commission as part of a registration statement or report, other than an annual report to shareholders or parts of that report incorporated by reference in a Form 10-K report, need not be furnished to each purchaser if the contents of the exhibits are identified and the exhibits are made available to the purchaser, upon his written request, prior to his purchase.

(iv) At a reasonable time prior to the purchase of securities by any purchaser that is not an accredited investor in a transaction under Rule 505 or 506, the issuer shall furnish the purchaser a brief description in writing of any written information concerning the offering that has been provided by the issuer to any accredited investor. The issuer shall furnish any portion or all of this information to the purchaser, upon his written request, prior to his purchase.

(v) The issuer shall also make available to each purchaser at a reasonable time prior to this purchase of securities in a transaction under Rule 505 or 506 the opportunity to ask questions and receive answers concerning the terms and conditions of the offering and to obtain any additional information which the issuer possesses or

(vi) For business combinations, in addition to information required by paragraph (b)(2) of this Rule 502, the issuer shall provide to each purchaser at the time the plan is submitted to security holders, or, with an exchange, during the course of the transaction and prior to sale, written information about any terms or arrangements of the proposed transaction that are materially different from those for all other security holders.

(c) *Limitation on manner of offering.* Except as provided in Rule 504(b)(1), neither the issuer nor any person acting on its behalf shall offer or sell the securities by any form of general solicitation or general advertising, including, but not limited to, the following:

(1) Any advertisement, article, notice or other communication published in any newspaper, magazine, or similar media or broadcast over television or radio; and

(2) Any seminar or meeting whose attendees have been invited by any general solicitation or general advertising.

(d) *Limitations on resale.* Except as provided in Rule 504(b)(1), securities acquired in a transaction under Regulation D shall have the status of securities acquired in a transaction under section 4(2) of the Act and cannot be resold without registration under the Act or an exemption therefrom. The issuer shall exercise reasonable care to assure that the purchasers of the securities are not underwriters within the meaning of section 2(11) of the Act, which reasonable care shall include, but not be limited to, the following:

(1) Reasonable inquiry to determine if the purchaser is acquiring the securities for himself or for other persons;

(2) Written disclosure to each purchaser prior to sale that the securities have not been registered under the Act and, therefore, cannot be resold unless they are registered under the Act or unless an exemption from registration is available; and

(3) Placement of a legend on the certificate or other document that evidences the securities stating that the securities have not been registered under the Act and setting forth or referring to the restrictions on transferability and sale of the securities.

Rule 503. Filing of Notice of Sales.

(a) The issuer shall file with the Commission five copies of a notice on Form D at the following times:

(1) No later than 15 days after the first sale of securities in an offering under Regulation D;

(2) Every six months after the first sale of securities in an offering under Regulation D, unless the final notice required by paragraph (a)(3) of this Rule 503 has been filed; and

(3) No later than 30 days after the last sale of securities in an offering under Regulation D.

(b) If the offering is completed within the 15 day period described in paragraph (a)(1) of this Rule 503 and if the notice is filed no later than the end of that period but after the completion of the offering, then only one notice need be filed to comply with paragraphs (a)(1) and (3) of this Rule 503.

(c) One copy of every notice on Form D shall be manually signed by a person duly authorized by the issuer.

(d) If sales are made under Rule 505, the notice shall contain an undertaking by the issuer to furnish to the Commission, upon the written request of its staff, the information furnished by the issuer under Rule 502(b)(2) to any purchaser that is not an accredited investor.

(e) If more than one notice for an offering is required to be filed under paragraph (a) of this Rule 503, notices after the first notice need only report the issuer's name and the information required by Part C and any material change in the facts from those set forth in Parts A and B of the first notice.

(f) A notice on Form D shall be considered filed with the Commission under paragraph (a) of this Rule 503:

(1) As of the date on which it is received at the Commission's principal office in Washington, D. C.; or

(2) As of the date on which the notice is mailed by means of United States registered or certified mail to the Commission's Office of Small Business Policy, Division of Corporation Finance, at the Commission's principal office in Washington, D. C., if the notice is delivered to such office after the date on which it is required to be filed.

Rule 504. Exemption for Limited Offers and Sales of Securities Not Exceeding $500,000.

(a) *Exemption.* Offers and sales of securities that satisfy the conditions in paragraph (b) of this Rule 504 by an issuer that is not subject to the reporting requirements of section 13 or 15(d) of the Exchange Act and that is not an investment company shall be exempt from the provisions of section 5 of the Act under section 3(b) of the Act.

(b) *Conditions to be met.*

(1) *General conditions.* To qualify for exemption under this Rule 504, offers and sales must satisfy the terms and conditions of Rule 501 through Rule 503, except that the provisions of Rule 502(c) and (d) shall not apply to offers and sales of securities under this Rule 504 that are made exclusively in one or more states each of which provides for the registration of the securities and requires the delivery of a disclosure document before sale and that are made in accordance with those state provisions.

(2) *Specific conditions.*

(i) *Limitation on aggregate offering price.* The aggregate offering price for an offering of securities under this Rule 504, as defined in Rule 501(c), shall not exceed

$500,000, less the aggregate offering price for all securities sold within the twelve months before the start of and during the offering of securities under this Rule 504 in reliance on any exemption under section 3(b) of the Act or in violation of section 5(a) of the Act.

Note 1: The calculation of the aggregate offering price is illustrated as follows:

Example 1. If an issuer sold $200,000 of its securities on June 1, 1982 under this Rule 504 and an additional $100,000 on September 1, 1982, the issuer would be permitted to sell only $200,000 more under this Rule 504 until June 1, 1983. Until that date the issuer must count both prior sales towards the $500,000 limit. However, if the issuer made its third sale on June 1, 1983, the issuer could then sell $400,000 of its securities because the June 1, 1982 sale would not be within the preceding twelve months.

Example 2. If an issuer sold $100,000 of its securities on June 1, 1982 under this Rule 504 and an additional $4,500,000 on December 1, 1982 under Rule 505, the issuer could not sell any of its securities under this Rule 504 until December 1, 1983. Until then the issuer must count the December 1, 1982 sale towards the limit of $500,000 within the preceding twelve months.

Note 2: If a transaction under this Rule 504 fails to meet the limitation on the aggregate offering price, it does not affect the availability of this Rule 504 for the other transactions considered in applying such limitation. For example, if the issuer in *Example 1* made its third sale on May 31, 1983, in the amount of $250,000, this Rule 504 would not be available for that sale, but the exemption for the prior two sales would be unaffected.

Rule 505. Exemption for Limited Offers and Sales of Securities Not Exceeding $5,000,000.

(a) *Exemption.* Offers and sales of securities that satisfy the conditions in paragraph (b) of this Rule 505 by an issuer that is not an investment company shall be exempt from the provisions of section 5 of the Act under section 3(b) of the Act.

(b) *Conditions to be met.*

(1) *General conditions.* To qualify for exemption under this Rule 505, offers and sales must satisfy the terms and conditions of Rules 501 through 503.

(2) *Specific conditions.*

(i) *Limitation on aggregate offering price.* The aggregate offering price for an offering of securities under this Rule 505, as defined in Rule 501(c), shall not exceed $5,000,000, less the aggregate offering price for all securities sold within the twelve months before the start of and during the offering of securities under this Rule 505 in reliance on any exemption under section 3(b) of the Act or in violation of section 5(a) of the Act.

Note: The calculation of the aggregate offering price is illustrated as follows:

Example 1. If an issuer sold $2,000,000 of its securities on June 1, 1982 under this Rule 505 and an additional $1,000,000 on September 1, 1982, the issuer would be permitted to sell only $2,000,000 more under this Rule 505 until June 1, 1983. Until that date the issuer must count both prior sales towards the $5,000,000 limit. However, if the issuer made its third sale on June 1, 1983, the issuer could then sell $4,000,000 of its securities because the June 1, 1982 sale would not be within the preceding twelve months.

Example 2. If an issuer sold $500,000 of its securities on June 1, 1982 under Rule 504 and an additional $4,500,000 on December 1, 1982 under this Rule 505, then the issuer could not sell any of its securities under this Rule 505 until June 1, 1983. At that time it could sell an additional $500,000 of its securities.

(ii) *Limitation on number of purchasers.* The issuer shall reasonably believe that there are no more than 35 purchasers of securities from the issuer in any offering under this Rule 505.

Note: See Rule 501(e) for the calculation of the number of purchasers and Rule 502(a) for what may or may not constitute an offering under this section.

(iii) *Disqualifications.* No exemption under this Rule 505 shall be available for the securities of any issuer described in Rule 252(c), (d), (e), or (f) of Regulation A, except that for purposes of this Rule 505 only:

(A) The term "filing of the notification required by Rule 255" as used in Rule 252(c), (d), (e) and (f) shall mean the first sale of securities under this Rule 505;

(B) The term "underwriter" as used in Rule 252(d) and (e) shall mean a person that has been or will be paid directly or indirectly remuneration for solicitation of purchasers in connection with sales of securities under this Rule 505; and

(C) Paragraph (b)(2)(iii) of this Rule 505 shall not apply to any issuer if the Commission determines, upon a showing of good cause, that it is not necessary under the circumstances that the exemption be denied. Any such determination shall be without prejudice to any other action by the Commission in any other proceeding or matter with respect to the issuer or any other person.

Rule 506. Exemption for Limited Offers and Sales Without Regard to Dollar Amount of Offering.

(a) *Exemption.* Offers and sales of securities by an issuer that satisfy the conditions in paragraph (b) of this Rule 506 shall be deemed to be transactions not involving any public offering within the meaning of section 4(2) of the Act.

(b) *Conditions to be met.*

(1) *General conditions.* To qualify for exemption under this Rule 506, offers and sales must satisfy all the terms and conditions of Rules 501 through 503.

(2) *Specific conditions.*

(i) *Limitation on number of purchasers.* The issuer shall reasonably believe that there are no more than 35 purchasers of securities from the issuer in any offering under this Rule 506.

Note: See Rule 501(e) for the calculation of the number of purchasers and Rule 502(a) for what may or may not constitute an offering under this Rule 506.

(ii) *Nature of purchasers.* The issuer shall reasonably believe immediately prior to making any sale that each purchaser who is not an accredited investor either alone or with his purchaser representative(s) has such knowledge and experience in financial and business matters that he is capable of evaluating the merits and risks of the prospective investment.

Appendix A

FORM D

U.S. SECURITIES AND EXCHANGE COMMISSION
Washington, D. C. 20549

OMB Approval
OMB 3235-0076
Expires December 31, 1984

SEC USE ONLY

NOTICE OF SALES OF SECURITIES
PURSUANT TO REGULATION D OR SECTION 4(6)

SEC USE ONLY
SERIAL
21-

Nature of this filing with respect to this offering.

INSTRUCTION: Please check the box(es) corresponding to the exemptive provision applicable to this offering.

Rule 504 ☐   Rule 505 ☐   Rule 506 ☐   Section 4(6) ☐

INSTRUCTION: Circle "N" for a new filing or "A" for an amended filing.

ORIGINAL 1 N/A   COMBINED ORIGINAL AND FINAL 2 N/A   SIX-MONTH UPDATE 3 N/A   FINAL 4 N/A

INSTRUCTIONS: The issuer shall file with the Commission five copies of this notice at the following times: (a) no later than 15 days after the first sale of securities in an offering under Regulation D or Section 4(6); (b) every six months after the first sale of securities in an offering under Regulation D or Section 4(6), unless a final notice has been filed; and (c) no later than 30 days after the last sale of securities in an offering under Regulation D or Section 4(6), *except that if the offering is completed within the 15-day period described in "(a)" above, and if the notice is filed no later than the end of that period but after the completion of the offering, then only one notice need be filed*. If more than one notice for an offering is required to be filed, notices after the first notice need only report the issuer's name, information in response to Part C and any material changes from the facts previously reported in Parts A and B. This notice shall be deemed to be filed with the Commission for purposes of the rule as of the date on which the notice is received by the Commission, or if delivered to the Commission after the date on which it is due, as of the date on which it is mailed by means of United States registered or certified mail to the Office of Small Business Policy, Division of Corporation Finance, U.S. Securities and Exchange Commission, Washington, D.C. 20549.

A. Basic Identification of Issuer.

INSTRUCTION: State the address of the issuer's executive offices and, if different, the address at which the issuer's principal business operations are conducted or proposed to be conducted.

NAME			
ADDRESS OF EXECUTIVE OFFICES			
CITY		STATE	ZIP
AREA CODE	TELEPHONE NUMBER		
ADDRESS OF PRINCIPAL BUSINESS OPERATIONS			
CITY		STATE	ZIP
AREA CODE	TELEPHONE NUMBER		

INSTRUCTION: Please list the full name and address of the following persons: each promoter of the issuer involved in the offering of securities as to which sales pursuant to Regulation D or Section 4(6) are reported on this notice, the issuer's chief executive officer, and each of the issuer's affiliates. Indicate the status of each person named by placing an "X" in the applicable box(es) opposite such person's name. The term "promoter" includes . . .

(a) Any person who, acting alone or in conjunction with one or more other persons, directly or indirectly takes the initiative in founding and organizing the business or enterprise of an issuer; or

(b) Any person who, in connection with the founding or organizing of the business or enterprise of an issuer, directly or indirectly receives in consideration of services or property, or both services and property, 10 percent or more of any class of securities of the issuer or 10 percent or more of the proceeds from the sale of any class of securities. However, a person who receives such securities or proceeds either solely as brokerage commissions or solely in consideration of property shall not be deemed a promoter within the meaning of this paragraph if such person does not otherwise take part in founding and organizing the enterprise.

SEC 1972 (3-82)

FORM D

**NOTICE OF SALES OF SECURITIES
PURSUANT TO REGULATION D OR SECTION 4(6)**

Page 2

CEO	Aff	Pro

NAME

ADDRESS   CITY   STATE   ZIP

CEO	Aff	Pro

NAME

ADDRESS   CITY   STATE   ZIP

1. Has the issuer filed any periodic reports pursuant to Section 13 or 15(d) of the Securities Exchange Act of 1934?   YES ☐   NO ☐

   If yes, please indicate the file number of the docket in which the periodic reports are filed. _____

2. Please indicate the issuer's IRS employer identification number. If an application for such number is pending, please enter "00-0000000."

3. Please briefly describe the issuer's business.

   _____
   _____
   _____

4. Please indicate the issuer's type of business organization.
   a. corporation   b. partnership   c. business trust   d. other, *please specify* _____

5. Please indicate the issuer's Standard Industrial Classification (SIC) at the 3 or 4 digit level. If the issuer has more than one SIC, please enter the issuer's primary SIC. If a 3 digit SIC is given, enter "X" in the left-most box.

6. In what year was the issuer incorporated or organized?

7. In what state is the issuer incorporated or organized? Please enter the standard two letter U.S. Postal Service abbreviation. Enter "CN" if the issuer is incorporated or organized in Canada; "FN" if the issuer is incorporated or organized in another foreign jurisdiction.

8. Has the issuer been assigned a CUSIP number for its securities?   YES ☐   NO ☐

   If yes, please specify the first six (6) digits. If no, please enter "000000."

9. Please check the appropriate box for each exchange or market, if any, where the issuer's securities are traded.
   American Stock Exchange . . . . a. ☐
   New York Stock Exchange . . . . b. ☐
   Other National Securities Exchanges . . . . c. ☐
   Over-the-Counter (including
      National Association of Securities Dealers Automated Quotations System) . . . d. ☐
   Other   *Please Specify* . . . . e. ☐

   SEC USE ONLY

   _____
   _____

   None. . . . . f. ☐

Appendix A

| FORM D | NOTICE OF SALES OF SECURITIES PURSUANT TO REGULATION D OR SECTION 4(6) | Page 3 |

B. Statistical Information About the Issuer

INSTRUCTION: Please enter the letter for the appropriate response to each item in Part B in the box indicated. If the issuer's first fiscal year has not yet ended, furnish the requested information as of a date, or as to a period ending on a date, no more than 90 days prior to the first sale of securities in this offering.

1. What were the issuer's gross revenues for its most recently ended fiscal year? ☐

   a. $500,000 or less   b. $500,001 – $1,000,000   c. $1,000,001 – $3,000,000
   d. $3,000,001 – $5,000,000   e. $5,000,001 – $25,000,000   f. $25,000,001 – $100,000,000
   g. Over $100,000,000

2. What were the issuer's total consolidated assets as of the end of its latest fiscal year? ☐

   a. $500,000 or less   b. $500,001 – $1,000,000   c. $1,000,001 – $3,000,000
   d. $3,000,001 – $5,000,000   e. $5,000,001 – $25,000,000   f. $25,000,001 – $100,000,000
   g. Over $100,000,000

3. What was the issuer's net income, or income before partners' compensation, for its most recently ended fiscal year? ☐

   a. None or net loss   b. $1 – $50,000   c. $50,001 – $250,000   d. $250,001 – $1,000,000
   e. $1,000,001 – $5,000,000   f. Over $5,000,000

4. What was the issuer's shareholders' or partners' equity at the end of its latest fiscal year? ☐

   a. Negative   b. $1 – $50,000   c. $50,001 – $250,000   d. $250,001 – $1,000,000
   e. $1,000,001 – $3,000,000   f. $3,000,001 – $10,000,000   g. Over $10,000,000

5. How many shareholders or partners did the issuer have at the end of its latest fiscal year? ☐

   a. 0 – 4   b. 5 – 9   c. 10 – 24   d. 25 – 99   e. 100 – 299
   f. 300 – 499   g. 500 or more

6. What percentage of shares outstanding were held by non-affiliated shareholders at the end of the issuer's latest fiscal year? 1/ ☐

   a. None   b. Less than 5.0%   c. 5.0% – 9.9%   d. 10.0% – 24.9%
   e. 25.0% – 49.9%   f. 50.0% – 74.9%   g. 75.0% or more   h. Not applicable

7. How many shares were outstanding at the end of the issuer's latest fiscal year? ☐

   a. 500,000 or less   b. 500,001 – 1,500,000   c. 1,500,001 – 2,500,000
   d. 2,500,001 – 3,500,000   e. 3,500,001 – 5,000,000   f. Over 5,000,000   g. Not applicable

8. How many full-time equivalent employees did the issuer have at the end of its latest fiscal year? 2/ ☐

   a. None   b. 1 – 5   c. 6 – 10   d. 11 – 20   e. 21 – 50   f. 51 – 100
   g. 101 – 500   h. 500 or more

1/ A non-affiliated person is defined to be anyone other than a person that directly or indirectly, through one or more intermediaries, controls or is controlled by the issuer or is under common control with such person.

2/ Full-time equivalent employees is defined to equal the sum of the number of full-time employees plus the number of part-time employees working 25 or more hours per typical work week.

Appendix A

FORM D

NOTICE OF SALES OF SECURITIES PURSUANT TO REGULATION D OR SECTION 4(6)

Page 4

C. Section 3(b) or 4(6) Sales Limit and Other Information About the Offering

INSTRUCTION: If a response to any item is "none" or "zero," please enter zero ("0") in the corresponding space.

1. Type and aggregate offering price of securities intended to be sold pursuant to Regulation D or Section 4(6) in this offering.

    a. Debt .... $ _____
    b. Equity .... $ _____
    c. Convertible .... $ _____

2. Number of accredited and non-accredited investors who have purchased securities in this offering in reliance on Rules 505 or 506 and aggregate dollar amounts of their purchases to date. For sales in reliance on Rule 504 or Section 4(6), please enter the number of persons who have purchased securities and aggregate dollar amounts of their purchases to date on the accredited investor lines.

	Number of Investors (A)	Aggregate Dollar Amount (B)
Accredited investors	_____	$ _____
Non-accredited investors	_____	_____
Total	_____	$ _____

3. If this offering is being made pursuant to Rule 504 or 505, report by exemption and type of security (*i.e., debt, equity, convertible*) the dollar amount of all Section 3(b) sales of securities (*other than sales reported in Item C.2 above*) occurring from twelve (12) months prior to the first sale of securities in this offering to date.

	Type (A)	Dollar Amount (B)
Rule 505	_____	$ _____
Regulation A	_____	_____
Rule 504	_____	_____
Total		$ _____

4. Please list the full name and address of each person who has been or will be paid or given directly or indirectly any commission or similar remuneration for solicitation of purchasers in connection with sales of securities in this offering pursuant to Regulation D or Section 4(6). If a person to be listed is an associated person of a broker or dealer registered with the Commission and/or with a state or states, then please also list the name of that broker or dealer. If more than five (5) persons to be listed are associated persons of a broker or dealer registered with the Commission and/or a state or states, then the issuer may list the name and address of only such broker or dealer. Please also list, using the standard two-letter Postal Service abbreviation the state or states in which each person, or if an associated broker or dealer is listed, each such broker or dealer, intends to or is offering securities in this offering; if all states, enter "all."

NAME			
ADDRESS	CITY	STATE	ZIP
NAME OF ASSOCIATED BROKER OR DEALER			
STATES			

SEC USE ONLY
8 - ☐☐☐☐☐

NAME			
ADDRESS	CITY	STATE	ZIP
NAME OF ASSOCIATED BROKER OR DEALER			
STATES			

SEC USE ONLY
8 - ☐☐☐☐☐

Appendix A

FORM D   NOTICE OF SALES OF SECURITIES   **Page 5**
PURSUANT TO REGULATION D OR SECTION 4(6)

5. a. Aggregate offering price of securities, from C.1 above $ ☐ _____

   b. Furnish a reasonably itemized statement of all expenses in connection with the issuance and distribution of the securities being offered in this offering. Please exclude any amounts relating solely to the organizational expenses of the issuer. Insofar as practicable, give amounts for the categories listed below. The information may be given as subject to future contingencies. If the expenditure in any category is not known, furnish an estimate and place an "X" in the box to the left of the amount given.

      a. Blue Sky Fees and Expenses . . . . $ ☐ _____
      b. Transfer Agents' Fees . . . . ☐ _____
      c. Printing and Engraving Costs . . . . ☐ _____
      d. Legal Fees . . . . ☐ _____
      e. Accounting Fees . . . . ☐ _____
      f. Engineering Fees . . . . ☐ _____
      g. Sales Commissions *(including Finders' Fees)* . . . . ☐ _____
      h. Other Expenses *(Identify)*

      _____ ☐ _____
      _____ ☐ _____

                Total $ ☐ _____

   c. Enter the difference between the aggregate offering price in 5.a. and total costs in 5.b. This difference is the "adjusted gross proceeds to the issuer." $ ☐ _____

6. Indicate below the amount of the adjusted gross proceeds to the issuer *(other than amounts specified in Item 5.b. above)* proposed to be used or used for each of the purposes listed below. If the amount to be used for any purpose is not known, furnish an estimate and place an "X" in the box to the left of the amount given.

		Payments to officers, directors and affiliates (A)	Payments to others (B)
a.	Salaries and fees	$ ☐ _____	$ ☐ _____
b.	Purchase of real estate	☐ _____	☐ _____
c.	Purchase, rental or leasing and installation of machinery and equipment	☐ _____	☐ _____
d.	Construction or leasing of plant building and facilities	☐ _____	☐ _____
e.	Development expense *(product development, research, patent costs, etc.)*	☐ _____	☐ _____
f.	Purchase of raw materials, inventories, supplies, etc.	☐ _____	☐ _____
g.	Selling, advertising, and other sales promotion	☐ _____	☐ _____
h.	Acquisition of other businesses *(including the value of securities involved in this offering which may be used in exchange for the assets or securities of another issuer pursuant to a merger)*	☐ _____	☐ _____
i.	Repayment of loans	☐ _____	☐ _____
	Other — *please specify*		
j.	_____	☐ _____	☐ _____
k.	_____	☐ _____	☐ _____
l.	_____	☐ _____	☐ _____
m.	_____	☐ _____	☐ _____
	Total	$ ☐ _____	$ ☐ _____

| FORM D | **NOTICE OF SALES OF SECURITIES PURSUANT TO REGULATION D OR SECTION 4(6)** | Page 6 |

D. Undertaking by issuers filing pursuant to Rule 505.

The undersigned issuer hereby undertakes to furnish to the Securities and Exchange Commission, upon the written request of its staff, the information furnished by the issuer to any non-accredited person pursuant to paragraph (b)(2) of Rule 502.

ISSUER _____

SIGNATURE _____

NAME _____

TITLE _____

E. The issuer has duly caused this notice to be signed on its behalf by the undersigned duly authorized person.

DATE OF NOTICE: _____

ISSUER _____

SIGNATURE _____

NAME _____

TITLE _____

INSTRUCTION: Print the name and title of the signing representative under his signature. One copy of every notice on Form D shall be manually signed. Any copies not manually signed shall bear typed or printed signatures.

——————————————**ATTENTION**——————————————
Intentional misstatements or omissions of fact constitute Federal Criminal Violations (See 18 U.S.C. 1001).

Appendix A

FORM D Continuation Sheet	NOTICE OF SALES OF SECURITIES PURSUANT TO REGULATION D OR SECTION 4(6)	Page 7
Item of Form *(identify)*	Answer	

Appendix B

UNDERWRITING AGREEMENT

1981

SHEARSON LOEB RHOADES INC.
As Representative of the several Underwriters
14 Wall Street
New York, New York 10005

Dear Sirs:

    Matrix Science Corporation, a Delaware corporation (the "Company"), proposes to issue and sell to the several Underwriters named in Schedule I hereto (the "Underwriters") 100,000 shares of Common Stock, $.01 par value (such class of stock being herein called the "Common Stock"), of the Company. Such 100,000 shares of Common Stock are herein called the "Company Shares." Certain shareholders of the Company named in Schedule II hereto (the "Selling Shareholders") propose severally to sell to the several Underwriters an additional 900,000 shares of Common Stock. Such 900,000 shares of Common Stock are herein called the "Selling Shareholder Shares." The Company Shares and the Selling Shareholder Shares are herein called the "Firm Shares." In addition, to cover over-allotments in connection with the sale of the Firm Shares, the Company proposes to grant to the Underwriters (as hereinafter defined) an option to purchase up to an additional 100,000 shares of Common Stock. The shares of Common Stock sold by the Company pursuant to such option are herein called the "Option Shares." The Firm Shares and any Option Shares are herein collectively called the "Stock."

Source: Matrix Science Corporation, 1981

The Company and the Selling Shareholders hereby confirm their agreements with respect to the purchase of the Stock by the several Underwriters. You represent and warrant that you are acting as the representative (the "Representative") of the Underwriters and that you have been authorized by each of the other Underwriters to enter into this Underwriting Agreement on its behalf and to act for it in the manner herein provided.

1. *Representations and Warranties.*

    (a) The Company represents and warrants to each Underwriter that:

    (i) Each of the Company and Matrix Exports, Inc. (the "Subsidiary"), has been duly incorporated and is validly existing as a corporation in good standing under the laws of the respective jurisdiction of its incorporation, with all necessary corporate power and authority to own its properties and conduct its business as described in the prospectus (as hereinafter defined); each of the Company and the Subsidiary is duly qualified to do business as a foreign corporation and is in good standing in each jurisdiction wherein the character of the business conducted by it or the location of the property owned or leased by it requires it to be qualified to do business as a foreign corporation.

    (ii) All the outstanding capital stock of the Subsidiary has been duly authorized and validly issued and is fully paid and nonassessable. The Company owns, and at the time the registration statement (as hereinafter defined) becomes effective, will so own, free and clear of any claim, lien, encumbrance or liability, all the issued and outstanding capital stock of the Subsidiary.

    (iii) The Company has no subsidiaries other than Matrix Exports, Inc., a California corporation, which operates as a domestic international sales corporation.

    (iv) The Company has caused to be prepared in conformity with the requirements of the Securities Act of 1933, as amended (the "1933 Act"), and the rules and regulations (the "Rules and Regulations") of the Securities and Exchange Commission (the "Commission") and filed with the Commission in Washington, D.C., a registration statement on Form S-1, File No. 2- (including a form of preliminary prospectus), and has caused to be so prepared and has filed and will so cause to be prepared and will file amendments thereto (including amended forms of the preliminary prospectus which may or may not have been included as part of a filed amendment to the registration statement) for the registration of the Stock under the 1933 Act. Copies of such registration statement (as hereinafter defined) and amendments (including all forms of preliminary prospectus) have been delivered to you as Representative of the Underwriters. Such registration statement, including all prospectuses included as a part thereof, all documents incorporated by reference therein and all financial schedules and exhibits thereto, as amended at the time when it shall become effective, are herein called the "Registration Statement," and the term "Prospectus" as used herein shall mean the final prospectus included as a part of the Registration Statement on file with the Commission when it becomes effective (except that if the prospectus filed by the Company pursuant to Rule 424(b) under the 1933 Act shall differ from said prospectus included in the Registration Statement, the term "Prospectus" as used herein shall mean the prospectus so filed pursuant to Rule 424(b) from and after the date on which it shall have been first used). The term "Preliminary Prospectus" as used herein means any preliminary prospectus (as defined in Rule 433 under the 1933 Act) included at any time as part of the Registration Statement.

    (v) The Commission has not issued any order preventing or suspending the use of any Preliminary Prospectus, and each Preliminary Prospectus, at the time of the filing thereof with the Commission, did not include any untrue statement of a material fact or omit to state a material fact required to be stated therein or necessary in order to make the statements therein, in the light of the circumstances under which they were made, not misleading; provided, however, that none of the representations and warranties in this subparagraph shall apply to statements in, or omissions from, any Preliminary Prospectus which are based upon and conform to written information furnished to the Company by or on behalf of any of the Selling Shareholders or Underwriters (which, for purposes of this paragraph, shall include information furnished by the Representative with respect to any Underwriter) specifically for use with reference to such Underwriter or Selling Shareholder in the preparation of such Preliminary Prospectus.

Appendix B

(vi) When the Registration Statement shall become effective, and at all times subsequent thereto, the Registration Statement and Prospectus, and all amendments thereof and supplements thereto, will comply in all material respects with the provisions of the 1933 Act and the Rules and Regulations. The Registration Statement (as amended, if the Company shall have filed with the Commission any post-effective amendment thereto) will not contain any untrue statement of a material fact or omit to state a material fact required to be stated therein or necessary to make the statements therein not misleading; the Prospectus (as amended or supplemented, if the Company shall have filed with the Commission any amendment thereof or supplement thereto) will not contain any untrue statement of a material fact or omit to state a material fact required to be stated therein or necessary to make the statements therein not misleading; provided, however, that none of the representations and warranties in this subparagraph shall apply to statements in, or omissions from, the Registration Statement or the Prospectus or any amendment thereof or supplement thereto which are based upon and conform to written information furnished to the Company by or on behalf of any of the Selling Shareholders or Underwriters (which, for purposes of this paragraph, shall include information furnished by the Representative with respect to any Underwriter) specifically for use with reference to such Underwriter or Selling Shareholder in the preparation of the Registration Statement or the Prospectus or any such amendment or supplement. There is no contract or document required to be described in the Registration Statement or Prospectus or to be filed as an exhibit to the Registration Statement which is not described or filed as required.

(vii) Arthur Andersen & Co., the accountants who have certified the financial statements filed and to be filed with the Commission as part of the Registration Statement and the Prospectus, are, as to the Company, independent public accountants within the meaning of the 1933 Act and the Rules and Regulations.

(viii) The authorized and outstanding capital stock of the Company as of December 11, 1980 is as set forth under the caption "Capitalization" in the Prospectus. The Company has full power and authority to issue, sell and deliver the Company Shares and the Option Shares in accordance with and upon the terms and conditions set forth in this Underwriting Agreement and in the Registration Statement and Prospectus; and all corporate action required to be taken by the Company for the due and proper authorization, issuance and sale of the Company Shares and the Option Shares has been validly and sufficiently taken. The outstanding shares of Common Stock are duly authorized, validly issued, fully paid and nonassessable. The capital stock of the Company conforms to the description thereof contained in the Prospectus.

(ix) Subsequent to the respective dates as of which information is given in the Registration Statement and Prospectus, neither the Company nor the Subsidiary has incurred any material liability or obligation, direct or contingent, or entered into any material transaction, whether or not in the ordinary course of business, and there has not been any change in the capital stock, or any increase in the long-term debt, or any issuance of options, warrants, convertible securities or other rights to purchase the capital stock of the Company or the Subsidiary, or any material adverse change in the general affairs, business, capitalization, financial position or net worth of any such corporation; and no such corporation has become a party to, nor has its business or property become the subject of, any litigation the outcome of which would have a material adverse impact on the business or financial position of such corporation, and no material loss or damage (whether or not insured) to the property of the Company or the Subsidiary which is material to the business or financial position of the Company has been sustained.

(x) Neither the Company nor the Subsidiary is in violation of its certificate or articles of incorporation, charter, bylaws or other governing documents, or is in default in the performance of any material obligation, agreement or condition contained in any indenture or loan agreement or in any bond, debenture, note or any other evidence of indebtedness or in any lease, license or other material contract. The execution and delivery of this Underwriting Agreement, the fulfillment of the terms hereof and the consummation of the transactions herein contemplated will not conflict with or result in a breach of, or default under, the certificate or articles of incorporation, charter, bylaws or other governing documents of the Company or the Subsidiary, or any material agreement, indenture or other instrument to which the Company or the Subsidiary is a party or by which it is bound, or any law, administrative regulation or court decree by which the Company or the Subsidiary may be bound or result in the creation or imposition of any lien, charge, claim or encumbrance upon any properties or assets of the Company or any Subsidiary. Except as required by the 1933 Act, the Securities Exchange Act of 1934, as amended, and applicable state securities or blue sky laws, no consent, approval, authorization or order of any governmental agency or governmental authority is required on the part of the Company or the Subsidiary in connection with the consummation of the transactions contemplated by this Underwriting Agreement.

(xi) The consolidated financial statements and schedules (including the related notes) of the Company and the Subsidiary, included or incorporated by reference in the Registration Statement and the Prospectus, present fairly the financial position of the Company and the Subsidiary, consolidated results of operations and changes in consolidated financial position of the Company and the Subsidiary, as of the dates and for the periods therein set forth. All such financial statements and schedules (including the related notes) have been prepared in accordance with generally accepted accounting principles applied on a basis consistent with that of the preceding periods throughout the periods involved.

(xii) On each Closing Date (as hereinafter defined), the Stock will have been duly authorized and validly issued, will be fully paid and nonassessable and will conform to the description thereof contained in the Prospectus. There are no pre-emptive rights or other rights to subscribe for or to purchase, or any restriction upon the voting or transfer of, any share of Stock pursuant to the Company's certificate of incorporation, bylaws or any agreement or other instrument to which the Company or the Subsidiary is a party.

(xiii) The Company has full right, power and authority to enter into this Underwriting Agreement, and this Underwriting Agreement has been duly authorized, executed and delivered by the Company and constitutes the valid and binding agreement of the Company enforceable in accordance with its terms, except as may be limited by the application of insolvency or similar laws affecting the rights of creditors generally and judicial limitations on the right of specific performance, and except as enforceability of indemnification provisions hereof may be limited by federal securities laws.

(xiv) Each of the Company and the Subsidiary has marketable title in fee simple, free and clear of all liens, encumbrances, equities, charges or claims, to all of the property, real and personal, described in the Registration Statement and Prospectus as being owned by it or them; and, except as otherwise stated in the Registration Statement and Prospectus, has valid and binding leases to the real and/or personal property described in the Registration Statement and Prospectus as under lease to them.

(xv) Except as otherwise stated in the Registration Statement and Prospectus, there are no actions, suits or proceedings pending before any court or governmental agency, authority or body to which the Company or the Subsidiary is a party or to which the business or property of the Company or the Subsidiary may be subect which, if decided adversely, would have a material adverse effect on the business or financial position of the Company or the Subsidiary, as the case may be, and no such action, suit or proceeding is threatened.

(xvi) Neither the Company nor the Subsidiary is in violation of any law, ordinance, governmental rule or regulation or court decree to which it may be subject or has failed to obtain any license, permit, franchise or other governmental authorization necessary to the ownership of its property or to the conduct of its business, which violation or failure would materially adversely affect the business, operations, affairs, properties, prospects, profits or condition (financial or otherwise) of the Company or the Subsidiary, as the case may be.

(xvii) The Company has not taken and will not take, directly or indirectly, any action designed to cause or result in, or which has constituted or which might reasonably be expected to constitute, the stabilization or manipulation of the price of the shares of Common Stock to facilitate the sale or resale of the Stock.

(xviii) Neither the Company nor the Subsidiary has, directly or indirectly, at any time during the past five years (i) made any unlawful contribution to any candidate for political office, or failed to disclose fully any contribution in violation of law, or (ii) made any payment to

Appendix B

any federal, state or foreign governmental officer or official, or other person charged with similar public or quasi-public duties, other than payments required or permitted by the laws of the United States or any jurisdiction thereof.

(xix) Each of the Company and the Subsidiary owns or possesses all the patents, patent applications, trademarks, service marks, trade names, trademark registrations, service mark registrations, copyrights, licenses, inventions, trade secrets and rights necessary for the present conduct of its business, and they are complying therewith, and the expiration of any of such patents, patent applications, trademarks, service marks, trade names, trademark registrations, service mark registrations, copyrights, licenses, inventions, trade secrets and rights, would not materially adversely affect the operations of the Company or the Subsidiary.

(b) Each Selling Shareholder represents and warrants to, and agrees with, each Underwriter that:

(i) Such Selling Shareholder has full right, power and authority to enter into this Underwriting Agreement, the Power of Attorney (the "Power of Attorney") and the Custody Agreement (the "Custody Agreement") hereinafter referred to and at the date hereof such Selling Shareholder has, and at the time of delivery of the Selling Shareholder Shares to the Underwriters hereunder, such Selling Shareholder will have, full right, power and authority to sell and deliver the Selling Shareholder Shares to be sold by such Selling Shareholder to the Underwriters, and at the date hereof such Selling Shareholder is, and at the time of delivery of the Selling Shareholder Shares to the Underwriters such Selling Shareholder will be, the lawful owner of and has, and will have, marketable title to such shares free and clear of any claims, liens, encumbrances or liabilities.

(ii) The execution and delivery of this Underwriting Agreement, the Power of Attorney and the Custody Agreement, the fulfillment of the terms herein and therein set forth and the consummation of the transactions herein and therein contemplated will not conflict with or constitute a breach of, or default under, any agreement or other instrument by which such Selling Shareholder is bound, or any law, administrative regulation or court decree. This Underwriting Agreement, the Power of Attorney and the Custody Agreement have been duly authorized, validly executed and delivered by such Selling Shareholder and each constitutes the valid and binding agreement of such Selling Shareholder enforceable in accordance with its terms, except as may be limited by the application of insolvency or similar laws affecting the rights of creditors generally and judicial limitations on the right of specific performance, and except as enforceability of the indemnification provisions hereof may be limited by federal securities laws.

(iii) When the Registration Statement shall become effective, and at all times subsequent thereto, the Registration Statement and Prospectus (as amended, if any post-effective amendment thereto has been filed) and all amendments thereof and supplements thereto, will not contain any untrue statement of a material fact regarding such Selling Shareholder or omit to state a material fact regarding such Selling Shareholder required to be stated therein or necessary in order to make the statements therein regarding such Selling Shareholder not misleading, and such Selling Shareholder is, and shall be, unaware of any material misstatement in or omission from the Registration Statement and Prospectus or of any material adverse information regarding the business or operations of the Company or its Subsidiaries which is not set forth in the Registration Statement and Prospectus.

(iv) Such Selling Shareholder has not taken and will not take, directly or indirectly, any action designed to cause or result in, or which has constituted or which might reasonably be expected to constitute, the stabilization or manipulation of the price of the Common Stock to facilitate the sale or resale of the Stock.

(v) Certificates in negotiable form representing all of the Selling Shareholder Shares to be sold by such Selling Shareholder hereunder have been placed in custody under a Custody Agreement, in the form heretofore furnished to you, duly executed and delivered by such Selling Shareholder to United California Bank, as custodian (the "Custodian"), and such Selling Shareholder has duly executed and delivered a Power of Attorney, in the form heretofore furnished to you, appointing Joseph S. O'Flaherty as such Selling Shareholder's attorney-in-fact (the "Attorney-in-Fact") with authority to execute and deliver this Underwriting Agreement on behalf of such Selling Shareholder, to authorize the delivery of the Selling Shareholder Shares to be sold by such Selling Shareholder hereunder and otherwise to act on behalf of such Selling Shareholder in connection with the transactions contemplated by this Underwriting Agreement and the Custody Agreement.

(vi) The Selling Shareholder Shares represented by the certificates held in custody for such Selling Shareholder under the Custody Agreement are subject to the interests of the Underwriters hereunder, and the arrangements made by such Selling Shareholder for such custody, as well as the appointment by such Selling Shareholder of the Attorney-in-Fact, are, to that extent, irrevocable. Each Selling Shareholder specifically agrees that the obligations of the Selling Shareholders hereunder shall not be terminated by operation of law, whether by the death or incapacity of any individual Selling Shareholder or, in the case of an estate or trust, by the death of any executor or trustee or the termination of such estate or trust, or by the occurrence of any other event. If any individual Selling Shareholder or any such executor or trustee should die or become incapacitated, or if any such estate or trust should be terminated, or if any other such event should occur, before the delivery of the Selling Shareholder Shares hereunder, certificates representing the Selling Shareholder Shares shall be delivered by or on behalf of such Selling Shareholder in accordance with the terms and conditions of this Underwriting Agreement and of the Custody Agreement, and the actions taken by the Attorney-in-Fact pursuant to the Power of Attorney shall be as valid as if such death, incapacity, termination, dissolution or other event had not occurred, whether or not the Custodian or the Attorney-in-Fact shall have received notice of such death, incapacity, termination, dissolution or other event.

2. *Purchase of the Stock by the Underwriters.*

(a) Subject to the terms and conditions and upon the basis of the representations and warranties herein set forth, the Company agrees to issue and sell the Company Shares and each Selling Shareholder agrees to sell the number of Selling Shareholder Shares set forth opposite its name in Schedule II hereto, to the Underwriters and each of the Underwriters agrees, severally and not jointly, to purchase at a purchase price of $ per share, the aggregate number of Firm Shares set opposite such Underwriter's name in Schedule I hereto. The Underwriters agree to offer the Firm Shares to the public as set forth in the Prospectus.

(b) Each Underwriter shall be obligated to purchase from the Company and each Selling Shareholder that number of Firm Shares which represents the same proportion of the number of Firm Shares to be sold by the Company and each Selling Shareholder as the number of Firm Shares set forth opposite the name of such Underwriter in Schedule I hereto represents of the total number of Firm Shares to be purchased by all of the Underwriters pursuant to this Underwriting Agreement. The respective purchase obligations of the Underwriters shall be rounded among the Underwriters to avoid fractional shares, as the Representative may determine.

(c) In addition, the Company hereby grants to the Underwriters for a period of 30 days from the date hereof an option to purchase from the Company solely for the purpose of covering over-allotments in the sale of Firm Shares, all or any portion of the Option Shares, at the purchase price per share of Stock set forth above. Option Shares shall be purchased severally and not jointly, for the accounts of the several Underwriters in proportion to the number of Firm Shares set opposite such Underwriter's name in Schedule I hereto, except that the respective purchase obligations of each Underwriter shall be adjusted by the Representative so that no Underwriter shall be obligated to purchase Option Shares other than in 100 share amounts.

If one or more of the Underwriters shall fail or refuse (otherwise than for a reason sufficient to justify the termination of this Underwriting Agreement under the provisions of Section 5 or 10 hereof) to purchase and pay for the number of shares of Stock agreed to be purchased by such Underwriter or Underwriters and the number of such shares shall not exceed 10% of the Stock, then, upon tender to the Representative of such shares in accordance with the terms hereof, each of the non-defaulting Underwriters shall purchase and pay for (in addition to the number of shares of Stock which it has severally agreed to purchase hereunder) that proportion of the number of shares of Stock which the defaulting Underwriter or Underwriters shall have so failed or refused to purchase which the number of shares of Stock agreed to be purchased by such non-defaulting Underwriter bears to the aggregate number of shares of Stock so agreed to be purchased by all such non-defaulting Underwriters. In such case, the Representative shall have the right to postpone each Closing Date specified in Section 3 hereof to a date not exceeding seven full business days after the date originally fixed as such Closing

Date pursuant to said Section 3 in order that any necessary changes in the Registration Statement, the Prospectus or any other documents or arrangements may be made.

If one or more of the Underwriters shall fail or refuse (otherwise than for a reason sufficient to justify the termination of this Underwriting Agreement under the provisions of Section 5 or 10 hereof) to purchase and pay for the number of shares of Stock agreed to be purchased by such Underwriter or Underwriters and the number of such shares shall exceed 10% of the Stock, then, upon tender to the Representative of such shares in accordance with the terms hereof (unless within 48 hours after such default arrangements satisfactory to the Representative shall have been made for the purchase of the defaulted Stock by a substituted Underwriter or Underwriters), this Underwriting Agreement will terminate without liability on the part of any non-defaulting Underwriter or on the part of the Company or the Selling Shareholders except for the expenses to be paid or caused to be paid by the Company pursuant to Section 4 hereof. As used in this Underwriting Agreement, the term "Underwriter" includes any person substituted for an Underwriter under this paragraph. Nothing in this paragraph, and no action taken hereunder, shall relieve any defaulting Underwriter from liability in respect of any default of such Underwriter under this Underwriting Agreement.

3. *Delivery of and Payment for Stock.*

Delivery of certificates for the Firm Shares to be purchased by the Underwriters from the Company and the Selling Shareholders and payment therefore shall be made at the offices of Shearson Loeb Rhoades Inc. located in New York, New York (or such other place as mutually may be agreed upon), at such time and date, not earlier than the fifth full business day following the effective date of the Registration Statement, but not later than ten business days after such effective date (or nine such days if the tenth shall be a Friday), as you shall designate by at least 48 hours prior notice to the Company (such date and time being called the "First Closing Date," which is subject to extension as provided in Sections 2 and 5 hereof).

At any time during the term thereof, the option to purchase Option Shares granted in Section 2 hereof may be exercised by written notice to the Company from the Representative. Such notice shall set forth the aggregate number of Option Shares as to which the option is being exercised and the time and date, not earlier than either the First Closing Date or the second business day after the day on which the option shall have been exercised nor later than the fifth business day after the date of such exercise, as determined by the Representative, when the Option Shares are to be delivered (such date and time being herein called the "Second Closing Date"), delivery and payment for such Option Shares to be at the offices set forth above for delivery and payment of the Firm Shares. (The First Closing Date and the Second Closing Date are sometimes herein individually called the "Closing Date" and collectively called the "Closing Dates.")

Delivery of certificates for the Stock shall be made by or on behalf of the Company and by or on behalf of the Custodian, to you, for the respective accounts of the Underwriters, against payment by you, for the several accounts of the Underwriters, of the purchase price therefor by certified or official bank check payable in New York Clearing House funds to the order of the Company or the Custodian, as the case may be. The certificates for such shares shall be registered in such names and denominations as you shall have requested at least two full business days prior to each Closing Date, and shall be made available for checking and packaging at a location in New York, New York as may be designated by you at least one full business day prior to each Closing Date. Time shall be of the essence and delivery at the time and place specified in this Underwriting Agreement is a further condition to the obligations of each Underwriter.

4. *Covenants of the Company and the Selling Shareholders.*

(a) The Company covenants and agrees that:

(i) Whether or not this Underwriting Agreement becomes effective or the sale of the Stock to the Underwriters is consummated, the Company will pay or cause to be paid (A) all expenses (including original issue stock transfer taxes, if any, and fees of counsel other than counsel for the Underwriters, but excluding all stock transfer taxes and expenses incurred by the Underwriters on their own behalf which shall be paid by the Underwriters) incurred in connection with the delivery to the several Underwriters of the Stock; (B) all expenses and fees (except fees and expenses of counsel for the Underwriters) in connection with the preparation, printing, filing, delivery and shipping of the Registration Statement (including the financial statements therein and all amendments and exhibits thereto), each Preliminary Prospectus, the Prospectus and the Prospectus as amended or supplemented and the printing, delivery and shipping of this Underwriting Agreement and other underwriting documents, including Underwriters' Questionnaires, Underwriters' Powers of Attorney, Blue Sky Memoranda, Agreement Among Underwriters and the Selected Dealer Agreement; (C) all filing fees, reasonable counsel fees and expenses incurred in connection with the qualification of the Stock for offering and sale by the Underwriters or by dealers under the securities or blue sky laws of the states and other jurisdictions which you, as the Representative of the Underwriters, shall designate in accordance with subparagraph (vi) of this Section 4(a); and (D) the filing fee of the National Association of Securities Dealers, Inc.

(ii) The Company will use its best efforts to cause the Registration Statement to become effective and, upon notification from the Commission that the Registration Statement has become effective, will so advise you and the Selling Shareholders promptly and in writing, if requested. The Company will advise you promptly of the issuance by the Commission or any state or regulatory body of any stop order or other order suspending the effectiveness of the Registration Statement or of the institution of any proceedings for that purpose, will use its best efforts to prevent the issuance of any stop order or other such order and, should a stop order or other such order be issued, to obtain as soon as possible the lifting thereof. The Company will notify you promptly of any request by the Commission for any amendment of or supplement to the Registration Statement or the Prospectus or for additional information, and will not file any amendment or supplement to the Registration Statement or the Prospectus, whether prior to or after the effective date of the Registration Statement, of which you have not been furnished a copy prior to the filing thereof or file any such amendment or supplement to which you have reasonably objected.

(iii) If, at any time when a prospectus relating to the Stock is required to be delivered under the 1933 Act, any event shall have occurred as a result of which, in the opinion of counsel for the Company or counsel for the Underwriters, the Prospectus, as then amended or supplemented, includes an untrue statement of a material fact or omits to state a material fact required to be stated therein or necessary to make the statements therein not misleading or if it is necessary at any time to amend or supplement the Prospectus to comply with the 1933 Act, the Company will notify you promptly and prepare and file with the Commission an appropriate amendment or supplement.

(iv) The Company will deliver to each of the Underwriters, from time to time and without charge, as many copies of any Preliminary Prospectus and of the Prospectus (and, in the event of an amendment or supplement to the Prospectus pursuant to the provisions of this Underwriting Agreement, of such amended or supplemented Prospectus) as you, as the Representative of the Underwriters, may reasonably request for the purposes contemplated by the 1933 Act, which Prospectuses, as from time to time amended or supplemented, the Company authorizes the Underwriters, all members of any selling group which may be formed in connection with the distribution of the Stock and all dealers to whom any of the Stock may be sold by the Underwriters or by members of any selling group to use as permitted by the 1933 Act and in connection with the sale of the Stock.

(v) The Company will furnish to you copies of the Registration Statement, two of which will be signed and four of which will include all exhibits, and all amendments and supplements to any of such documents, in each case as soon as available and in such additional quantities as you request.

(vi) The Company will take or cause to be taken all necessary action, and furnish to whomever you may direct such proper information, as may be lawfully required in qualifying the Stock for offering and sale by the Underwriters or by dealers under the securities or blue sky laws of any states or other jurisdictions which you, as the Representative of the Underwriters, shall designate to the Company or its counsel; provided, however, that in no event shall the Company be obligated to qualify as a foreign corporation, or execute a general consent for service of process, in any jurisdiction in which it is not now so qualified.

(vii) The Company will make generally available to its security holders and deliver to you, as the Representative of the Underwriters, as soon as practicable and in any event not later than

45 days after the end of its fiscal quarter in which the first anniversary date of the effective date of the Registration Statement occurs, a consolidated statement of earnings (which need not be audited but which shall satisfy the provisions of Section 11(a) of the 1933 Act) of the Company and the Subsidiary covering a period of at least 12 consecutive months.

(viii) The Company will, for a period of five years from the effective date of the Registration Statement, furnish to its shareholders and to you, as the Representative of the Underwriters, as soon as the same shall be sent to shareholders generally, copies of any annual or interim reports of the Company, including:

(A) as soon as practicable after the end of each fiscal year, one copy of the annual independent accountants' report, including therein the accountants' certificate, the consolidated balance sheet of the Company and its Subsidiaries and the related consolidated statements of income, shareholders' equity and changes in consolidated financial position;

(B) one copy of any report, application or document (other than exhibits, which, however, will be furnished on request) which the Company shall file with the Commission or any securities exchange; and

(C) as soon as the same shall be sent to shareholders generally, copies of each communication which shall be sent to shareholders.

(ix) The Company will apply the net proceeds of the sale of the Company Shares and the Option Shares as set forth under the caption "Use of Proceeds" in the Prospectus and will file such reports with the Commission with respect to the sale of the Company Shares and the Option Shares and the application of the proceeds therefrom in accordance with Rule 463 adopted by the Commission under the 1933 Act.

(x) The Company covenants and agrees that it will not, during the 90 days following the effective date of the Registration Statement, except with the prior written consent of the Representative, offer for sale, sell, distribute or otherwise dispose of any shares of Common Stock, or sell or grant options, rights or warrants with respect to any shares of Common Stock, otherwise than in accordance with this Underwriting Agreement or as contemplated in the Prospectus.

(b) Each of the Selling Shareholders covenants and agrees that he will not, during the 90 days following the effective date of the Registration Statement, except with the prior written consent of the Representative, offer for sale, sell, distribute or otherwise dispose of any shares of Common Stock, or sell or grant options, rights or warrants with respect to any shares of Common Stock, otherwise than in accordance with this Underwriting Agreement or as contemplated in the Prospectus.

5. *Conditions of Underwriters' Obligations.*

(a) The obligations of the Underwriters hereunder are subject to the accuracy of and compliance with all representations and warranties of the Company and of the Selling Shareholders contained herein and other statements made on the part of the Company and the Selling Shareholders herein as of the date hereof and as of each Closing Date, to the performance by the Company and each of the Selling Shareholders of their respective obligations hereunder and to the following further conditions:

(i) The Registration Statement shall have become effective at or before 5:00 P.M., New York City time, on the date of this Underwriting Agreement or such later time and date as you, as the Representative of the Underwriters, shall approve; no stop order suspending the effectiveness of the Registration Statement or any amendment or supplement thereto shall have been issued and be in effect; and no proceedings for the issuance of such an order shall be pending or threatened; and any request of the Commission for inclusion of additional information in the Registration Statement or the Prospectus or otherwise shall have been complied with to your reasonable satisfaction.

(ii) You shall not have advised the Company or the Selling Shareholders that the Registration Statement or Prospectus, or any amendment thereof or supplement thereto, contains an untrue statement of fact which, in the opinion of Messrs. Willkie Farr & Gallagher, counsel for the Underwriters, is material or that the Registration Statement, as amended or supplemented, or Prospectus, as amended or supplemented, omits to state a fact which, in the opinion of such counsel, is material and is required to be stated therein or is necessary to make the statements therein not misleading.

(iii) On or prior to the date of this Underwriting Agreement there shall have been furnished to you, as the Representative of the Underwriters, a letter or letters, in form and substance satisfactory to counsel for the Underwriters, pursuant to which each officer and director of the Company and each Selling Shareholder shall have agreed not to offer for sale, sell, distribute or otherwise dispose of any shares of Common Stock during the 90 days following the effective date of the Registration Statement, except with the prior written consent of the Representative.

(iv) On or prior to each Closing Date, the form and validity of the Stock, the legality and sufficiency of the corporate proceedings and matters relating to the organization of each of the Company and its Subsidiary and other matters incident to the issuance of the Stock, the form of Registration Statement and the Prospectus and of any amendments thereof or supplements thereto filed prior to such Closing Date (other than financial statements and other financial data included therein), the authorization, execution and delivery of this Underwriting Agreement by the Company and the Selling Shareholders, the authorization, execution and delivery of the Custody Agreement and the Power of Attorney by the Selling Shareholders and the description of the Stock contained in the Prospectus shall have been approved by Messrs. Willkie Farr & Gallagher, counsel for the Underwriters, and the Company and the Selling Shareholders shall have furnished to such counsel such documents as they may have reasonably requested for the purpose of enabling them to pass upon such matters and counsel for the Underwriters shall have furnished to you as Representative, an opinion as to the form and validity of the Stock, the form of Registration Statement and the Prospectus and of any amendments thereof or supplements thereto filed prior to such Closing Date, the authorization, execution and delivery of this Underwriting Agreement by the Company and the description of the Stock contained in the Prospectus.

(v) On each Closing Date there shall have been furnished to you, as the Representative of the Underwriters, the favorable opinion (addressed to the Underwriters) of Messrs. Hedlund, Hunter & Lynch, counsel for the Company, dated such Closing Date and in form and substance satisfactory to counsel for the Underwriters, with photostatic or photo-offset copies thereof for each of the other Underwriters, to the effect that:

(A) Each of the Company and the Subsidiary has been duly incorporated and is validly existing as a corporation in good standing under the laws of the respective jurisdiction of its incorporation with all necessary power and authority to own its properties and conduct its business as it is described in the Prospectus, and is duly qualified to do business as a foreign corporation in good standing in each other jurisdiction in which the location of its properties or the character of its operations makes such qualification necessary or in which the consequences of a failure to qualify would have a materially adverse effect on the business of the Company as now conducted or on the results of its operations.

(B) All the outstanding capital stock of the Subsidiary has been duly authorized and validly issued and is fully paid and nonassessable, and the Company owns, free and clear of any claim, lien, encumbrance or liability, all the issued and outstanding capital stock of the Subsidiary.

(C) The authorized and outstanding capital stock of the Company is as described under the caption "Capitalization" in the Prospectus. The Company has all requisite power and authority to issue, sell and deliver the Company Shares and Option Shares in accordance with and upon the terms and conditions set forth in this Underwriting Agreement and in the Registration Statement and Prospectus. The outstanding shares of Common Stock have been, and the Stock, upon issuance and delivery and payment therefor in the manner herein described, will be, duly authorized, validly issued, fully paid and nonassessable. The capital stock of the Company conforms in all material respects to the description thereof contained under the caption "Description of Common Stock" in the Prospectus.

(D) The certificates evidencing the Stock comply as to form with the applicable provisions of the Delaware Corporation Law.

(E) There are no preemptive or other rights to subscribe for or to purchase, nor any restriction upon the voting or transfer of, any shares of the Stock pursuant to the Company's certificate of incorporation or by-laws or any agreement or other outstanding instrument to

Appendix B

which the Company or its Subsidiary is a party or by which any of them may be bound.

(F) This Underwriting Agreement has been duly authorized, executed and delivered by the Company and this Underwriting Agreement constitutes the valid and binding agreement of the Company enforceable in accordance with its terms, except as may be limited by the application of insolvency or similar laws affecting the rights of creditors generally and judicial limitations on the right of specific performance and except that the enforceability of indemnification provisions may be limited by federal securities laws.

(G) Neither the Company nor the Subsidiary is in violation of any material term or condition of, or in default under, nor will the execution or delivery hereof or the performance by the Company of its obligations hereunder result in a violation of any of the terms or conditions of, or constitute a default under, the certificate or articles of incorporation, charter, by-laws or other governing documents of the Company or the Subsidiary, or the provisions of any indenture, agreement or instrument of which such counsel has knowledge to which the Company or the Subsidiary is a party or by which it may be bound, nor will the performance by the Company of its obligations hereunder violate any law or any order, rule or regulation applicable to the Company or the Subsidiary of any court, or of any federal or state regulatory body or administrative agency having jurisdiction over the Company or the Subsidiary or over any of their properties (except that no opinion need be expressed as to qualification of the Stock under state securities or blue sky laws) or result in the creation or imposition of any lien, charge, claim or encumbrance upon any of the properties or assets of the Company or of the Subsidiary that would have a material adverse effect on the business, affairs, property or financial condition of the Company.

(H) No consent, approval, authorization or other order of any regulatory or other governmental body or administrative agency (other than under the 1933 Act, the Securities Exchange Act of 1934, as amended, and the securities and blue sky laws of any state or other jurisdiction) is required on the part of the Company for the performance of its obligations hereunder.

(I) The Registration Statement has become effective under the 1933 Act and, to the best knowledge of such counsel, no stop order suspending the effectiveness of the Registration Statement has been issued and no proceedings for that purpose have been instituted or are pending before or threatened by the Commission under the 1933 Act; the Registration Statement, the Prospectus and each amendment or supplement thereto (except for the financial statements and other financial data, as to which counsel need express no opinion) comply in all material respects as to form with the requirements of the 1933 Act and the Rules and Regulations; and nothing has come to the attention of such counsel that would lead them to believe that either the Registration Statement and any such amendment or supplement thereto or the Prospectus and any amendment or supplement thereto (except for the financial statements and other financial data, as to which counsel need express no opinion) contain any untrue statement of a material fact or omit to state a material fact required to be stated therein, or necessary to make the statements therein, in light of the circumstances under which they were made, not misleading.

(J) Based on the knowledge of such counsel acquired through discussions with executives of the Company and such counsel's participation in the preparation of the Registration Statement and the Prospectus, such counsel have no reason to believe that there is any pending or threatened litigation or governmental proceedings required to be dsecribed in the Prospectus which is not described as required, or any contract or document required to be described in the Registration Statement or Prospectus or to be filed as an exhibit to the Registration Statement which is not described or filed as required.

In expressing their opinion as to questions of law of jurisdictions other than the State of Delaware, California or the United States, such counsel may rely upon an opinion (dated the Closing Date, addressed to the Underwriters and in form satisfactory to you, with signed or conformed copies for each of the other Underwriters) of counsel acceptable to Messrs. Willkie Farr & Gallagher. Such opinion of counsel for the Company shall state that the opinion of such other counsel is in form and substance satisfactory to counsel for the Company and, in their opinion, you and they are justified in relying on such other opinion.

(vi) On each Closing Date there shall have been furnished to you, as the Representative of the Underwriters, the favorable opinion (addressed to the Underwriters) of Messrs. Hedlund, Hunter & Lynch, counsel for the Selling Shareholders, dated such Closing Date, and in form and substance satisfactory to counsel for the Underwriters, with photostatic or photo-offset copies thereof for each of the other Underwriters, to the effect that:

(A) This Underwriting Agreement has been duly executed and delivered by or on behalf of each of the Selling Shareholders and constitutes a valid and legally binding agreement of each such Selling Shareholder, enforceable in accordance with its terms, except as may be limited by the application of insolvency or similar laws affecting the rights of creditors generally and judicial limitations on the right of specific performance and except as the enforceability of indemnification provisions may be limited by federal securities laws.

(B) A Power of Attorney and the Custody Agreement have been duly authorized, executed and delivered by each of the Selling Shareholders and each constitutes a valid and legally binding agreement of such Selling Shareholder enforceable in accordance with its terms, except as may be limited by the application of insolvency or similar laws affecting the rights of creditors generally and judicial limitations on the right of specific performance and except as the enforceability of indemnification provisions may be limited by federal securities laws.

(C) Marketable title to the Selling Shareholder Shares sold by each Selling Shareholder hereunder, free and clear of all liens, security interests, claims and encumbrances whatsoever, has been transferred to, and is vested in, the Underwriters who have severally purchased such shares hereunder.

(D) To the knowledge of such counsel, no consent, approval, authorization or other order of any regulatory body, administrative agency or other governmental body (other than under the 1933 Act or the securities or blue sky laws of any state or other jurisdiction) is required on the part of any Selling Shareholder for the sale of the Selling Shareholder Shares to the Underwriters under this Underwriting Agreement.

In expressing their opinion as to questions of law of jurisdictions other than the State of Delaware, California or the United States, such counsel may rely upon an opinion (dated the Closing Date, addressed to the Underwriters and in form satisfactory to you, with signed or conformed copies for each of the other Underwriters) of counsel acceptable to Messrs. Willkie Farr & Gallagher. Such opinion of counsel for the Company shall state that the opinion of such other counsel is in form and substance satisfactory to counsel for the Selling Shareholder and, in their opinion, you and they are justified in relying on such other opinion.

(vii) On each Closing Date there shall have been furnished to you, as Representative of the Underwriters, a certificate, dated such Closing Date, signed by the President and Chief Financial Officer of the Company to the effect that: (A) the representations and warranties of the Company in this Underwriting Agreement are materially correct on and as of the date of this Underwriting Agreement and on and as of each Closing Date, as if made on and as of such Closing Date and the Company has complied materially with all the agreements and satisfied all the conditions to be performed or satisfied by it hereunder at or prior to such Closing Date; (B) no stop order suspending the effectiveness of the Registration Statement has been issued and no proceedings for that purpose have been instituted or are pending or, to the best of their knowledge, are contemplated under the 1933 Act; (C) the signers of said certificate have carefully examined the Registration Statement and the Prospectus and, in their opinion: (I) as of the effective date of the Registration Statement and as of such Closing Date, the Registration Statement and the Prospectus did not and do not contain any untrue statement of a material fact or omit to state a material fact required to be stated therein or necessary to make the statements therein not misleading; (II) since the effective date of the Registration Statement no event has occurred which should have been set forth in an amendment or supplement to the Prospectus which has not been set forth in such an amendment or supplement; and (III) subsequent to the respective dates as of which information is given in the Registration Statement and Prospectus, and except as set forth in the Prospectus, neither the Company nor the Subsidiary has incurred any material liability or obligation, direct or contingent, or entered into any material transaction, whether or not in the ordinary course of business, and there has not been any change in the capital stock, or any increase in the long-term debt, or any issuance of options, warrants, convertible securities or other rights to purchase the capital stock of the Company or the Subsidiary, or any material adverse change in the general affairs, business, capitalization, financial position or net worth of the Company or the Subsidiary; and (D) except as otherwise stated in the Registration Statement and Prospectus, there are no actions, suits or proceedings pending before any court or governmental agency, authority or body or, to their knowledge, threatened, to which the Company or the Subsidiary is a party or to which the business or property of the Company or the Subsidiary is subject which, if adversely decided, would have a material adverse effect on the business or financial position of the Company or the Subsidiary, as the case may be.

(viii) On each Closing Date there shall have been furnished to you, as the Representative of the Underwriters, a certificate, dated such Closing Date, signed by or on behalf of the Selling Shareholders, to the effect that the representations and warranties of the Selling Shareholders in this Underwriting Agreement are materially correct on and as of the date of this Underwriting Agreement and on and as of each Closing Date, as if made on and as of such Closing Date and that the Selling Shareholders have complied with all the agreements and satisfied all the conditions on their part to be performed or satisfied at or prior to such Closing Date.

(ix) The representations and warranties of the Company and the Selling Shareholders herein shall be materially true and correct on and as of each Closing Date, as if made on and as of such Closing Date, and all agreements herein contained to be performed or complied with by the Company and the Selling Shareholders at or prior to such Closing Date shall have been performed or complied with.

(x) On each Closing Date, the Company shall have delivered to the Representative a letter of Arthur Andersen & Co., dated such Closing Date, confirming that they are independent public accountants within the meaning of the 1933 Act and are in compliance with the applicable requirements relating to the qualifications of accountants under Rule 2-01 of Regulation S-X of the Commission and stating as of the date of such letter (or, with respect to matters involving changes or developments since the respective dates as of which specified financial information is given in the Prospectus, as of a date not more than five days prior to the date of such letter), the conclusions and findings of said firm with respect to the financial information and other matters covered by its letter delivered to the Representative concurrently with the execution of this Underwriting Agreement, and the effect of the letter so to be delivered on such Closing Date shall be to confirm in all material respects the conclusions and findings set forth in such prior letter.

(xi) You shall have been furnished such additional certificates and other evidence as you or Messrs. Willkie Farr & Gallagher, counsel for the Underwriters, may reasonably request showing fulfillment of the conditions contained in this Section 5.

All such opinions, certificates, letters and documents will be in compliance with the provisions hereof only if they are reasonably satisfactory to you and to said counsel for the Underwriters. All statements contained in any certificate, letter or other document delivered pursuant hereto by or on behalf of the Company or any Selling Shareholders shall be deemed to constitute representations and warranties of the Company or such Selling Shareholder, as the case may be.

If any of the conditions specified in this Section 5 shall not have been fulfilled when and as required by this Underwriting Agreement to be fulfilled, this Underwriting Agreement and all obligations of the Underwriters hereunder may be cancelled at, or at any time prior to, each Closing Date, by you, as the Representative of the Underwriters. Any such cancellation shall be without liability of the Underwriters to the Company or the Selling Shareholders. Notice of such cancellation shall be given to the Company and the Selling Shareholders at the addresses specified in Section 12 hereof, in writing, or by telegraph or telephone and confirmed in writing.

6. *Conditions of the Company's and Selling Shareholders' Obligations.*

The obligation of the Company and the Selling Shareholders to deliver the Firm Shares or Option Shares, as the case may be, shall be subject to the conditions that no stop order suspending the effectiveness of the Registration Statement shall be in effect at any Closing Date, and no proceedings therefor shall be pending or threatened by the Commission at any Closing Date.

In case the conditions specified in this Section 6 shall not be fulfilled, this Underwriting Agreement may be terminated by the Company by notice to the Representative. Any such termination shall be without liability of the Company or the Selling Shareholders to the Underwriters, except as otherwise provided in Section 7 hereof, and without liability of the Underwriters to the Company or the Selling Shareholders.

7. *Certain Liabilities of the Company.*

If this Underwriting Agreement shall be cancelled or terminated by the Underwriters on any of the grounds referred to or specified in Section 5 or 10 hereof, or because of any failure or refusal on the part of the Company or the Selling Shareholders to comply with any of the terms or to fulfill any of the conditions of this Underwriting Agreement, or if the Company, pursuant to the provisions hereof, shall cancel or terminate this Underwriting Agreement or for any reason be unable to perform its obligations hereunder, the Company nevertheless shall pay the costs and expenses pursuant to Section 4 hereof and shall reimburse the Underwriters severally for all out-of-pocket expenses (including reasonable fees and disbursements of their counsel) incurred by them in connection with the contemplated purchase, offer and sale of the Stock; provided, however, that the Company shall not be obligated to reimburse the Underwriters for such out-of-pocket expenses in the event of a termination or cancellation of this Underwriting Agreement by the Underwriters pursuant to clauses (b), (c) and (d) of the second paragraph of Section 10 hereof.

8. *Indemnification.*

(a) The Company agrees to indemnify and hold harmless each Underwriter, each Selling Shareholder and each person, if any, who controls any Underwriter or Selling Shareholder within the meaning of the 1933 Act against any loss, claim, damage or liability, joint or several, to which such Underwriter, such Selling Shareholder or such controlling person may become subject, under the 1933 Act or otherwise, insofar as such loss, claim, damage or liability (or actions in respect thereof) arises out of or is based upon (i) any untrue statement or alleged untrue statement made by the Company in Section 1(a) hereof, or (ii) any untrue statement or alleged untrue statement of a material fact contained (A) in the Registration Statement (including the Prospectus as part thereof) or any amendment thereof, or (B) in any blue sky application or other document executed by the Company specifically for that purpose or based upon written information furnished by the Company filed in any state or other jurisdiction in order to qualify any or all of the Stock under the securities laws thereof (any such application, document or information being hereinafter called a "Blue Sky Application"), or (iii) the omission or alleged omission to state in the Registration Statement (including the Prospectus as a part thereof) or any amendment thereof or in any Blue Sky Application a material fact required to be stated therein or necessary to make the statements therein not misleading, or (iv) any untrue statement or alleged untrue statement of a material fact contained in any Preliminary Prospectus, if used in conformity with applicable law and prior to the effective date of the Registration Statement, or in the Prospectus (as amended or as supplemented, if the Company shall have filed with the Commission any amendment thereof or supplement thereto), or the omission or alleged omission to state therein a material fact required to be stated therein or necessary in order to make the statements therein not misleading; and will reimburse each Underwriter, each Selling Shareholder and each such controlling person for any legal or other expenses reasonably incurred by such Underwriter, such Selling Shareholder or such controlling person in connection with investigating or defending any such loss, claim, damage, liability or action; provided, however, that the Company will not be liable in any such case to the extent that any such loss, claim, damage or liability arises out of or is based upon an untrue statement or alleged untrue statement or omission or alleged omission made in reliance upon and in conformity with written information furnished to the Company through you by or on behalf of any Underwriter or to the Company by or on behalf of any Selling Shareholder, as the case may be, specifically for use in the preparation of the Registration Statement or any such post-effective

Appendix B

amendment thereof or any such Blue Sky Application or any such Preliminary Prospectus or the Prospectus or any such amendment thereof or supplement thereto; and further provided, however, that the foregoing indemnity agreement is subject to the condition that, insofar as it relates to any untrue statement, alleged untrue statement, omission or alleged omission made in any Preliminary Prospectus but eliminated or remedied in the Prospectus, such indemnity agreement shall not inure to the benefit of any Underwriter or Selling Shareholder from whom the person asserting any loss, liability, claim or damage purchased the Stock which is the subject thereof (or to the benefit of any person who controls such Underwriter or Selling Shareholder), if a copy of the Prospectus was not sent or given to such person with or prior to the written confirmation of the sale of such Stock to such person. This indemnity agreement will be in addition to any liability which the Company may otherwise have. The indemnity agreement of the Company contained in this subparagraph (a) and the representations and warranties of the Company contained in Section 1 hereof shall remain operative and in full force and effect regardless of any investigation made by or on behalf of any indemnified party and shall survive the delivery of, and payment for, the Stock.

(b) Each Underwriter severally, but not jointly, agrees to indemnify and hold harmless the Company and each Selling Shareholder, each of the Company's directors, each of the Company's officers who signed the Registration Statement, and each person, if any, who controls the Company or any Selling Shareholder within the meaning of the 1933 Act, against any loss, claim, damage or liability to which the Company, such Selling Shareholder or any such director or officer or controlling person may become subject, under the 1933 Act or otherwise, insofar as such loss, claim, damage or liability (or actions in respect thereof) arises out of or is based upon (i) any untrue statement or alleged untrue statement of a material fact contained (A) in the Registration Statement (including the Prospectus as a part thereof) or any post-effective amendment thereof, or (B) in any Blue Sky Application, or (ii) the omission or alleged omission to state in the Registration Statement (including the Prospectus as a part thereof) or any post-effective amendment thereof or in any Blue Sky Application a material fact required to be stated therein or necessary to make the statements therein not misleading, or (iii) any untrue statement or alleged untrue statement of a material fact contained in any Preliminary Prospectus, if used prior to the effective date of the Registration Statement, or in the Prospectus (as amended or as supplemented, if the Company shall have filed with the Commission any amendment thereof or supplement thereto), or the omission or alleged omission to state therein a material fact required to be stated therein or necessary in order to make the statements therein, in the light of the circumstances under which they were made, not misleading, in each case to the extent, but only to the extent, that such untrue statement or alleged untrue statement or omission or alleged omission was made in reliance upon and in conformity with written information furnished to the Company through you by or on behalf of such Underwriter specifically for use in the preparation of the Registration Statement or any such post-effective amendment thereof or any such Blue Sky Application or any such Preliminary Prospectus or the Prospectus or any such amendment thereof or supplement thereto; and will reimburse any legal or other expenses reasonably incurred by the Company, or each Selling Shareholder or any such director or officer or controlling person in connection with investigating or defending any such loss, claim, damage, liability or action. This indemnity agreement is in addition to any liability which such Underwriter may otherwise have. This indemnity agreement of each Underwriter contained in this subparagraph (b) shall remain operative and in full force and effect regardless of any investigation made by or on behalf of any indemnified party and shall survive the delivery of, and payment for, the Stock.

(c) Each Selling Shareholder, to the extent of such Selling Shareholder's proportionate share (based upon the number of Selling Shareholder Shares sold by such Selling Shareholder as compared with the aggregate number of Selling Shareholder Shares sold by all Selling Shareholders), agrees to indemnify and hold harmless the Company, each of its directors, each of its officers who signed the Registration Statement, each person who controls the Company within the meaning of the 1933 Act, each Underwriter and each person who controls an Underwriter against any loss, claim, damage or liability to which the Company, any Underwriter or any such director or officer or controlling person may become subject, under the 1933 Act or otherwise, insofar as such loss, claim, damage or liability (or actions in respect thereof) arise out of or are based upon (i) any untrue statement or alleged untrue statement of a material fact contained (A) in the Registration Statement (including the Prospectus as a part thereof) or any post-effective amendment thereof, or (B) in any Blue Sky Application, or (ii) the omission or alleged omission to state in the Registration Statement (including the Prospectus as a part thereof) or any post-effective amendment thereof or in any Blue Sky Application a material fact required to be stated therein or necessary to make the statements therein not misleading, or (iii) any untrue statement or alleged untrue statement of a material fact contained in any Preliminary Prospectus, if used prior to the effective date of the Registration Statement, or in the Prospectus (as amended or as supplemented, if the Company shall have filed with the Commission any amendment thereof or supplement thereto), or the omission or alleged omission to state therein a material fact required to be stated therein or necessary in order to make the statements therein not misleading, in each case to the extent, but not only to the extent, that such untrue statement or alleged untrue statement or omission or alleged omission was made in reliance upon and in conformity with written information furnished to the Company by or on behalf of such Selling Shareholder specifically for use in the preparation of the Registration Statement or any such post-effective amendment thereof or any such Blue Sky Application or any such Preliminary Prospectus or the Prospectus or any such amendment thereof or supplement thereto; and will reimburse any legal or other expenses reasonably incurred by the Company, or any Underwriter or any such director or officer or controlling person in connection with investigating or defending any such loss, claim, damage, liability or action. This indemnity agreement is in addition to any liability which such Selling Shareholder may otherwise have. The indemnity agreement of each Selling Shareholder contained in this subparagraph (c) shall remain operative and in full force and effect regardless of any investigation made by or on behalf of any indemnified party and shall survive the delivery of, and payment for, the Stock.

(d) Promptly after receipt by an indemnified party under this Section 8 of notice of the commencement of any action, suit or proceeding, such indemnified party will, if a claim in respect thereof is to be made against any indemnifying party under this Section 8, notify in writing the indemnifying party of the commencement thereof; the omission so to notify the indemnifying party will relieve it from any liability under this Section 8 as to the particular item for which indemnification is then being sought, but not from any other liability which it may have to any indemnified party. In case any such action, suit or proceeding is brought against any indemnified party, and it notifies an indemnifying party of the commencement thereof, the indemnifying party will be entitled to participate therein and, to the extent that it may wish, jointly with any other indemnifying party similarly notified, to assume the defense thereof, with counsel who shall be reasonably satisfactory to such indemnified party, and after notice from the indemnifying party to such indemnified party of its election so to assume the defense thereof, the indemnifying party will not be liable to such indemnified party under this Section 8 for any legal or other expenses subsequently incurred by such indemnified party in connection with the defense thereof other than reasonable costs of investigation. Any such indemnifying party shall not be liable to any such indemnified party on account of any settlement of any claim or action effected without the consent of such indemnifying party; provided, however, that if, in the reasonable judgment of the Representative it is advisable for the Representative, such Underwriters and controlling persons to be represented by separate counsel, the Representative shall have the right to employ a single counsel to represent the Representative and all Underwriters and their controlling persons, who may be subject to liability arising out of any claim in respect of which indemnity may be sought by the Representative, the Underwriters or any controlling person thereof against the Company or the Selling Shareholders herein, in which event the fees and expenses of such separate counsel shall be borne by the Company or the Selling Shareholders, as the case may be.

9. *Contribution.*

In order to provide for just and equitable contribution in any case in which any Underwriter (or person who controls such Underwriter within the meaning of the 1933 Act) makes claim for indemnification pursuant to Section 8 hereof but it is judicially determined (by entry of a final judgment or decree by a court of competent jurisdiction and the expiration of time to appeal or the denial of the last right of appeal) that such indemnification may not be enforced in such case, notwithstanding the fact that the provisions of Section 8 hereof so provide for indemnification in such case, then, and in each such case, (a) the Company and each of its directors and each of its officers who has signed the Registration Statement and each person who controls the Company, in the aggregate, (b) the several Underwriters and each person who controls any Underwriter, in the aggregate, and (c) the Selling Shareholders and each person who controls any Selling Shareholder, in the aggregate, shall contribute to the aggregate losses, claims, damages or liabilities to which they may be subject (after contribution from all others) in such proportion so that the Underwriters and their controlling persons are responsible for the portion represented by the percentage that the underwriting discount per

Appendix B

share appearing on the cover page of the Prospectus bears to the public offering price per share appearing thereon, and the Company and its officers and directors, and controlling persons, and the Selling Shareholders and controlling persons in the aggregate, are responsible for the remaining portion; provided, however, that no person guilty of a fraudulent misrepresentation (within the meaning of Section 11(f) of the 1933 Act) shall be entitled to contribution from any person who is not guilty of such fraudulent misrepresentation. The foregoing contribution agreement shall in no way affect the contribution liabilities of any persons having liability under Section 11 of the 1933 Act other than the Company, officers and directors of the Company, the Selling Shareholders and the Underwriters and persons controlling the Company, the Selling Shareholders or the Underwriters. The provisions of the Agreement Among Underwriters shall govern contribution among the several Underwriters. In no case shall any Underwriter (except as may be provided in the Agreement Among Underwriters) be responsible for any amount in excess of its pro rata share based on the number of shares purchased by it.

Promptly after receipt by any party to this Underwriting Agreement of notice of the commencement of any action, suit or proceeding, such person will, if a claim for contribution in respect thereof is to be made against another party (the "contributing party"), notify the contributing party of the commencement thereof; but the omission so to notify the contributing party will not relieve the contributing party from any liability which it may have to any party other than for contribution. Any notice given pursuant to Section 8 hereof shall be deemed to be like notice hereunder. In case any such action, suit or proceeding is brought against any party, and such person notifies a contributing party of the commencement thereof, the contributing party will be entitled to participate therein with the notifying party and any other contributing party similarly notified.

10. *Effective Date and Termination.*

This Underwriting Agreement shall become effective at 11:00 A.M., New York City time, on the first full business day following the day upon which the Registration Statement shall have become effective, or at such earlier time after such effective date as you, in your discretion, shall first release the Stock for sale to the public. For the purposes of this Section 10, the Stock shall be deemed to have been released for sale to the public upon release by you for publication of a newspaper advertisement relating to the Stock or upon release by you of communications offering the Stock for sales to securities dealers, whichever shall first occur. By giving notice as hereinafter specified before the time this Underwriting Agreement becomes effective, either you, as Representative of the several Underwriters, by notifying the Company and the Selling Shareholders or the Company by notifying you and the Selling Shareholders, may prevent this Underwriting Agreement from becoming effective but the giving of such notice shall not affect the obligations of the Company under Section 7 hereof.

Until the First Closing Date, this Underwriting Agreement may be terminated by you as Representative at your option or when directed so to do by a majority in interest of the several Underwriters, by giving notice to the Company and the Selling Shareholders, if (a) the Company or any Subsidiary shall have sustained a loss by fire, flood, accident or other calamity which is material to the property, business or financial condition of the Company or such Subsidiary, as the case may be, or (b) trading in securities generally on the New York Stock Exchange shall have been suspended or minimum prices shall have been established on such Exchange by the Commission or by such Exchange, or (c) a general banking moratorium shall have been declared by Federal or state authorities, or (d) if there shall have been such a material change in general economic, political or financial conditions or if the effect of international conditions on the financial markets in the United States shall be such as, in your judgment or in the judgment of such majority in interest of the several Underwriters, makes it inadvisable to proceed with the delivery of the Stock.

Any termination of this Underwriting Agreement pursuant to this Section 10 shall be without liability of the Company or the Selling Shareholders to the Underwriters, except as otherwise provided in Section 7 hereof, and without liability of the Underwriters to the Company or the Selling Shareholders.

Any notice referred to above may be given at the address specified in Section 12 hereof in writing or by telegraph or telephone, and if by telegraph or telephone, shall be immediately confirmed in writing.

11. *Survival of Indemnities, Contribution, Warranties and Representations.*

The respective indemnity agreements of the Company, the Selling Shareholders and the Underwriters contained in Section 8 hereof, the contribution provisions set forth in Section 9 hereof and the representations and warranties of the Company and the Selling Shareholders set forth in Section 1(a) and 1(b) hereof, shall remain operative and in full force and effect regardless of any termination or cancellation of this Underwriting Agreement or any investigation made by or on behalf of any of the Underwriters, the Selling Shareholders, the Company or any of its directors and officers, or any controlling person referred to in said Sections 8 and 9, and shall survive the delivery of, and payment for, the Stock.

Any successor of any Underwriter or of any Selling Shareholder or of the Company or of any such controlling person or any legal representative of such controlling person, as the case may be, shall be entitled to the benefit of the respective indemnity and contribution agreements.

12. *Notices.*

Except as otherwise provided in this Underwriting Agreement, (a) whenever notice is required by the provisions of this Underwriting Agreement to be given to the Company, such notice shall be in writing addressed to the Company at 435 Maple Avenue, Torrance, California 90503, Attention: Joseph S. O'Flaherty; (b) whenever notice is required by the provisions of this Underwriting Agreement to be given to the Selling Shareholders, such notice shall be in writing addressed to Joseph S. O'Flaherty; and (c) whenever notice is required by the provisions of this Underwriting Agreement to be given to the several Underwriters, such notice shall be in writing addressed to the Underwriters in care of Shearson Loeb Rhoades Inc., 14 Wall Street, Ninth Floor, New York, New York 10005; Attention: Investment Banking Division.

13. *Information Furnished by Underwriters.*

The statements set forth in the last paragraph on the cover page and under the caption "Underwriting" in any Preliminary Prospectus and in the Prospectus, except for the statements made in the paragraph under the caption "Underwriting" in the Prospectus relating to sales or dispositions by the Company or certain individuals, and, to the extent the same relate to any of the Underwriters, in any Blue Sky Application, constitute the written information furnished by or on behalf of any Underwriter referred to in subparagraphs (v) and (vi) of Section 1(a) and paragraphs (a) and (b) of Section 8 hereof.

14. *Persons Entitled to Benefit of Agreement.*

This Underwriting Agreement is made solely for the benefit of the several Underwriters, the Selling Shareholders, the Company, any officer, director or controlling person referred to in Sections 8 and 9 hereof, and their respective successors and assigns, and no other person shall acquire or have any right by virtue of this Underwriting Agreement. The term "successors and assigns", as used in this Underwriting Agreement, shall not include any purchaser (as such purchaser) from any of the Underwriters of any of the Stock.

Appendix B

15. *Governing Law.*

This Underwriting Agreement shall be governed by and construed in accordance with the laws of the State of New York.

Please confirm, by signing and returning to us four counterparts of this Underwriting Agreement, that you are acting on behalf of yourselves and the other several Underwriters and that the foregoing correctly sets forth the Underwriting Agreement among the Company and the several Underwriters.

                    Very truly yours,

                    MATRIX SCIENCE CORPORATION

            By: ....
                    Chairman of the Board and
                    Chief Executive Officer

                    SELLING SHAREHOLDERS

            By: ....
                    Individually and as Attorney-in-fact for
                    the Selling Shareholders named
                    in Schedule II hereto.

Confirmed as of the date first above mentioned:

SHEARSON LOEB RHOADES INC.
   as Representative

By: ....
            Authorized Officer

Acting severally on behalf of itself and the other several Underwriters named in Schedule I hereto.

Appendix C

FORM S-1

SECURITIES AND EXCHANGE COMMISSION

REGISTRATION STATEMENT
Under
The Securities Act of 1933.

....
(Exact name of registrant as specified in its charter)

....
(State or other jurisdiction of incorporation or organization)

....
(Primary Standard Industrial Classification Code Number)

....
(I.R.S. Employer Identification No.)

Source: Ticor Print Network/Jeffries Banknote Company *Securities Regulations Handbook*, updated to January 31, 1983

....
(Address, including zip code, and telephone number,
including area code, of registrant's principal executive offices)

....
(Name, address, including zip code, and telephone number,
including area code, of agent for service)

Approximate date of commencement of proposed sale to the public................

If any of the securities being registered on this Form are to be offered on a delayed or continuous basis pursuant to Rule 415 under the Securities Act of 1933 check the following box. ☐

CALCULATION OF REGISTRATION FEE

Title of each class of securities to be registered	Amount to be registered	Proposed maximum offering price per unit	Proposed maximum aggregate offering price	Amount of registration fee

GENERAL INSTRUCTIONS

I. Eligibility Requirements for Use of Form S-1

This Form shall be used for the registration under the Securities Act of 1933 ("Securities Act") of securities of all registrants for which no other form is authorized or prescribed, except that this Form shall not be used for securities of foreign governments or political subdivisions thereof.

II. Application of General Rules and Regulations

A. Attention is directed to the General Rules and Regulations under the Securities Act, particularly those comprising Regulation C thereunder. That Regulation contains general requirements regarding the preparation and filing of the registration statement.

B. Attention is directed to Regulation S-K for the requirements applicable to the content of the nonfinancial statement portions of registration statements under the Securities Act. Where this Form directs the registrant to furnish information required by Regulation S-K and the item of Regulation S-K so provides, information need only be furnished to the extent appropriate.

III. Exchange Offers

If any of the securities being registered are to be offered in exchange for securities of any other issuer the prospectus shall also include the information which would be required by Item 11 if the securities of such other issuer were registered on this Form. There shall also be included the information concerning such securities of such other issuer which would be called for by Item 9 if such securities were being registered. In connection with this instruction, reference is made to Rule 409.

PART I.

INFORMATION REQUIRED IN PROSPECTUS

Item 1. Forepart of the Registration Statement and Outside Front Cover Page of Prospectus.

Appendix C

Set forth in the forepart of the registration statement and on the outside front cover page of the prospectus the information required by Item 501 of Regulation S-K.

Item 2. Inside Front and Outside Back Cover Pages of Prospectus.

Set forth on the inside front cover page of the prospectus or, where permitted, on the outside back cover page, the information required by Item 502 of Regulation S-K.

Item 3. Summary Information, Risk Factors and Ratio of Earnings to Fixed Charges.

Furnish the information required by Item 503 of Regulation S-K.

Item 4. Use of Proceeds.

Furnish the information required by Item 504 of Regulation S-K.

Item 5. Determination of Offering Price.

Furnish the information required by Item 505 of Regulation S-K.

Item 6. Dilution.

Furnish the information required by Item 506 of Regulation S-K.

Item 7. Selling Security Holders.

Furnish the information required by Item 507 of Regulation S-K.

Item 8. Plan of Distribution.

Furnish the information required by Item 508 of Regulation S-K.

Item 9. Description of Securities to Be Registered.

Furnish the information required by Item 202 of Regulation S-K.

Item 10. Interests of Named Experts and Counsel.

Furnish the information required by Item 509 of Regulation S-K.

Item 11. Information with Respect to the Registrant.

Furnish the following information with respect to the registrant:

(a) Information required by Item 101 of Regulation S-K, description of business;

(b) Information required by Item 102 of Regulation S-K, description of property;

(c) Information required by Item 103 of Regulation S-K, legal proceedings;

(d) Where common equity securities are being offered, information required by Item 201 of Regulation S-K, market price of and dividends on the registrant's common equity and related stockholder matters;

(e) Financial statements meeting the requirements of Regulation S-X (Schedules required under Regulation S-X shall be filed as "Financial Statement Schedules" pursuant to Item 16, Exhibits and Financial Statement Schedules, of this Form), as well as any financial information required by Rule 3.05 and Article 11 of Regulation S-X:

(f) Information required by Item 301 of Regulation S-K, selected financial data:

(g) Information required by Item 302 of Regulation S-K, supplementary financial information;

(h) Information required by Item 303 of Regulation S-K, management's discussion and analysis of financial condition and results of operations;

(i) Information required by Item 304 of Regulation S-K, disagreements with accountants on accounting and financial disclosure;

(j) Information required by Item 401 of Regulation S-K, directors and executive officers;

(k) Information required by Item 402 of Regulation S-K, management remuneration and transactions; and

(l) Information required by Item 403 of Regulation S-K, security ownership of certain beneficial owners and management.

Item 12. Disclosure of Commission Position on Indemnification for Securities Act Liabilities.

Furnish the information required by Item 510 of Regulation S-K.

PART II.
INFORMATION NOT REQUIRED IN PROSPECTUS

Item 13. Other Expenses of Issuance and Distribution.

Furnish the information required by Item 511 of Regulation S-K.

Item 14. Indemnification of Directors and Officers.

Furnish the information required by Item 702 of Regulation S-K.

Item 15. Recent Sales of Unregistered Securities.

Furnish the information required by Item 701 of Regulation S-K.

Item 16. Exhibits and Financial Statement Schedules.

(a) Subject to the rules regarding incorporation by reference, furnish the exhibits as required by Item 601 of Regulation S-K.

(b) Furnish the financial statement schedules required by Regulation S-K and Item 11(e) of this Form. These schedules shall be lettered or numbered in the manner described for exhibits in paragraph (a).

Item 17. Undertakings.

Furnish the undertakings required by Item 512 of Regulation S-K.

SIGNATURES

Pursuant to the requirements of the Securities Act of 1933, the registrant has duly caused this registration statement to be signed on its behalf by the undersigned, thereunto duly authorized, in the City of ...., and State of ...., on ...., 19......... .

Appendix C

....
(Registrant)

By ....
(Signature and Title)

Pursuant to the requirements of the Securities Act of 1933, this registration statement has been signed by the following persons in the capacities and on the dates indicated.

....
(Signature)   (Title)   (Date)

Instructions. 1. The registration statement shall be signed by the registrant, its principal executive officer or officers, its principal financial officer, its controller or principal accounting officer and by at least a majority of the board of directors or persons performing similar functions. If the registrant is a foreign person, the registration statement shall also be signed by its authorized representative in the United States. Where the registrant is a limited partnership, the registration statement shall be signed by a majority of the board of directors of any corporate general partner signing the registration statement.

2. The name of each person who signs the registration statement shall be typed or printed beneath his signature. Any person who occupies more than one of the specified positions shall indicate each capacity in which he signs the registration statement. Attention is directed to Rule 402 concerning manual signatures and to Item 601 of Regulation S-K concerning signatures pursuant to powers of attorney.

INSTRUCTIONS AS TO SUMMARY PROSPECTUSES

1. A summary prospectus used pursuant to Rule 431, shall at the time of its use contain such of the information specified below as is then included in the registration statement. All other information and documents contained in the registration statement may be omitted.

(a) As to Item 1, the aggregate offering price to the public, the aggregate underwriting discounts and commissions and the offering price per unit to the public;

(b) As to Item 4, a brief statement of the principal purposes for which the proceeds are to be used;

(c) As to Item 7, a statement as to the amount of the offering, if any, to be made for the account of security holders;

(d) As to Item 8, the name of the managing underwriter or underwriters and a brief statement as to the nature of the underwriter's obligation to take the securities; if any securities to be registered are to be offered otherwise than through underwriters, a brief statement as to the manner of distribution; and, if securities are to be offered otherwise than for cash, a brief statement as to the general purposes of the distribution, the basis upon which the securities are to be offered, the amount of compensation and other expenses of distribution, and by whom they are to be borne;

(e) As to Item 9, a brief statement as to dividend rights, voting rights, conversion rights, interest, maturity;

(f) As to Item 11, a brief statement of the general character of the business done and intended to be done, the selected financial data (Item 301 of Regulation S-K) and a brief statement of the nature and present status of any material pending legal proceedings; and

(g) A tabular presentation of notes payable, long term debt, deferred credits, minority interests, if material, and the equity section of the latest balance sheet filed, as may be appropriate.

2. The summary prospectus shall not contain a summary or condensation of any other required financial information except as provided above.

3. Where securities being registered are to be offered in exchange for securities of any other issuer, the summary prospectus also shall contain that information as to Items 9 and 11 specified in paragraphs (e) and (f) above which would be required if the securities of such other issuer were registered on this Form.

4. The Commission may, upon the request of the registrant, and where consistent with the protection of investors, permit the omission of any of the information herein required or the furnishing in substitution therefor of appropriate information of comparable character. The Commission may also require the inclusion of other information in addition to, or in substitution for, the information herein required in any case where such information is necessary or appropriate for the protection of investors.

Appendix D

FORM S-18
SECURITIES AND EXCHANGE COMMISSION
REGISTRATION STATEMENT UNDER
THE SECURITIES ACT OF 1933

....
(Exact name of registrant as specified in charter)

....
(State or other jurisdiction   (Primary Standard   (I.R.S. Employer
 of incorporation or   Industrial Classification   Identification No.)
 organization)   Code Number)

....
(Address, including zip code, and telephone number, including area code,
of registrant's principal executive offices)

....
(Address of principal place of business or intended principal place of business)

....
(Name, address, including zip code, and telephone number,
including area code, of agent for service)

Source: Ticor Print Network/Jeffries Banknote Company *Securities Regulations Handbook*, updated to January 31, 1983

Approximate date of commencement of proposed sale to the public ....

CALCULATION OF REGISTRATION FEE

Title of each class securities to be registered	Amount to be registered	Proposed maximum offering price per unit	Proposed maximum aggregate offering price	Amount of registration fee

The registrant hereby amends this registration statement on such date or dates as may be necessary to delay its effective date until the registrant shall file a further amendment which specifically states that this registration statement shall thereafter become effective in accordance with Section 8(a) of the Securities Act of 1933 or until the registration statement shall become effective on such date as the Commission, acting pursuant to said Section 8(a), may determine.*

* Inclusion of this paragraph is optional. See Rule 473. (Each page of this document, including exhibits and attachments, shall be numbered sequentially from this page, as page 1, through the last page of the document.)

GENERAL INSTRUCTIONS

I. Rule as to use of Form S-18.

A. This form is to be used for the registration of securities not to exceed an aggregate offering price of $5 million which are to be sold for cash, installments for cash and/or cash assessments and assumptions by partners of partnership debt, by the registrant, or for the account of security holders in accordance with paragraph B, provided such registrant:

(1) Is organized under the laws of the United States or Canada or any State or Province thereof, and has or proposes to have its principal business operations in the United States, if a domestic issuer, or Canada or the United States if a Canadian issuer;

(2) Is not subject to the reporting provisions of the Securities Exchange Act of 1934 pursuant to Section 12 or 15(d) of that Act;

(3) Is not an investment company;

(4) Is not an insurance company which is exempt from the provisions of Section 12 of the Securities Exchange Act of 1934 in reliance upon Section 12(g)(2)(G) thereof; and

(5) Is not a majority owned subsidiary of a registrant which does not meet the qualifications for use of the form, as specified herein.

B. This form may be used for the registration of securities to be sold for the account of any person other than the registrant, provided: (i) the aggregate offering price of such securities does not exceed $1.5 million and (ii) the aggregate offering price of such securities together with the aggregate offering price of any securities to be sold by the registrant does not exced $5 million.

C. For purposes of computing the $5 million ceiling specified above, there shall be included in the aggregate offering price of the securities registered herein, the aggregate offering price of all securities sold: (i) by the registrant within one year prior to the commencement of the proposed offering in violation of Section 5(a) of the Securities Act; (ii) by the registrant within one year prior to the commencement of the proposed offering pursuant to a registration statement filed on Form S-18; and (iii) which would be deemed integrated with the proposed offering. (*See:* Securities Act Release No. 4552 (November 6, 1962) [27 FR 11316].) In computing the $5 million ceiling, the aggregate price of all securities sold which fall in more than one of the above described categories need be counted only once.

Appendix D

D. Notwithstanding the provisions of paragraph (A)(2), a registrant which has had a prior offering on Form S-18 may, during the remainder of the fiscal year in which the prior registration statement was made effective, use the form to register additional securities until the offering limit as computed in paragraph C has been met.

II. Place of Filing.

A. At the election of the registrant, all registration statements on Form S-18 and related papers filed with the Commission shall be filed either at its principal office in Washington, D. C. or in the Regional Office for the region in which the registrant's principal business operations are conducted, or are proposed to be conducted. The registration statement of any registrant having or proposing to have its principal business operations in Canada may be filed with the Regional Office nearest the place where the registrant's principal business operations are conducted, or are proposed to be conducted; *Provided, however,* That if the offering is to be made through a principal underwriter located in the United States, the offering statement may be filed with the Regional Office for the region in which such underwriter has its principal office. Such material may be filed by delivery to the Commission through the mails or otherwise. Questions concerning the appropriate place of filing may be directed to the Commission's Regional Offices.

B. The Commission will endeavor to process Form S-18 registration statements at the place of filing. However, due to workload or other special consideration, the Commission may refer processing to a different Commission office.

C. All post-effective amendments to the Form S-18 registration statement shall be filed in the office where the corresponding Form S-18 registration statement was declared effective.

III. Application of General Rules and Regulations.

A. Attention is directed to the General Rules and Regulations under the Act, particularly those comprising Regulation C, which contains general requirements regarding the preparation and filing of a registration statement.

B. Attention is directed to Rule 463 and Form SR which is required to be filed by first-time registrants under the Securities Act showing sales of registered securities and the use of proceeds therefrom. Form SR shall be filed at the same office where the registration statement was declared effective.

C. Attention is directed to Regulation S-K relating to registration statement content. Where this form specifically references an item within that Regulation, the information need only be furnished to the extent appropriate. Special attention also is directed to paragraphs (b) and (c) of § 229.10 of Regulation S-K which outline the Commission's policies on projections and securities ratings, respectively.

D. Attention is directed to disclosure provisions set forth in the Industry Guides which are listed in Rule 801 of Regulation S-K. These Industry Guides represent Division practices with respect to the disclosure to be provided by the affected industries in registration statements.

E. Attention is directed to Rule 15c2-8 regarding prior delivery of preliminary prospectuses by registrants not subject to the reporting requirements of the Exchange Act.

F. Attention is directed to Form S-11 which relates to the registration of securities of certain real estate companies, and particularly Item 13 [Investment Policies of Registrant], Item 14 [Description of Real Estate], and Item 15 [Operating Data] contained therein. To the extent that these items offer enhanced guide lines for disclosure by real estate entities, registrants engaged or to be engaged in real estate operations may wish to consider these items for use in a Form S-18 offering.

PART I.
INFORMATION REQUIRED IN PROSPECTUS

Item 1. Forepart of the Registration Statement and Outside Front Cover Page of Prospectus.

Set forth in the forepart of the registration statement and on the outside front cover page of the prospectus the information required by Item 501 of Regulation S-K.

Item 2. Inside Front and Outside Back Cover Pages of Prospectus.

Set forth on the inside front cover page of the prospectus or, where permitted, on the outside back cover page, the information required by Item 502 of Regulation S-K.

Item 3. Summary Information and Risk Factors.

Furnish the information required by Item 503(a), (b), and (c) of Regulation S-K.

Item 4. Use of Proceeds.

Furnish the information required by Item 504 of Regulation S-K.

Item 5. Determination of Offering Price.

Furnish the information required by Item 505 of Regulation S-K.

Item 6. Dilution.

Furnish the information required by Item 506 of Regulation S-K.

Item 7. Selling Security Holders.

Furnish the information required by Item 507 of Regulation S-K.

Item 8. Plan of Distribution.

Furnish the information required by Item 508 of Regulation S-K, except the information specified in Item 508(c)(1), (3), and (d).

Item 9. Legal Proceedings.

Furnish the information required by Item 103 of Regulation S-K.

Item 10. Directors and Executive Officers.

Furnish the information required by Item 401 of Regulation S-K.

Item 11. Security Ownership of Certain Beneficial Owners and Management.

Furnish the information required by Item 403 of Regulation S-K.

Item 12. Description of the Securities To Be Registered.

Furnish the information required by Item 202 of Regulation S-K.

Appendix D

Item 13. Interest of Named Experts and Counsel.

Furnish the information required by Item 509 of Regulation S-K.

Item 14. Statement as to Indemnification.

Furnish the information required by Item 510 of Regulation S-K.

Item 15. Organization Within 5 Years.

If the registrant was organized within the past five years, furnish the following information:

(a) State the names of the promoters, the nature and amount of anything of value (including money, property, contracts, options or rights of any kind) received or to be received by each promoter directly or indirectly from the registrant, and the nature and amount of any assets, services or other consideration therefor received or to be received by the registrant. The term "promoter" is defined in Rule 405 under the Act.

(b) As to any assets acquired or to be acquired by the registrant from a promoter, state the amount at which acquired or to be acquired and the principal followed or to be followed in determining the amount. Identify the persons making the determination and state their relationship, if any, with the registrant or any promoter. If the assets were acquired by the promoter within two years prior to their transfer to the registrant, state the cost thereof to the promoter.

(c) List all parents of the registrant showing the basis of control and as to each parent, the percentage of voting securities owned or other basis of control by its immediate parent if any.

Instruction. Include the registrant and show the percentage of its voting securities owned or other basis of control by its immediate parent.

Item 16. Description of Business.

(a) *General development of business.* Describe the general development of the business of the registrant, its subsidiaries and any predecessor(s) during the past five years, or such shorter period as the registrant may have been engaged in business. Information shall be disclosed for earlier periods if material to an understanding of the general development of the business.

(1) In describing developments, information shall be given as to matters such as the following: the year in which the registrant was organized and its form of organization; the nature and results of any bankruptcy, receivership or similar proceedings with respect to the registrant or any of its significant subsidiaries; the nature and results of any other material reclassification, merger or consolidation of the registrant or any of its significant subsidiaries; the acquisition or disposition of any material amount of assets otherwise than in the ordinary course of business; and any material changes in the mode of conducting the business.

Instruction. The following requirement in paragraph (2) applies only to registrants (including predecessors) which have not received revenue from operations during each of the three fiscal years immediately prior to the filing of the registration statement.

(2) Describe, if formulated, the registrant's plan of operation for the remainder of the fiscal year, if the registration statement is filed prior to the end of the registrant's second fiscal quarter. Describe, if formulated, the registrant's plan of operation for the remainder of the fiscal year and for the first six months of the next fiscal year if the registration statement is filed subsequent to the end of the second fiscal quarter. If such information is not available, the reasons for its not being

available shall be stated. Disclosure relating to any plan should include such matters as:

(i) A statement in narrative form indicating the registrant's opinion as to the period of time that the proceeds from the offering will satisfy cash requirements and whether in the next six months it will be necessary to raise additional funds to meet the expenditures required for operating the business of the registrant. The specific reasons for such opinion shall be set forth and categories of expenditures and sources of cash resources shall be identified; however, amounts of expenditure and cash resources need not be provided. In addition, if the narrative statement is based on a cash budget, such budget should be furnished to the commission as supplemental information, but not as a part of the registration statement.

(ii) An explanation of material product research and development to be performed during the period covered in the plan.

(iii) Any anticipated material acquisition of plant and equipment and the capacity thereof.

(iv) Any anticipated material changes in number of employees in the various departments such as research and development production, sales or administration.

(v) Other material areas which may be peculiar to the registrant's business.

(b) *Narrative description of business.*

(1) Describe the business done and intended to be done by the registrant and its subsidiaries. Such description should include, if material to an understanding of the registrant's business, a discussion of:

(a) the principal products produced and services rendered and the principal markets for and methods of distribution of such products and services.

(b) the status of a product or service if the issuer has made public information about a new product or service which would require the investment of a material amount of the assets of the registrant or is otherwise material.

(c) the estimated amount spent during each of the last two fiscal years on company-sponsored research and development activities determined in accordance with generally accepted accounting principles. In addition, state the estimated dollar amount spent during each of such years on material customer-sponsored research activities relating to the development of new products, services or techniques or the improvement of existing products, services or techniques.

(d) the number of persons employed by the registrant indicating the number employed full time.

(e) the material effects that compliance with Federal, State and local provisions which have been enacted or adopted regulating the discharge of materials into the environment, or otherwise relating to the protection of the environment, may have upon the capital expenditures, earnings and competitive position of the registrant and its subsidiaries. The registrant shall disclose any material estimated capital expenditures for environmental control facilities for the remainder of its current fiscal year and for such further periods as the registrant may deem material.

(2) The registrant should also describe those distinctive or special characteristics of the registrant's operations or industry which may have a material impact upon the registrant's future financial performance. Examples of factors which might be discussed include dependence on one or a few major customers or suppliers (including suppliers of raw materials or financing), existing or probable governmental regulation, expiration of material labor contracts or patents, trademarks, licenses, franchises, concessions or royalty agreements, unusual competitive conditions in the

industry, cyclicality of the industry and anticipated raw material or energy shortages to the extent management may not be able to secure a continuing source of supply.

(c) *Segment data.* If the registrant is required to include segment information in its financial statements, such information may be disclosed in the description of business or in the financial statements. If such information is included in the financial statements, an appropriate cross reference shall be included in the description of business.

Item 17. Description of Property.

State briefly the location and general character of the principal plants, and other materially important physical properties of the registrant and its subsidiaries. If any such property is not held in fee or is held subject to any major encumbrance, so state and briefly describe how held.

Instruction. What is required is information essential to an investor's appraisal of the securities being registered. Such information should be furnished as will reasonably inform investors as to the suitability, adequacy, productive capacity and extent of utilization of the facilities used in the enterprise. Detailed descriptions of the physical characteristics of individual properties or legal descriptions by metes and bounds are not required and should not be given.

Item 17A. Description of Property — Issuers Engaged or to be Engaged in Significant Mining Operations.

(a) *Definitions:* The following definitions apply to registrants engaged or to be engaged in significant mining operations:

(1) *Reserve:* That part of a mineral deposit which could be economically and legally extracted or produced at the time of the reserve determination. *Note:* Reserves are customarily stated in terms of "ore" when dealing with metalliferous minerals; when other materials such as coal, oil shale, tar sands, limestone, etc. are involved, an appropriate term such as "recoverable coal" may be substituted.

(2) *Proven (Measured) Reserves:* Reserves for which (a) quantity is computed from dimensions revealed in outcrops, trenches, workings, or drill holes; grade and/or quality are computed from the results of detailed sampling and (b) the sites for inspection, sampling and measurement are spaced so closely and the geologic character is so well defined that size, shape, depth, and mineral content of reserves are well-established.

(3) *Probable (Indicated) Reserves:* Reserves for which quantity and grade and/or quality are computed from information similar to that used for proven (measured) reserves, but the sites for inspection, sampling, and measurement are farther apart or are otherwise less adequately spaced. The degree of assurance, although lower than that for proven (measured) reserves, is high enough to assume continuity between points of observation.

(4) (i) *Exploration Stage* — includes all issuers engaged in the search for mineral deposits (reserves) which are not in either the development or production stage.

(ii) *Development Stage* — includes all issuers engaged in the preparation of an established commercially mineable deposit (reserves) for its extraction which are not in the production stage.

(iii) *Production Stage* — includes all issuers engaged in the exploitation of a mineral deposit (reserve).

Instruction. Mining companies in the exploration stage should not refer to themselves as development stage companies in the financial statements, even though such companies should comply with FASB Statement No. 7, if applicable.

(b) *Mining Operations Disclosure* — Furnish the following information as to each of the mines, plants and other significant properties owned or operated, or presently intended to be owned or operated, by the registrant:

(1) The location of and means of access to the property.

(2) A brief description of the title, claim, lease or option under which the registrant and its subsidiaries have or will have the right to hold or operate the property, indicating any conditions which the registrant must meet in order to obtain or retain the property. If held by leases or options, the expiration dates of such leases or options should be stated. Appropriate maps may be used to portray the locations of significant properties.

(3) A brief history of previous operations, including the names of previous operators, insofar as known.

(4)(a) A brief description of the present condition of the property, the work completed by the registrant on the property, the registrant's proposed program of exploration and development, and the current state of exploration and/or development of the property. Mines should be identified as either open-pit or underground. If the property is without known reserves and the proposed program is exploratory in nature, a statement to that effect shall be made.

(b) The age, details as to modernization and physical condition of the plant and equipment, including subsurface improvements and equipment. Further, the total cost for each property and its associated plant and equipment should be stated. The source of power utilized with respect to each property should also be disclosed.

(5) A brief description of the rock formations and mineralization of existing or potential economic significance on the property, including the identity of the principal metallic or other constituents insofar as known. If proven (measured) or probable (indicated) reserves have been established, state (i) the estimated tonnages and grades (or quality, where appropriate) of such classes of reserves, and (ii) the name of the person making the estimates and the nature of his relationship to the registrant.

Instructions. 1. It should be stated whether the reserve estimate is of in-place material or of recoverable material. Any in-place estimate should be qualified to show the anticipated losses resulting from mining methods and beneficiation or preparation.

2. The summation of proven (measured) and probable (indicated) ore reserves is acceptable if the difference in degree of assurance between the two classes of reserves cannot be reliably defined.

3. Estimates other than proved (measured) or probable (indicated) reserves, and any estimated values of such reserves shall not be disclosed unless such information is required to be disclosed by foreign or state law; provided, however, that where such estimates previously have been provided to a person (or any of its affiliates) that is offering to acquire, merge, or consolidate with, the registrant or otherwise to acquire the registrant's securities, such estimates may be included.

(6) If technical terms relating to geology, mining or related matters whose definitions cannot be readily found in conventional dictionaries (as opposed to technical dictionaries or glossaries) are used, an appropriate glossary should be included in the registration statement.

(7) Detailed geologic maps and reports, feasibility studies and other highly technical data should not be included in the registration statement but should be, to

Appendix D

the degree appropriate and necessary for the Commission's understanding of the registrant's presentation of business and property matters, furnished as supplemental information.

(c) *Supplemental Information:*

(1) If an estimate of proven (measured) or probable (indicated) reserves is set forth in the registration statement, furnish:

(i) maps drawn to scale showing any mine workings and the outlines of the reserve blocks involved together with the pertinent sample-assay thereon.

(ii) all pertinent drill data and related maps;

(iii) the calculations whereby the basic sample-assay or drill data were translated into the estimates made of the grade and tonnage of reserves in each block and in the complete reserve estimate.

Instructions. Maps and other drawings submitted to the staff should include: 1. A legend or explanation showing, by means of pattern or symbol, every pattern or symbol used on the map or drawing; the use of the symbols used by the U.S. Geological Survey is encouraged;

2. A graphical bar scale should be included; additional representations of scale such as "one inch equals one mile" may be utilized provided the original scale of the map has not been altered;

3. A north arrow on maps;

4. An index map showing where the property is situated in relationship to the state or province, etc., in which it was located;

5. A title of the map or drawing and the date on which it was drawn;

6. In the event interpretive data is submitted in conjunction with any map, the identity of the geologist or engineer that prepared such data;

7. Any drawing should be simple enough or of sufficiently large scale to clearly show all features on the drawing.

(2) Furnish a complete copy of every material engineering, geological or metallurgical report concerning the registrant's property, including governmental reports, which are known and available to the registrant. Every such report should include the name of its author and the date of its preparation, if known to the registrant.

Any of the above-required reports as to which the staff has access need not be submitted. In this regard, issuers should consult with the staff prior to filing the registration statement. Any reports not submitted should be identified in a list furnished to the staff. This list should also identify any known governmental reports concerning the registrant's property.

(3) Furnish copies of all documents such as title documents, operating permits and easements needed to support representations made in the registration statement.

Item 17B. Supplementary Financial Information about Oil and Gas Producing Activities.

Registrants engaged in oil and gas producing activities shall follow the disclosure standards specified in paragraph (c) of Item 302 of Regulation S-K with respect to such activities.

Item 18. Interest of Management and Others in Certain Transactions.

Describe briefly any transactions during the previous two years or any presently proposed transactions, to which the registrant or any of its subsidiaries was or is to be a party, in which any of the following persons had or is to have a direct or indirect material interest, naming such person and stating his relationship to the issuer, the nature of his interest in the transaction and, where practicable, the amount of such interest:

(1) Any director or officer of the issuer;

(2) Any nominee for election as a director;

(3) Any security holder named in answer to Item 11; or

(4) Any relative or spouse of any of the foregoing persons, or any relative of such spouse, who has the same house as such persons or who is a director or officer of any parent or subsidiary of the registrant.

Instructions. 1. See Instruction 2 to Item 20(a)(i). No information need to be given in response to this Item as to any remuneration or other transaction reported in response to Item 20 or specifically excluded from Item 20.

2. No information need be given in answer to this Item as to any transaction where:

(a) the rates or charges involved in the transaction are determined by competitive bids, or the transaction involves the rendering of services as a common or contract carrier, or public utility, at rates or charges fixed in conformity with law or governmental authority;

(b) the transaction involves services as a bank depositary of funds, transfer agent, registrar, trustee under a trust indenture, or similar services;

(c) the amount involved in the transaction or a series of similar transactions, including all periodic installments in the case of any lease or other agreement of providing for periodic payments or installments, does not exceed $40,000; or

(d) the interest of the specified person arises solely from the ownership of securities of the issuer and the specified person receives no extra or special benefit not shared on a pro rata basis by all holders of securities of the class.

3. It should be noted that this item calls for disclosure of indirect, as well as direct, material interests in transactions. A person who has a position or relationship with a firm, corporation, or other entity, which engages in a transaction with the issuer or its subsidiaries may have an indirect interest in such transaction by reason of such position or relationship. However, a person shall be deemed not to have a material indirect interest in a transaction within the meaning of this Item where:

(a) the interest arises only (i) from such person's position as a director of another corporation or organization (other than a partnership) which is a party to the transaction or (ii) from the direct or indirect ownership by such person and all other persons specified in subparagraphs (1) through (3) above, in the aggregate, of less than a 10 percent equity interest in another person (other than a partnership) which is a party to the transaction, or (iii) from both such position and ownership.

(b) the interest arises only from such person's position as a limited partner in a partnership in which he and all other persons specified in (1) through (4) above had an interest of less than 10 percent; or

(c) the interest of such person arises solely from the holding of an equity interest (including a limited partnership interest but excluding a general partnership interest) or a creditor interest in another person which is a party to the transaction with the issuer or any of its subsidiaries and the transaction is not material to such other person.

4. Include the name of each person whose interest in any transaction is described and the nature of the relationships by reason of which such interest is required to be described. The amount of the interest of any specified person shall be computed without regard to the amount of the profit or loss involved in the transaction. Where it is not practicable to state the approximate amount of the interest, the approximate amount involved in the transaction shall be disclosed.

5. Information should be included as to any material underwriting discounts and commissions upon the sale of securities by the registrant where any of the specified persons was or is to be a principal underwriter or is a controlling person, or member, of a firm which was or is to be a principal underwriter. Information need not be given concerning ordinary management fees paid by underwriters to a managing underwriter pursuant to an agreement amoung underwriters the parties to which do not include the registrant or its subsidiaries.

6. As to any transaction involving the purchase or sale of assets by or to the registrant or any subsidiary, otherwise than in the ordinary course of business, state the cost of the assets to the purchaser and if acquired by the seller within two years prior to the transaction, the cost thereof to the seller.

7. Information shall be furnished in answer to this item with respect to transactions not excluded above which involve remuneration from the registrant or its subsidiaries, directly or indirectly, to any of the specified persons for services in any capacity unless the interest of such persons arises solely from the ownership individually and in the aggregate of less than 10% of any class of equity securities of another corporation furnishing the services to the registrant or its subsidiaries.

8. The foregoing instructions specify certain transactions and interests as to which information may be omitted in answering this item. There may be situations where, although the foregoing instructions do not expressly authorize nondisclosure, the interest of a specified person in the particular transaction or series of transaction is not a material interest. In that case, information regarding such interest and transaction is not required to be disclosed in response to this item. The materiality of any interest or transaction is to be determined on the basis of the significance of the information to investors in light of all of the circumstances of the particular transaction. The importance of the interest to the person having the interest, the relationship of the parties to the transaction to each other and the amount involved in the transaction are among the factors to be considered in determining the significance of the information to investors.

Item 19. Certain Market Information.

Furnish the information required by Item 201(a)(2) of Regulation S-K.

Item 20. Remuneration of Directors and Officers.

(a) Furnish the information required in the table below in substantially the tabular form specified, concerning all remuneration paid or distributed through the latest practicable date to, or accrued through such date for the account of, the following persons for services in all capacities to the registrant and its subsidiaries during the registrant's last fiscal year.

(i) each of the five highest paid persons who are officers or directors of the registrant whose aggregate remuneration exceeded $50,000 naming each such person.

(ii) all directors and officers of the registrant as a group, without naming them.

Name of individual or identity of group	Capacities in which remuneration was received	Aggregate remuneration

Instructions. 1. Information is to be included as to all options, securities, or other property given for services, annuity, pension, or retirement benefits; bonus or profit sharing plans; future remuneration; or personal benefits. In case of remuneration paid or to be paid otherwise than in cash, if it is impracticable to determine the cash value thereof, state in a note to the table the nature and amount thereof.

2. This item applies to any person who was a director or officer of the registrant at any time during the period specified. However, information need not be given for

any portion of the period during which such person was not a director or officer of the registrant.

3. This item is to be answered on an accrual basis if practicable; if not so answered, state the basis used.

4. If the registrant has not completed a full fiscal year since its organization or if it acquired or is to acquire the majority of its assets from a predecessor within the current fiscal year, the information shall be given for the current fiscal year, estimating future payments, if necessary. To the extent that such remuneration is to be computed upon the basis of a percentage of profits, it will suffice to state such percentage without estimating the amount of such profits to be paid.

5. Personal benefits. Disclosure shall be provided as to the value of personal benefits which are not directly related to job performance, other than those provided to broad categories of employees and which do not discriminate in favor of officers or directors, furnished by the registrant or its subsidiaries directly or through third parties to each of the specified persons and groups, or benefits furnished by the registrant or its subsidiaries to other persons which indirectly benefit the specified persons.

(a) *Valuation.* Such benefits shall be valued on the basis of the registrant's and subsidiaries' aggregate actual incremental costs; however, if such aggregate costs are significantly less than the aggregate amounts the recipient would have had to pay to obtain the benefits, appropriate disclosure, including the aggregate value to the recipient, should be made in a footnote to the table.

(b) *Conditional exclusion of personal benefits.* If the registrant cannot determine without reasonable effort or expense the specific amount of certain personal benefits, or the extent to which benefits are personal rather than business, the amount of such personal benefits may be omitted from the table provided the following condition is met:

Inquiry. After reasonable inquiry, the registrant has concluded that the aggregate amounts of such personal benefits which cannot be specifically or precisely ascertained do not in any event exceed $10,000 as to each person or, in the case of a group, $10,000 for each person in the group and has concluded that the information set forth in the table is not rendered materially misleading by virtue of the omission of the value of such personal benefits.

(c) *Footnote disclosure.* If as to a person named in the table an amount representing personal benefits included in the table exceeds 10 percent of the aggregate amount disclosed or $25,000, whichever is less, include a footnote to the table stating the dollar amount or percentage of the amount disclosed represented by such personal benefits and briefly describing the kinds of such benefits.

6. Information relating to any pension or retirement benefits need not be disclosed if the amounts to be paid are computed on an actuarial basis under any plan which provides for fixed benefits in the event of retirement at a specified age or after a specified number of years of service.

7. Information need not be included as to payments to be made for, or benefits to be received from, group life or accident insurance, group hospitalization or similar group payments or benefits. If it is impracticable to state the amount of remuneration payments proposed to be made, the aggregate amount set aside or accrued to date in respect of such payments should be stated.

(b) Furnish the following information as to options to purchase securities from the registrant or any of its subsidiaries which are outstanding as of a specified date not more than 30 days prior to the date of filing of the registration statement held by (1) each director and executive officer named in answer to paragraph (a), above, naming each such person, and (2) all directors and officers as a group without naming them:

(i) the title and amount of the securities called for by such options;

(ii) the purchase price of the securities called for and the expiration dates of such options; and

(iii) the market value of the securities called for by such options as of the latest practicable date.

Instructions. 1. The term "options" as used in this item includes all options, warrants, and rights other than those issued to security holders on a pro rata basis.

2. The extension of options shall be deemed the granting of options within the meaning of this item.

3. Where the total market value of securities called for by all outstanding options as of the specified date referred to in this item does not exceed $10,000 for any director or executive officer named in answer to paragraph (a), above, or $50,000 for all officers and directors as a group this item need not be answered with respect to options held by such person or group.

4. In case a number of options are outstanding having different prices and expiration dates, the options may be grouped by prices and date. If this produces more than five separate groups, then there may be shown only the range of the expiration dates and the average purchase prices, i.e., the aggregate purchase price of all securities of the same class called for by all outstanding options to purchase securities of that class divided by the number of securities of such class so called for.

Item 21. Financial Statements.

(a) General

(1) The financial statements of the registrant, or the registrant and its predecessors or any businesses to which the registrant is a successor, which are to be filed as part of the registration statement shall be prepared in accordance with generally accepted accounting principles (GAAP) in the United States or in the case of a Canadian registrant, a reconciliation to such U.S. GAAP shall be included in a note or schedule to the financial statements.

(2) Regulation S-X, Form and Content of and Requirements for Financial Statements, shall not apply to the preparation of such financial statements, except that the report and qualifications of the independent accountant shall comply with the requirements of Article 2 of Regulation S-X, and registrants engaged in oil and gas producing activities shall follow the financial accounting and reporting standards specified in Article 4.10 of Regulation S-X with respect to such activities. However, to the extent that Article 10 (Interim Financial Statements), Article 11.01 (Pro Forma Presentation Requirements) and Article 11.02 (Pro Forma Preparation Requirements) offer enhanced guidelines for the preparation, presentation and disclosure of condensed financial statements and pro forma financial information, registrants may wish to consider these items for use in a Form S-18 offering.

(3) The Commission may, upon the informal written request of the registrant, and where consistent with the protection of investors, permit the omission of one or more of the financial statements herein required or the filing in substitution therefor of appropriate statements of comparable character. The Commission may also by informal written notice require the filing of other financial statements in addition to, or in substitution for, the statements herein required in any case where such statements are necessary or appropriate for an adequate presentation of the financial condition of any person whose financial statements are required, or whose statements are otherwise necessary for the protection of investors.

(b) Consolidated Balance Sheets

(1) The registrant and its subsidiaries consolidated shall file an audited balance sheet as of the end of the most recent fiscal year, or as of a date within 135 days of the date of filing the registration statement if the registrant (including predecessors) existed for a period less than one fiscal year.

(2) When the filing date of the registration statement falls after 134 days subsequent to the end of the registrant's most recent fiscal year a balance sheet as of an interim date within 135 days of the filing date also shall be included in the registration statement. Such balance sheet need not be audited and may be in condensed form.

(c) Consolidated Statements of Income, Changes in Financial Condition and Stockholder's Equity.

(1) There shall be filed for the registrant and its subsidiaries consolidated statements of income, changes in financial position and stockholders equity for each of the two fiscal years preceding the date of the most recent audited balance sheet being filed (or for such shorter period as the registrant has been in business), and for the interim period, if any, between the end of the most recent fiscal year and the date of the most recent balance sheet being filed. These statements should be audited to the date of the most recent audited balance sheet being filed. Any interim financial statements may be in condensed form.

(2) If an income statement is filed for an interim period there shall also be filed, except for registrants in the development stage as defined by GAAP, an income statement for a comparable period of the prior year.

(3) In connection with any unaudited statement for an interim period a statement shall be made that all adjustments necessary to a fair statement of the results for such period have been included. If all such adjustments are of a normal recurring nature, a statement to that effect shall be made; otherwise, there shall be furnished information describing in appropriate detail the nature and amount of any adjustments other than normal recurring adjustments entering into the determination of the results shown.

(d) Financial Statements of Businesses Acquired or to be Acquired.

(1) Financial statements for the periods specified in (3) below should be furnished if any of the following conditions exist:

(i) Consummation of a significant business combination accounted for as a purchase has occurred or is probable (for purposes of this rule, the term "purchase" encompasses the purchase of an interest in a business accounted for by the equity method); or

(ii) Consummation of a significant business combination to be accounted for as a pooling of interests is probable.

(2) A business combination shall be considered significant if a comparison of the most recent annual financial statements of the business acquired or to be acquired and the registrant's most recent annual consolidated financial statements filed at or prior to the date of acquisition indicates that the business would be a significant subsidiary pursuant to the conditions specified in Rule 405 of Regulation C.

(3)(i) The financial statements shall be furnished for the periods up to the date of acquisition, for those periods for which the registrant is required to furnish financial statements as specified in paragraph (b) and (c)(1).

(ii) The financial statements covering fiscal years shall be audited.

(iii) A separate audited balance sheet of the acquired business is not required when the registrant's most recent audited balance sheet filed is for a date after the acquisition was consummated.

Appendix D

(iv) If none of the conditions in the definitions of significant subsidiary in Rule 405 exceeds 20%, income statements of the acquired business for only the most recent fiscal year and any interim period need be filed.

(4) If consummation of more than one transaction has occurred or is probable, the tests of significance shall be made using the aggregate impact of the businesses and the required financial statements may be presented on a combined basis, if appropriate.

(5) This paragraph (d) shall not apply to a business which is totally held by the registrant prior to consummation of the transaction.

(e) Pro Forma Financial Information.

(1) Pro forma information shall be furnished if any of the following conditions exist (for purposes of this rule, the term "purchase" encompasses the purchase of an interest in a business accounted for by the equity method):

(i) During the most recent fiscal year or subsequent interim period for which a balance sheet is required by paragraph (b), a significant business combination accounted for as a purchase has occurred;

(ii) After the date of the most recent balance sheet filed pursuant to paragraph (b), consummation of a significant business combination to be accounted for by either the purchase method or pooling of interests method of accounting has occurred or is probable.

(2) The provisions of paragraph (d)(2), (4) and (5) apply to this paragraph (e).

(3) Pro forma statements shall ordinarily be in columnar form showing condensed historical statements, pro forma adjustments, and the pro forma results and should include the following:

(i) If the transaction was consummated during the most recent fiscal year or in the subsequent interim period, pro forma statements of income reflecting the combined operations of the entities for the latest fiscal year and interim period, if any; or

(ii) If consummation of the transaction has occurred or is probable after the date of the most recent balance sheet, a pro forma balance sheet giving effect to the combination as of the date of the most recent balance sheet required by paragraph (b). For a purchase, pro forma statements of income reflecting the combined operations of the entities for the latest fiscal year and interim period, if any, and for a pooling of interests, pro forma statements of income for all periods for which income statements of the registrant are required.

(f) Age of Financial Statements at Effective Date of Registration Statement.

(1) If the financial statements are as of a date 135 days or more prior to the date the registration statement is expected to become effective the financial statements shall be updated with a balance sheet as of an interim date within 135 days and with statements of income and changes in financial position for the interim period between the end of the most recent fiscal year and the date of the interim balance sheet. There shall also be filed, except for registrants in the development stage, an income statement for a corresponding period of the preceding fiscal year. Such interim financial statements need not be audited and may be in condensed form.

(2) When the anticipated effective date of the registration statement falls within 45 days subsequent to the end of the fiscal year, the registration statement need not include financial statements more current than as of the end of the third fiscal quarter of the most recently completed fiscal year: *Provided, however,* That if the audited financial statements for such fiscal year are available they must be included in the registration statement. If the anticipated effective date falls afer 45 days subsequent

to the end of the fiscal year the registration statement must include audited financial statements for the most recently completed fiscal year.

(3) When the filing date of the registration statement is near the end of a fiscal year and the audited financial statements for that fiscal year are not included in the registration statement, the registration statement shall be updated with such financial statements if they become available prior to the anticipated effective date.

(g) *Special Instructions for Real Estate Operations to be Acquired.*

If, during the period for which income statements are required, the registrant (a) has acquired one or more properties which in the aggregate are significant, or (b) since the date of the latest balance sheet required, has acquired or proposes to acquire one or more properties which in the aggregate are significant, the following shall be furnished with respect to such properties.

(1) Audited income statements (not including earnings per unit) for the two most recent years, which shall exclude items not comparable to the proposed future operations of the property such as mortgage interest, leasehold rental, depreciation, corporate expenses and Federal and state income taxes: *Provided, however,* That such audited statements need be presented for only the most recent fiscal year if (i) the property is not acquired from a related party; (ii) material factors considered by the registrant in assessing the property are described with specificity in the prospectus with regard to the property, including sources of revenue (including, but not limited to, competition in the rental market, comparative rents, occupancy rates) and expense (including, but not limited to, utility rates, *ad valorem* tax rates, maintenance expenses, capital improvements anticipated); and (iii) the registrant indicates in the prospectus that, after reasonable inquiry, the registrant is not aware of any material factors relating to that specific property other than those discussed in response to paragraph (1) (ii) of this section that would cause the reported financial information not to be necessarily indicative of future operating results.

(2) If the property is to be operated by the registrant there shall be furnished a statement showing the estimated taxable operating results of the registrant based on the most recent twelve month period including such adjustments as can be factually supported. If the property is to be acquired subject to a net lease the estimated taxable operating results shall be based on the rent to be paid for the first year of the lease. In either case, the estimated amount of cash to be made available by operations shall be shown. There shall be stated in an introductory paragraph the principal assumptions which have been made in preparing the statements of estimated taxable operating results and cash to be made available by operations.

(3) If appropriate under the circumstances, there shall be given in tabular form for a limited number of years the estimated cash distribution per unit showing the portion thereof reportable as taxable income and the portion representing a return of capital together with an explanation of annual variations, if any. If taxable net income per unit will become greater than the cash available for distribution per unit, that fact and approximate year of occurrence shall be stated, if significant.

(h) *Special Instructions for Limited Partnerships.*

(1) In addition to the financial reporting requirements in paragraphs (a) through (g), registrants which are limited partnerships are required also to file the balance sheets of the general partners as described in subparagraphs (2) through (4), below.

(2) Where a general partner of the limited partnership is a corporation there shall be filed an audited balance sheet of such corporation as of the end of its most recently completed fiscal year. Receivables from the parent or affiliate of the general partner (including notes receivable, but excluding trade receivables), should be presented as deductions from the shareholders' equity of the general partner. Where

a parent or affiliate of the general partner has committed itself to increase or maintain the general partner's capital then there shall also be filed an audited balance sheet of such parent or affiliate as of the end of its most recently completed fiscal year.

(3) Where a general partner of the limited partnership is a partnership there shall be filed an audited balance sheet of such partnership as of the end of its most recently completed fiscal year.

(4) Where a general partner of the limited partnership is a natural person there shall be filed, as supplemental information, a balance sheet of such natural person as of a recent date. Such balance sheet need not be audited. The assets and liabilities on such balance sheet should be carried at estimated fair market value, with provisions for estimated income taxes' on unrealized gains. The net worth of such general partner(s), based on the estimated fair market value of their assets and liabilities, singly or in the aggregate, shall be disclosed in the text of the prospectus.

(i) Special Instructions for Registrants Engaged in Mining Operations.

With respect to companies engaged or to be engaged in the mining business, attention is directed to the instruction to Item 17A concerning the appropriate classification of issuers engaged in the exploratory, development and production stage of mining.

PART II
INFORMATION NOT REQUIRED IN PROSPECTUS

Item 22. Indemnification of Directors and Officers.

Furnish the information called for Item 702 of Regulation S-K.

Item 23. Other Expenses of Issuance and Distribution.

Furnish the information called for by Item 511 of Regulation S-K.

Item 24. Recent Sales of Unregistered Securities.

Furnish the information called for by Item 701 of Regulation S-K.

Item 25. Exhibits.

Furnish the exhibits as required by Item 601 of Regulation S-K.

Item 26. Undertakings.

Furnish the undertakings required by Item 512 of Regulation S-K.

SIGNATURES

Pursuant to the requirements of the Securities Act of 1933, the registrant certifies that it has reasonable grounds to believe that it meets all of the requirements for filing on Form S-18 and has duly caused this registration statement to be signed on its behalf by the undersigned thereunto duly authorized, in the City of ...., State of ...., on ...., 19...... .

(Registrant) ....

By ....
(Signature and Title)

Pursuant to the requirements of the Securities Act of 1933, this registration statement has been signed by the following persons in the capacities and on the dates indicated.

(Signature) ....

(Title) ....

(Date) ....

Instructions. 1. The registration statement shall be signed by the registrant, its principal executive officer or officers, its principal financial officer, its controller or principal accounting officer and by at least the majority of the board of directors or persons performing similar functions. If the registrant is a Canadian person, the registration statement shall also be signed by its authorized representative in the United States. Where the registrant is a limited partnership, the registration statement shall be signed by a majority of the board of directors of any corporate general partner signing the registration statement.

2. The name of each person who signs the registration statement shall be typed or printed beneath his signature. Any person who occupies more than one of the specified positions shall indicate each capacity in which he signs the registration statement. Attention is directed to Rule 402 concerning manual signatures and to the exhibit requirements concerning signatures pursuant to powers of attorney.

Appendix E

SECURITIES AND EXCHANGE COMMISSION

Washington, D. C. 20549

FORM 10-K
ANNUAL REPORT PURSUANT TO SECTION 13 OR 15(d) OF THE SECURITIES EXCHANGE ACT OF 1934

GENERAL INSTRUCTIONS

A. Rule as to Use of Form 10-K.

This Form shall be used for annual reports pursuant to section 13 or 15(d) of the Securities Exchange Act of 1934 (the "Act") for which no other form is prescribed. Reports on this form shall be filed within 90 days after the end of the fiscal year covered by the report. However, all schedules required by Article 12 of Regulation S-X may, at the option of the registrant, be filed as an amendment to the report not later than 120 days after the end of the fiscal year covered by the report. Such amendment shall be filed under cover of Form 8.

Source: Ticor Print Network/Jeffries Banknote Company *Securities Regulations Handbook,* updated to January 31, 1983.

B. Application of General Rules and Regulations.

(1) The General Rules and Regulations under the Act contain certain general requirements which are applicable to reports on any form. These general requirements should be carefully read and observed in the preparation and filing of reports on this Form.

(2) Particular attention is directed to Regulation 12B which contains general requirements regarding matters such as the kind and size of paper to be used, the legibility of the report, the information to be given whenever the title of securities is required to be stated, and the filing of the report. The definitions contained in Rule 12b-2 should be especially noted. *See also* Regulations 13A and 15D.

C. Preparation of Report.

(1) This Form is not to be used as a blank form to be filled in, but only as a guide in the preparation of the report on paper meeting the requirements of Rule 12b-12. Except as provided in General Instruction G, the answers to the items shall be prepared in the manner specified in Rule 12b-13.

(2) Except where information is required to be given for the fiscal year or as of a specified date, it shall be given as of the latest practicable date.

(3) Attention is directed to Rule 12b-20, which states: "In addition to the information expressly required to be included in a statement or report, there shall be added such further material information, if any, as may be necessary to make the required statements, in the light of the circumstances under which they are made, not misleading."

D. Signature and Filing of Report.

(1) Three complete copies of the report, including financial statements, financial statement schedules, exhibits, and all other papers and documents filed as a part thereof, and five additional copies which need not include exhibits, shall be filed with the Commission. At least one complete copy of the report, including financial statements, financial statement schedules, exhibits, and all other papers and documents filed as a part thereof, shall be filed with each exchange on which any class of securities of the registrant is registered. At least one complete copy of the report filed with the Commission and one such copy filed with each exchange shall be manually signed. Copies not manually signed shall bear typed or printed signatures.

(2)(a) The report shall be signed by the registrant, and on behalf of the registrant by its principal executive officer or officers, its principal financial officer, its controller or principal accounting officer, and by at least the majority of the board of directors or persons performing similar functions. Where the registrant is a limited partnership, the report shall be signed by the majority of the board of directors of any corporate general partner who signs the report. (b) The name of each person who signs the report shall be typed or printed beneath his signature. Any person who occupies more than one of the specified positions shall indicate each capacity in which he signs the report. Attention is directed to Rule 12b-11 concerning manual signatures and signatures pursuant to powers of attorney.

E. Disclosure With Respect to Foreign Subsidiaries.

Information required by any item or other requirement of this form with respect to any foreign subsidiary may be omitted to the extent that the required disclosure would be detrimental to the registrant. However, financial statements and financial statement schedules, otherwise required, shall not be omitted pursuant to this Instruction. Where information is omitted pursuant to this Instruction, a statement shall be made that such information has been omitted and the names of the subsidiaries involved shall be separately furnished to the Commission. The Commission may, in its discretion, call for justification that the required disclosure would be detrimental.

Appendix E

F. Information as to Employee Stock Purchase, Savings and Similar Plans.

Attention is directed to Rule 15d-21 which provides that separate annual and other reports need not be filed pursuant to Section 15(d) of the Act with respect to any employee stock purchase, savings or similar plan if the issuer of the stock or other securities offered to employees pursuant to the plan furnishes to the Commission the information and documents specified in the Rule.

G. Information to be Incorporated by Reference.

(1) Attention is directed to Rule 12b-23 which provides for the incorporation by reference of information contained in certain documents in answer or partial answer to any item of a report.

(2) The information called for by Parts I and II of this Form [Items 1 through 9 or any portion thereof] may, at the registrant's option, be incorporated by reference from the registrant's annual report to security holders furnished to the Commission pursuant to Rule 14a-3(b) or Rule 14c-3(a) or from the registrant's annual report to security holders, even if not furnished to the Commission pursuant to Rule 14a-3(b) or Rule 14c-3(a), provided such annual report contains the information required by Rule 14a-3.

NOTE: In order to fulfill the requirements of Part I of Form 10-K the incorporated portion of the annual report to security holders must contain the information required by Items 1-3 of Form 10-K, to the extent applicable.

(3) The information called for by Part III [Items 10, 11, 12] shall be incorporated by reference from the registrant's definitive proxy statement (filed or to be filed pursuant to Regulation 14A) or definitive information statement (filed or to be filed pursuant to Regulation 14C) which involves the election of directors, if such definitive proxy statement or information statement is filed with the Commission not later than 120 days after the end of the fiscal year covered by the Form 10-K. However, if such definitive proxy or information statement is not filed with the Commission in the 120-day period, the Items comprising the Part III information must be filed as part of the Form 10-K, or as an amendment to the Form 10-K under cover of Form 8, not later than the end of the 120-day period. It should be noted that the information regarding executive officers required by Item 401 of Regulation S-K may be included in Part I of Form 10-K under an appropriate caption. *See* Instruction 4 to Item 401(b) of Regulation S-K.

(4) No item numbers or captions of items need be contained in the material incorporated by reference into the report. However, the registrant's attention is directed to Rule 12b-23(e) regarding the specific disclosure required in the report concerning information incorporated by reference. When the registrant combines all of the information in Parts I and II of this Form (Items 1 through 9) by incorporation by reference from the registrant's annual report to security holders and all of the information in Part III of this Form (Items 10, 11, 12) by incorporation by reference from a definitive proxy statement or information statement involving the election of directors, then, notwithstanding General Instruction C(1), this Form shall consist of the facing or cover page, those sections incorporated from the annual report to security holders, the proxy or information statement, and the information, if any, required by Part IV of this Form, signatures, and a cross reference sheet setting forth the item numbers and captions in Parts I, II and III of this Form and the page and/or pages in the referenced materials where the corresponding information appears.

H. Integrated Reports to Security Holders.

Annual reports to security holders may be combined with the required information of Form 10-K and will be suitable for filing with the Commission if the following conditions are satisfied:

(1) The combined report contains full and complete answers to all items required by Form 10-K. When responses to a certain item of required disclosure are separated within the combined report, an appropriate cross-reference should be made. If the information required by Part III of Form 10-K is omitted by virtue of General Instruction G, a definitive proxy or information statement shall be filed.

(2) The cover page and the required signatures are included. As appropriate, a cross-reference sheet should be filed indicating the location of information required by the items of the Form.

I. Registrants Filing on Form S-18.

If the registrant is subject to the reporting requirements of Section 15(d) of the Exchange Act and such obligation arises solely because the registrant has filed a registration statement on Form S-18 which has become effective during the last fiscal year, the registrant may comply with the disclosure requirements of Form S-18 Item 6, Description of Business; Item 10, Remuneration of Directors and Officers; and Item 13, Interest of Management and Others in Certain Transactions, in lieu of complying with the disclosure requirements of Item 1, Business, and Item 11, Management Remuneration and Transactions, herein. Item 6 of this Form, Selected Financial Data, may be omitted at the election of such registrant.

If a registrant remains subject to Section 15(d), or becomes subject to Section 12, after the year of its Form S-18 offering, it will then be required to comply with the general Form 10-K item requirements for its subsequent reports.

J. Omission of Information by Certain Wholly-Owned Subsidiaries.

If, on the date of the filing of its report on Form 10-K, the registrant meets the conditions specified in paragraph (1) below, then such registrant may furnish the abbreviated narrative disclosure specified in paragraph (2) below.

(1) Conditions for availability of the relief specified in paragraph (2) below.

(a) All of the registrant's equity securities are owned, either directly or indirectly, by a single person which is a reporting company under the Act and which has filed all the material required to be filed pursuant to section 13, 14, or 15(d) thereof, as applicable, and which is named in conjunction with the registrant's description of its business;

(b) During the preceding thirty-six calendar months and any subsequent period of days, there has not been any material default in the payment of principal, interest, a sinking or purchase fund installment, or any other material default not cured within thirty days, with respect to any indebtedness of the registrant or its subsidiaries, and there has not been any material default in the payment of rentals under material long-term leases; and

(c) There is prominently set forth, on the cover page of the Form 10-K, a statement that the registrant meets the conditions set forth in General Instruction I(1)(a) and (b) of Form 10-K and is therefore filing this Form with the reduced disclosure format.

(2) Registrants meeting the conditions specified in paragraph (1) above are entitled to the following relief:

(a) Such registrants may omit the information called for by Item 6, Selected Financial Data, and Item 7, Management's Discussion and Analysis of Financial Condition and Results of Operations provided that the registrant includes in the Form 10-K a management's narrative analysis of the results of operations explaining the reasons for material changes in the amount of revenue and expense items between the most recent fiscal year presented and the fiscal year immediately preceding it. Explanations of material changes should include, but not be limited to, changes in the various elements which determine revenue

Appendix E

and expense levels such as unit sales volume, prices charged and paid, production levels, production cost variances, labor costs and discretionary spending programs. In addition, the analysis should include an explanation of the effect of any changes in accounting principles and practices or method of application that have a material effect on net income as reported.

(b) Such registrants may omit the list of subsidiaries exhibit required by Item 601 of Regulation S-K.

(c) Such registrants may omit the information called for by the following otherwise required Items: Item 4, Security Ownership of Certain Beneficial Owners and Management; Item 10, Directors and Executive Officers of the Registrant; and Item 11, Management Remuneration and Transactions; and Item 12, Security Ownership of Certain Beneficial Owners and Management.

(d) In response to Item 1, Business, such registrant only need furnish a brief description of the business done by the registrant and its subsidiaries during the most recent fiscal year which will, in the opinion of management, indicate the general nature and scope of the business of the registrant and its subsidiaries, and in response to Item 2, Properties, such registrant only need furnish a brief description of the material properties of the registrant and its subsidiaries to the extent, in the opinion of the management, necessary to an understanding of the business done by the registrant and its subsidiaries.

PART I

[See General Instruction G(2)]

Item 1. Business.

Furnish the information required by Item 1 of Regulation S-K except that the discussion of the development of the registrant's business need only include developments since the beginning of the fiscal year for which this report is filed.

Item 2. Properties.

Furnish the information required by Item 102 of Regulation S-K.

Item 3. Legal Proceedings.

(a) Furnish the information required by Item 103 of Regulation S-K.

(b) As to any proceeding that was terminated during the fourth quarter of the fiscal year covered by this report, furnish information similar to that required by Item 103 of Regulation S-K, including the date of termination and a description of the disposition thereof with respect to the registrant and its subsidiaries.

Item 4. Submission of Matters to a Vote of Security Holders.

If any matter was submitted during the fourth quarter of the fiscal year covered by this report to a vote of security holders, through the solicitation of proxies or otherwise, furnish the following information:

(a) The date of the meeting and whether it was an annual or special meeting.

(b) If the meeting involved the election of directors, the name of each director elected at the meeting and the name of each other director whose term of office as a director continued after the meeting.

(c) A brief description of each other matter voted upon at the meeting and the number of affirmative votes and the number of negative votes cast with respect to each such matter.

(d) A description of the terms of any settlement between the registrant and any other participant (as defined in Rule 14a-11 of Regulation 14A under the Act) terminating any solicitation subject to Rule 14a-11, including the cost or anticipated cost to the registrant.

Instructions:

1. If any matter has been submitted to a vote of security holders otherwise than at a meeting of such security holders, corresponding information with respect to such submission shall be furnished. The solicitation of any authorization or consent (other than a proxy to vote at a stockholders' meeting) with respect to any matter shall be deemed a submission of such matter to a vote of security holders within the meaning of this item.

2. Paragraph (a) need be answered only if paragraph (b) or (c) is required to be answered.

3. Paragraph (b) need not be answered if (i) proxies for the meeting were solicited pursuant to Regulation 14A under the Act, (ii) there was no soliciation in opposition to the management's nominees as listed in the proxy statement, and (iii) all of such nominees were elected. If the registrant did not solicit proxies and the board of directors as previously reported to the Commission was re-elected in its entirety, a statement to that effect in answer to paragraph (b) will suffice as an answer thereto.

4. Paragraph (c) need not be answered as to procedural matters or as to the selection or approval of auditors.

5. If the registrant has furnished to its security holders proxy soliciting material containing the information called for by paragraph (d), the paragraph may be answered by reference to the information contained in such material.

6. If the registrant has published a report containing all of the information called for by this item, the item may be answered by a reference to the information contained in such report.

PART II

[See General Instruction G(2)]

Item 5. Market for Registrant's Common Equity and Related Stockholder Matters.

Furnish the information required by Item 201 of Regulation S-K.

Item 6. Selected Financial Data.

Furnish the information required by Item 301 of Regulation S-K.

Item 7. Management's Discussion and Analysis of Financial Condition and Results of Operation.

Furnish the information required by Item 303 of Regulation S-K.

Item 8. Financial Statements and Supplementary Data.

Furnish financial statements meeting the requirements of Regulation S-X, except Rule 3.05 and Article 11 thereof, and the supplementary financial information required by Item 302 of Regulation S-K. Financial statements of the registrant and its subsidiaries consolidated [as required by Rule 14a-3(b)] shall be filed under this Item. Other financial statements and schedules required under Regulation S-X may be filed as "Financial Statement Schedules" pursuant to Item 13. Exhibits, Financial Statement Schedules and Reports on Form 8-K, of this form.

Notwithstanding the above, if the issuer is subject to the reporting provisions of Section 15(d) and such obligation results solely from the issuer having filed a registration statement on Form S-18 which became effective under the Securities Act of 1933 during the last fiscal year, or such obligation applies as to the first or second fiscal year after the registration statement on Form S-18 became effective solely because the issuer had on the first day of the pertinent fiscal year 300 or more record holders of any of its securities to which the Form S-18 related, audited financial statements for the issuer, or for the issuer and its predecessors, may be presented as provided below. The report of the independent accountant shall in all events comply with the requirements of Article 2 of Regulation S-X.

(a) A Form 10-K filed for the fiscal year during which the registrant had a registration statement on Form S-18 become effective may include the following financial statements prepared in accordance with generally accepted accounting principles:

(1) A balance sheet as of the end of each of the two most recent fiscal years; and

(2) Consolidated statements of income, statements of changes in financial condition, and statements of other stockholders' equity for each of the two fiscal years preceding the date of the most recent audited balance sheet being filed.

(b) A Form 10-K filed for the first fiscal year after the registrant had a registration statement on Form S-18 become effective may include financial statements prepared as follows:

(1) Financial statements for the most recent fiscal year prepared in accordance with Regulation S-X, Form and Content of and Requirements for Financial Statements; and

(2) Financial statements previously disclosed in accordance with paragraph (a) for the prior year. These statements do not need to include the compliance items and schedules of Regulation S-X, but should be recast to show the same line items as are set forth for the most recent fiscal year.

(c) A Form 10-K filed for the second fiscal year after the registrant had a registration statement on Form S-18 become effective may include financial statements for the two most recent fiscal years prepared in accordance with Regulation S-X.

Item 9. Disagreements on Accounting and Financial Disclosure.

Furnish the information required by Item 304 of Regulation S-K.

PART III

[See General Instruction G(3)]

Item 10. Directors and Executive Officers of the Registrant.

Furnish the information required by Item 401 of Regulation S-K.

Item 11. Management Remuneration and Transactions.

Furnish the information required by Item 402 of Regulation S-K.

Item 12. Security Ownership of Certain Beneficial Owners and Managment.

Furnish the information required by Item 403 of Regulation S-K.

PART IV

Item 13. Exhibits, Financial Statement Schedules, and Reports on Form 8-K.

(a) List the following documents filed as a part of the report:

1. All financial statements;

2. Those financial statement schedules required by Item 8 of this Form, and by paragraph (d) below.

3. Those exhibits required by Item 601 of Regulation S-K and by paragraph (c) below. Where any financial statement, financial statement schedule, or exhibit is incorporated by reference, the incorporation by reference shall be set forth in the list required by this item. For purposes of all rules concerning incorporation by reference a financial statement schedule shall constitute an "exhibit." See Rule 12b-23.

(b) Reports on Form 8-K. State whether any reports on Form 8-K have been filed during the last quarter of the period covered by this report, listing the items reported, any financial statements filed and the dates of any such reports.

(c) Registrants shall file, as exhibits to this Form, the exhibits required by Item 601 of Regulation S-K.

(d) Registrants shall file, as financial statement schedules to this Form, the financial statements required by Regulation S-X which are excluded from the annual report to shareholders by Rule 14a-3(b)(1), including (1) separate financial statements of the registrant only (where consolidated financial statements of the registrant and its subsidiaries are included); (2) separate financial statements of subsidiaries not consolidated and fifty percent or less owned persons; (3) separate financial statements of consolidated majority-owned subsidiaries of the registrant engaged in diverse financial activities; (4) separate financial statements of affiliates whose securities are pledged as collateral; and (5) schedules.

SIGNATURES

[See General Instruction D]

Pursuant to the requirements of Section 13 or 15(d) of the Securities Exchange Act of 1934, the registrant has duly caused this report to be signed on its behalf by the undersigned, thereunto duly authorized.

(Registrant) ....

By (Signature and Title)* ....

Date..

Pursuant to the requirements of the Securities Exchange Act of 1934, this report has been signed below by the following persons on behalf of the registrant and in the capacities and on the dates indicated.

By (Signature and Title)*..

(Date)..

* * * * *

By (Signature and Title)*..

(Date)..

---

* Print the name and title of each signing officer under his signature.

Appendix E

Supplemental Information to be Furnished With Reports Filed Pursuant to Section 15(d) of the Act by Registrants Which Have Not Registered Securities Pursuant to Section 12 of the Act

(a) Except to the extent that the materials enumerated in (1) and/or (2) below are specifically incorporated into this Form by reference (in which case *see* Rule 12b-23(d)), every registrant which files an annual report on this Form pursuant to Section 15(d) of the Act shall furnish to the Commission for its information, at the time of filing its report on this Form, four copies of the following:

(1) Any annual report to security holders covering the registrant's last fiscal year; and

(2) Every proxy statement, form of proxy or other proxy soliciting material sent to more than ten of the registrant's security holders with respect to any annual or other meeting of security holders.

(b) The foregoing material shall not be deemed to be "filed" with the Commission or otherwise subject to the liabilities of Section 18 of the Act, except to the extent that the registrant specifically incorporates it in its annual report on this Form by reference.

(c) If no such annual report or proxy material has been sent to security holders, a statement to that effect shall be included under this caption. If such report or proxy material is to be furnished to security holders subsequent to the filing of the annual report of this Form, the registrant shall so state under this caption and shall furnish copies of such material to the Commission when it is sent to security holders.

Appendix F

FORM 10-Q

SECURITIES AND EXCHANGE COMMISSION
Washington, D.C. 20549

Quarterly Report Under Section 13 or 15(d)
of the Securities Exchange Act of 1934

For Quarter Ended ....

Commission file number ....

....
(Exact name of registrant as specified in its charter)

....
(State or other jurisdiction of   (I.R.S. Employer
incorporation or organization)   Identification No.)

Source: Ticor Print Network/Jeffries Banknote Company *Securities Regulations Handbook*, updated to January 31, 1983

....
(Address of principal executive offices)   (Zip Code)

....
(Registrant's telephone number, including area code)

....
(Former name, former address and former fiscal year, if changed since last report.)

Indicate by check mark whether the registrant (1) has filed all reports required to be filed by Section 13 or 15(d) of the Securities Exchange Act of 1934 during the preceding 12 months (or for such shorter period that the registrant was required to file such reports), and (2) has been subject to such filing requirements for the past 90 days. Yes____. No____.

APPLICABLE ONLY TO ISSUERS INVOLVED IN BANKRUPTCY PROCEEDINGS DURING THE PRECEDING FIVE YEARS:

Indicate by check mark whether the registrant has filed all documents and reports required to be filed by Sections 12, 13, or 15(d) of the Securities Exchange Act of 1934 subsequent to the distribution of securities under a plan confirmed by a court. Yes____. No____.

APPLICABLE ONLY TO CORPORATE ISSUERS:

Indicate the number of shares outstanding of each of the issuer's classes of common stock, as of the latest practicable date.

GENERAL INSTRUCTIONS

A. Rule as to Use of Form 10-Q.

1. Form 10-Q shall be used for quarterly reports under Section 13 or 15(d) of the Securities Exchange Act of 1934, filed pursuant to Rule 13a-13 or Rule 15d-13.

2. A report on this form shall be filed within 45 days after the end of each of the first three fiscal quarters of each fiscal year. No report need be filed for the fourth quarter of any fiscal year.

B. Application of General Rules and Regulations.

1. The General Rules and Regulations under the Act contain certain general requirements which are applicable to reports on any form. These general requirements should be carefully read and observed in the preparation and filing of reports on this form.

2. Particular attention is directed to Regulation 12B which contains general requirements regarding matters such as the kind and size of paper to be used, the legibility of the report, the information to be given whenever the title of securities is required to be stated, and the filing of the report. The definitions contained in Rule 12b-2 should be especially noted. See also Regulations 13A and 15D.

C. Preparation of Report.

1. This is not a blank form to be filled in. It is a guide copy to be used in preparing the report in accordance with Rules 12b-11 and 12b-12. The Commission does not furnish blank copies of this form to be filled in for filing.

2. These general instructions are not to be filed with the report. The instructions to the various captions of the form are also to be omitted from the report as filed.

D. Incorporation By Reference.

1. If the registrant makes available to its stockholders or otherwise publishes, within the period prescribed for filing the report, a document or statement containing

Appendix F

information meeting some or all of the requirements of Part I of this form, the information called for may be incorporated by reference from such published document or statement, in answer or partial answer to any item or items of Part I of this form, provided copies thereof are filed as an exhibit to Part I of the report on this form.

2. Other information may be incorporated by reference in answer or partial answer to any item or items of Part II of this form in accordance with the provisions of Rule 12b-23.

E. Integrated Reports to Security Holders.

Quarterly reports to security holders may be combined with the required information of Form 10-Q and will be suitable for filing with the Commission if the following conditions are satisfied:

1. The combined report contains full and complete answers to all items required by Part I of this form. When responses to a certain item of required disclosure are separated within the combined report, an appropriate cross-reference should be made.

2. If not included in the combined report, the cover page, appropriate responses to Part II, and the required signatures shall be included in the Form 10-Q. Additionally, as appropriate, a cross-reference sheet should be filed indicating the location of information required by the items of the form.

F. Filed Status of Information Presented.

1. Pursuant to Rule 13a-13(d) and Rule 15d-13(d), the information presented in satisfaction of the requirements of Items (1) and (2) of Part I of this form, whether included directly in a report on this form, incorporated therein by reference from a report, document or statement filed as an exhibit to Part I of this form pursuant to Instruction D(1) above, or contained in a statement regarding computation of per share earnings or a letter regarding a change in accounting principles filed as an exhibit to Part I pursuant to Item 601 of Regulation S-K, except as provided by Instruction F(2) below, shall not be deemed filed for the purpose of Section 18 of the Act or otherwise subject to the liabilities of that section of the Act but shall be subject to the other provisions of the Act.

2. Information presented in satisfaction of the requirements of this form other than those of Items (1) and (2) of Part I shall be deemed filed for the purpose of Section 18 of the Act; except that, where information presented in response to Item (1) or (2) of Part I (or as an exhibit thereto) is also used to satisfy Part II requirements through incorporation by reference, only that portion of Part I (or exhibit thereto) consisting of the information required by Part II shall be deemed so filed.

G. Signature and Filing of Report.

Three complete copies of the report, including any financial statements, exhibits or other papers or documents filed as a part thereof, and five additional copies which need not include exhibits, shall be filed with the Commission. At least one complete copy of the report, including any financial statements, exhibits or other papers or documents filed as a part thereof, shall be filed with each exchange on which any class of securities of the registrant is registered. At least one complete copy of the report filed with the Commission and one such copy filed with each exchange shall be manually signed on the registrant's behalf by a duly authorized officer of the registrant and by the principal financial or chief accounting officer of the registrant. Copies not manually signed shall bear typed or printed signatures. In the case where the principal financial officer or chief accounting officer is also duly authorized to sign on behalf of the registrant, one signature is acceptable provided that the registrant clearly indicates the dual responsibilities of the signatory.

H. Omission of Information by Certain Wholly-Owned Subsidiaries.

If, on the date of the filing of its report on Form 10-Q, the registrant meets the conditions specified in paragraph (1) below, then such registrant may omit the information called for in the items specified in paragraph (2) below.

1. Conditions for availability of the relief specified in paragraph (2) below:

   a. All of the registrant's equity securities are owned, either directly or indirectly, by a single person which is a reporting company under the Act and which has filed all the material required to be filed pursuant to section 13, 14 or 15(d) thereof, as applicable;

   b. During the preceding thirty-six calendar months and any subsequent period of days, there has not been any material default in the payment of principal, interest, a sinking or purchase fund installment, or any other material default not cured within thirty days, with respect to any indebtedness of the registrant or its subsidiaries, and there has not been any material default in the payment of rentals under material long-term leases; and

   c. There is prominently set forth, on the cover page of the Form 10-Q, a statement that the registrant meets the conditions set forth in General Instruction H(1)(a) and (b) of Form 10-Q and is therefore filing this Form with the reduced disclosure format.

2. Registrants meeting the conditions specified in paragraph (1) above are entitled to the following relief:

   a. Such registrants may omit the information called for by Item 2 of Part I, Management's Discussion and Analysis of Financial Condition and Results of Operations, provided that the registrant includes in the Form 10-Q a management's narrative analysis of the results of operations explaining the reasons for material changes in the amount of revenue and expense items between the most recent fiscal year-to-date period presented and the corresponding year-to-date period in the preceding fiscal year. Explanations of material changes should include, but not be limited to, changes in the various elements which determine revenue and expense levels such as unit sales volume, prices charged and paid, production levels, production cost variances, labor costs and discretionary spending programs. In addition, the analysis should include an explanation of the effect of any changes in accounting principles and practices or method of application that have a material effect on net income as reported.

   b. Such registrants may omit the information called for in the following Part II Items: Item 2, Changes in Securities; Item 3, Defaults Upon Senior Securities; and Item 4, Submission of Matters to a Vote of Security Holders.

PART I — FINANCIAL INFORMATION

Item 1. Financial Statements.

Provide the information required by Rule 10.01 of Regulation S-X.

Item 2. Management's Discussion and Analysis of Financial Condition and Results of Operations.

Furnish the information required by Item 303 of Regulation S-K.

Appendix F

PART II — OTHER INFORMATION

Instruction. The report shall contain the item numbers and captions of all applicable items of Part II, but the text of such items may be omitted provided the responses clearly indicate the coverage of the item. Any item which is inapplicable or to which the answer is negative may be omitted and no reference thereto need be made in the report. If substantially the same information has been previously reported by the registrant, an additional report of the information on this form need not be made. The term "previously reported" is defined in Rule 12b-2. A separate response need not be presented in Part II where information called for is already disclosed in the financial information provided in Part I and is incorporated by reference into Part II of the report by means of a statement to that effect in Part II which specifically identifies the incorporated information.

Item 1. Legal Proceedings.

Furnish the information required by Item 103 of Regulation S-K. As to such proceedings which have been terminated during the period covered by the report, provide similar information, including the date of termination and a description of the disposition thereof with respect to the registrant and its subsidiaries.

Instruction. A legal proceeding need only be reported in the 10-Q filed for the quarter in which it first became a reportable event and in subsequent quarters in which there have been material developments. Subsequent Form 10-Q filings in the same fiscal year in which a legal proceeding or a material development is reported should reference any previous reports in that year.

Item 2. Changes in Securities.

(a) If the constituent instruments defining the rights of the holders of any class of registered securities have been materially modified, give the title of the class of securities involved and state briefly the general effect of such modification upon the rights of holders of such securities.

(b) If the rights evidenced by any class of registered securities have been materially limited or qualified by the issuance or modification of any other class of securities, state briefly the general effect of the issuance or modification of such other class of securities upon the rights of the holders of the registered securities.

Instruction. Working capital restrictions and other limitations upon the payment of dividends are to be reported hereunder.

Item 3. Defaults Upon Senior Securities.

(a) If there has been any material default in the payment of principal, interest, a sinking or purchase fund installment, or any other material default not cured within 30 days, with respect to any indebtedness of the registrant or any of its significant subsidiaries exceeding 5 percent of the total assets of the registrant and its consolidated subsidiaries, identify the indebtedness and state the nature of the default. In the case of such a default in the payment of principal, interest, or a sinking or purchase fund installment, state the amount of the default and the total arrearage on the date of filing this report.

Instruction. This paragraph refers only to events which have become defaults under the governing instruments, i.e., after the expiration of any period of grace and compliance with any notice requirements.

(b) If any material arrearage in the payment of dividends has occurred or if there has been any other material delinquency not cured within 30 days, with respect to any class of preferred stock of the registrant which is registered or which ranks prior to any class of registered securities, or with respect to any class of preferred stock of any significant subsidiary of the registrant, give the title of the class and state the nature of the arrearage or delinquency. In the case of an arrearage in the payment of dividends, state the amount and the total arrearage on the date of filing this report.

Instruction. Item 3 need not be answered as to any default or arrearage with respect to any class of securities all of which is held by, or for the account of, the registrant or its totally held subsidiaries.

Item 4. Submission of Matters to a Vote of Security Holders.

If any matter has been submitted to a vote of security holders, through the solicitation of proxies or otherwise, furnish the following information:

(a) The date of the meeting and whether it was an annual or special meeting.

(b) If the meeting involved the election of directors, the name of each director elected at the meeting and the name of each other director whose term of office as a director continued after the meeting.

(c) A brief description of each other matter voted upon at the meeting and state the number of affirmative votes and the number of negative votes cast with respect to each such matter.

(d) A description of the terms of any settlement between the registrant and any other participant (as defined in Rule 14a-11 of Regulation 14A under the Act) terminating any solicitation subject to Rule 14a-11, including the cost or anticipated cost to the registrant.

Instructions:

1. If any matter has been submitted to a vote of security holders otherwise than at a meeting of such security holders, corresponding information with respect to such submission shall be furnished. The solicitation of any authorization or consent (other than a proxy to vote at a stockholders' meeting) with respect to any matter shall be deemed a submission of such matter to a vote of security holders within the meaning of this item.

2. Paragraph (a) need be answered only if paragraph (b) or (c) is required to be answered.

3. Paragraph (b) need not be answered if (i) proxies for the meeting were solicited pursuant to Regulation 14 under the Act, (ii) there was no solicitation in opposition to the management's nominees as listed in the proxy statement, and (iii) all of such nominees were elected. If the registrant did not solicit proxies and the board of directors as previously reported to the Commission was re-elected in its entirety, a statement to that effect in answer to paragraph (b) will suffice as an answer thereto.

4. Paragraph (c) need not be answered as to procedural matters or as to the selection or approval of auditors.

5. If the registrant has furnished to its security holders proxy soliciting material containing the information called for by paragraph (d), the paragraph may be answered by reference to the information contained in such material.

6. If the registrant has published a report containing all of the information called for by this item, the item may be answered by a reference to the information contained in such report.

Item 5. Other Information.

The registrant may, at its option, report under this item any information, not previously reported in a report on Form 8-K, with respect to which information is not otherwise called for by this form. If disclosure of such information is made under this item, it need not be repeated in a report on Form 8-K which would otherwise be required to be filed with respect to such information or in a subsequent report on Form 10-Q.

Item 6. Exhibits and Reports on Form 8-K.

(a) Furnish the exhibits required by Item 601 of Regulation S-K.

(b) Reports on Form 8-K. State whether any reports on Form 8-K have been filed during the quarter for which this report is filed, listing the items reported, any financial statements filed, and the dates of any such reports.

SIGNATURES*

Pursuant to the requirements of the Securities Exchange Act of 1934, the registrant has duly caused this report to be signed on its behalf by the undersigned thereunto duly authorized.

....
(Registrant)

Date... ....
(Signature)**

Date... ....
(Signature)**

---

*See General Instruction E.
**Print name and title of the signing officer under his signature.

Appendix G

GENERAL RULE 144 OF 1933 SECURITIES ACT

Rule 144. Persons deemed not to be engaged in a distribution and therefore not underwriters.

(a) *Definitions.* The following definitions shall apply for the purposes of this rule:

(1) An "affiliate" of an issuer is a person that directly, or indirectly through one or more intermediaries, controls, or is controlled by, or is under common control with, such issuer.

(2) The term "person" when used with reference to a person for whose account securities are to be sold in reliance upon this rule includes, in addition to such person, all of the following persons:

(A) Any relative or spouse of such person, or any relative of such spouse, any one of whom has the same home as such person;

(B) Any trust or estate in which such person or any of the persons specified in (A) collectively own ten percent or more of the total beneficial interest or of which any of such persons serves as trustee, executor or in any similar capacity; and

(C) Any corporation or other organization (other than the issuer) in which such person or any of the persons specified in (A) are the beneficial owners collectively of ten percent or more of any class of equity securities or ten percent or more of the equity interest.

Source: Ticor Print Network/Jeffries Banknote Company *Securities Regulations Handbook*, updated to January 31, 1983

(3) The term "restricted securities" means securities that are acquired directly or indirectly from the issuer, or from an affiliate of the Issuer, in a transaction or chain of transactions not involving any public offering, or securities acquired from the issuer that are subject to the resale limitations of Regulation D under the Act, or securities that are subject to the resale limitations of Regulation D and are acquired in a transaction or chain of transactions not involving any public offering.

(b) *Conditions to be Met.* Any affiliate or other person who sells restricted securities of an issuer for his own account, or any person who sells restricted or any other securities for the account of an affiliate of the issuer of such securities, shall be deemed not to be engaged in a distribution of such securities and therefore not to be an underwriter thereof within the meaning of Section 2(11) of the Act if all of the conditions of this rule are met.

(c) *Current Public Information.* There shall be available adequate current public information with respect to the issuer of the securities. Such information shall be deemed available if either of the following conditions are met:

(1) *Filing of Reports.* The issuer has securities registered pursuant to Section 12 of the Securities Exchange Act of 1934, has been subject to the reporting requirements of Section 13 of that Act for a period of at least 90 days immediately preceding the sale of the securities and has filed all the reports required to be filed thereunder during the 12 months preceding such sale (or for such shorter period that the issuer was required to file such reports); or has securities registered pursuant to the Securities Act of 1933, has been subject to the reporting requirements of Section 15(d) of the Securities Exchange Act of 1934 for a period of at least 90 days immediately preceding the sale of the securities and has filed all the reports required to be filed thereunder during the 12 months preceding such sale (or for such shorter period that the issuer was required to file such reports). The person for whose account the securities are to be sold shall be entitled to rely upon a statement in whichever is the most recent report, quarterly or annual, required to be filed and filed by the issuer that such issuer has filed all reports required to be filed by Section 13 or 15(d) of the Securities Exchange Act of 1934 during the preceding 12 months (or for such shorter period that the issuer was required to file such reports) and has been subject to such filing requirements for the past 90 days, unless he knows or has reason to believe that the issuer has not complied with such requirements. Such person shall also be entitled to rely upon a written statement from the issuer that it has complied with such reporting requirements unless he knows or has reason to believe that the issuer has not complied with such requirements.

(2) *Other Public Information.* If the issuer is not subject to Section 13 or 15(d) of the Securities Exchange Act of 1934, there is publicly available the information concerning the issuer specified in clauses (1) to (14), inclusive, and clause (16) of paragraph (a)(4) of Rule 15c2-11 under that Act or, if the issuer is an insurance company, the information specified in Section 12(g)(2)(G)(i) of that Act.

(d) *Holding Period for Restricted Securities.* If the securities sold are restricted securities, the following provisions apply:

(1) *General Rule.* The person for whose account the securities are sold shall have been the beneficial owner of the securities for a period of at least two years prior to the sale and, if the securities were purchased, the full purchase price or other consideration shall have been paid or given at least two years prior to the sale.

(2) *Promissory Notes, Other Obligations or Installment Contracts.* Giving the person from whom the securities were purchased a promissory note or other

obligation to pay the purchase price, or entering into an installment purchase contract with such person, shall not be deemed full payment of the purchase price unless the promissory note, obligation or contract —

(A) provides for full recourse against the purchaser of the securities;

(B) is secured by collateral, other than the securities purchased, having a fair market value at least equal to the purchase price of the securities purchased; and

(C) shall have been discharged by payment in full prior to the sale of the securities.

(3) *Short Sales, Puts or Other Options to Sell Securities.* In computing the two-year holding period the following periods shall be excluded:

(A) If the securities sold are equity securities, there shall be excluded any period during which the person for whose account they are sold had a short position in, or any put or other option to dispose of, any equity securities of the same class or any securities convertible into securities of such class; and

(B) If the securities sold are nonconvertible debt securities, there shall be excluded any period during which the person for whose account they are sold had a short position in, or any put or other option to dispose of, any nonconvertible debt securities of the same issuer.

(4) *Determination of Holding Period.* The following provisions shall apply for the purpose of determining the period securities have been held:

(A) *Stock Dividends, Splits and Recapitalizations.* Securities acquired from the issuer as a dividend or pursuant to a stock split, reverse split or recapitalization shall be deemed to have been acquired at the time as the securities on which the dividend or, if more than one, the initial dividend was paid, the securities involved in the split or reverse split, or the securities surrendered in connection with the recapitalization;

(B) *Conversions.* If the securities sold were acquired from the issuer for a consideration consisting solely of other securities of the same issuer surrendered for conversion, the securities so acquired shall be deemed to have been acquired at the same time as the securities surrendered for conversion;

(C) *Contingent Issuance of Securities.* Securities acquired as a contingent payment of the purchase price of an equity interest in a business, or the assets of a business, sold to the issuer or an affiliate of the issuer shall be deemed to have been acquired at the time of such sale if the issuer or affiliate was then committed to issue the securities subject only to conditions other than the payment of further consideration for such securities. An agreement entered into in connection with any such purchase to remain in the employment of, or not to compete with, the issuer or affiliate or the rendering of services pursuant to such agreement shall not be deemed to be the payment of further consideration for such securities.

(D) *Pledged Securities.* Securities which are bona fide pledged by any person other than the issuer when sold by the pledgee, or by a purchaser, after a default in the obligation secured by the pledge, shall be deemed to have been acquired when they were acquired by the pledgor, except that if the securities were pledged without recourse they shall be deemed to have been acquired by the pledgee at the time of the pledge or by the purchaser at the time of purchase.

Note. Securities sold by the pledgee shall be aggregated with those sold by the pledgor, as provided in paragraph (e)(3)(B) below.

(E) *Gifts of Securities.* Securities acquired from any person, other than the issuer, by gift shall be deemed to have been acquired by the donee when they were acquired by the donor;

Note. Securities sold by the donee shall be aggregated with those sold by the donor, as provided in paragraph (e)(3)(C) below.

(F) *Trusts.* Securities acquired from the settlor of a trust by the trust or acquired from the trust by the beneficiaries thereof shall be deemed to have been acquired when they were acquired by the settlor;

Note. Securities sold by the trust shall be aggregated with those sold by the settlor of the trust, as provided in paragraph (c)(3)(D) below.

(G) *Estates.* Securities held by the estate of a deceased person or acquired from such an estate by the beneficiaries thereof shall be deemed to have been acquired when they were acquired by the deceased person, except that no holding period is required if the estate is not an affiliate of the issuer or if the securities are sold by a beneficiary of the estate who is not such an affiliate.

Notes. 1. Securities sold by the estate shall be aggregated with those sold by the deceased person, as provided in paragraph (e)(3)(E) below, if the estate is an affiliate of the issuer.

2. While there is no holding period or amount limitation for estates and beneficiaries thereof which are not affiliates of the issuer, paragraphs (c), (f), (g), (h) and (i) of the rule apply to securities sold by such persons in reliance upon the rule.

(e) *Limitation on Amount of Securities Sold.* Except as hereinafter provided, the amount of securities which may be sold in reliance upon this rule shall be determined as follows:

(1) *Sales by Affiliates.* If restricted or other securities are sold for the account of an affiliate of the issuer, the amount of securities sold, together with all sales of restricted and other securities of the same class for the account of such person within the preceding three months, shall not exceed the greater of (i) one percent of the shares or other units of the class outstanding as shown by the most recent report or statement published by the issuer, or (ii) the average weekly volume of trading in such securities reported on all national securities exchanges and/or reported through the automated quotation system of a registered securities association during the four calendar weeks preceding the filing of the notice required by paragraph (h), or, if no such notice is required, the date of receipt of the order to execute the transaction by the broker or the date of execution of the transaction directly with a market maker, or (iii) the average weekly volume of trading in such securities reported through the consolidated transaction reporting system contemplated by Rule 11Aa3-1 under the Securities Exchange Act of 1934 during the four-week period specified in subdivision (ii) of this subparagraph.

(2) *Sales by persons other than affiliates.* The amount of restricted securities sold for the account of any person other than an affiliate of the issuer, together with all other sales of restricted securities of the same class for the account of such person within the preceding three months, shall not exceed the amount specified in paragraphs (e)(1)(i), (1)(ii) or (1)(iii) of this section, whichever is applicable, unless the conditions of paragraph (k) of this rule are satisfied.

(3) *Determination of amount.* For the purpose of determining the amount of securities specified in paragraphs (e)(1) and (2) of this rule, the following provisions shall apply:

(A) Where both convertible securities and securities of the class into which they are convertible are sold, the amount of convertible securities sold shall be deemed to be the amount of securities of the class into which they are convertible for the purpose of determining the aggregate amount of securities of both classes sold;

(B) The amount of securities sold for the account of a pledgee thereof, or for the account of a purchaser of the pledged securities, during any period of three months within two years after a default in the obligation secured by the pledge, and the amount of securities sold during the same three-month period for the account of the pledgor shall not exceed, in the aggregate, the amount specified in paragraph (1) or (2) above, whichever is applicable;

(C) The amount of securities sold for the account of a donee thereof during any period of three months within two years after the donation, and the amount of securities sold during the same three-month period for the account of the donor, shall not exceed, in the aggregate, the amount specified in subparagraph (1) or (2) of this paragraph, whichever is applicable;

(D) Where securities were acquired by a trust from the settlor of the trust, the amount of such securities sold for the account of the trust during any period of three months within two years after the acquisition of the securities by the trust, and the amount of securities sold during the same three-month period for the account of the settlor, shall not exceed, in the aggregate, the amount specified in subparagraph (1) or (2) of this paragraph, whichever is applicable;

(E) The amount of securities sold for the account of the estate of a deceased person, or for the account of a beneficiary of such estate, during any period of three months and the amount of securities sold during the same period for the account of the deceased person prior to his death shall not exceed, in the aggregate, the amount specified in subparagraph (1) or (2) of this paragraph, whichever is applicable; **Provided,** That no limitation on amount shall apply if the estate or beneficiary thereof is not an affiliate of the issuer;

(F) When two or more affiliates or other persons agree to act in concert for the purpose of selling securities of an issuer, all securities of the same class sold for the account of all such persons during any period of three months shall be aggregated for the purpose of determining the limitation on the amount of securities sold;

(G) Securities sold pursuant to an effective registration statement under the Act or pursuant to an exemption provided by Regulation A under the Act or in a transaction exempt pursuant to Section 4 of the Act and not involving any public offering need not be included in determining the amount of securities sold in reliance upon this rule.

(f) *Manner of Sale.* The securities shall be sold in "brokers' transactions" within the meaning of section 4(4) of the Act or in transactions directly with a "market maker," as that term is defined in section 3(a)(38) of the Securities Exchange Act of 1934, and the person selling the securities shall not (1) solicit or arrange for the solicitation of orders to buy the securities in anticipation of or in connection with such transaction, or (2) make any payment in connection with the offer or sale of the securities to any person other than the broker who executes an order to sell the securities. The requirements of this paragraph, however, shall not apply to securities sold for the account of the estate of a deceased person or for the account of a beneficiary of such estate provided the estate or beneficiary thereof is not an affiliate of the issuer; nor shall they apply to securities sold for the account of any person other than an affiliate of the issuer provided the conditions of paragraph (k) of this rule are satisfied.

(g) *Brokers' Transactions.* The term "brokers' transactions" in Section 4(4) of the Act shall for the purposes of this rule be deemed to include transactions by a broker in which such broker —

(1) does no more than execute the order or orders to sell the securities as agent for the person for whose account the securities are sold; and receives no more than the usual and customary broker's commission;

(2) neither solicits nor arranges for the solicitation of customers' orders to buy the securities in anticipation of or in connection with the transaction; provided, that the foregoing shall not preclude (*i*) inquiries by the broker *of* other brokers or dealers who have indicated an interest in the securities within the preceding 60 days, (*ii*) inquiries by the broker of his customers who have indicated an unsolicited bona fide interest in the securities within the preceding 10 business days; or (*iii*) the publication by the broker of bid and ask quotations for the security in an inter-dealer quotation system provided that such quotations are incident to the maintenance of a bona fide inter-dealer market for the security for the broker's own account and that the broker has published bona fide bid and ask quotations for the security in an inter-dealer quotation system on each of at least twelve days within the preceding thirty calendar days with no more than four business days in succession without such two-way quotations;

Note to Subparagraph g(2)(ii): The broker should obtain and retain in his files written evidence of indications of bona fide unsolicited interest by his customers in the securities at the time such indications are received.

(3) after reasonable inquiry is not aware of circumstances indicating that the person for whose account the securities are sold is an underwriter with respect to the securities or that the transaction is a part of a distribution of securities of the issuer. Without limiting the foregoing, the broker shall be deemed to be aware of any facts or statements contained in the notice required by paragraph (h) below.

Notes. 1. The broker, for his own protection, should obtain and retain in his files a copy of the notice required by paragraph (h).

2. The reasonable inquiry required by paragraph (g)(3) above should include, but not necessarily be limited to, inquiry as to the following matters:

a. The length of time the securities have been held by the person for whose account they are to be sold. If practicable, the inquiry should include physical inspection of the securities;

b. The nature of the transaction in which the securities were acquired by such person;

c. The amount of securities of the same class sold during the past three months by all persons whose sales are required to be taken into consideration pursuant to paragraph (e) above;

d. Whether such person intends to sell additional securities of the same class through any other means;

Appendix G

e. Whether such person has solicited or made any arrangement for the solicitation of buy orders in connection with the proposed sale of securities;

f. Whether such person has made any payment to any other person in connection with the proposed sale of the securities; and

g. The number of shares or other units of the class outstanding, or the relevant trading volume.

(h) *Notice of Proposed Sale.* If the amount of securities to be sold in reliance upon the rule during any period of three months exceeds 500 shares or other units or has an aggregate sale price in excess of $10,000, three copies of a notice on Form 144 shall be filed with the Commission at its principal office in Washington, D.C.; and if such securities are admitted to trading on any national securities exchange, one copy of such notice shall also be transmitted to the principal exchange on which such securities are so admitted. The Form 144 shall be signed by the person for whose account the securities are to be sold and shall be transmitted for filing concurrently with either the placing with a broker of an order to execute a sale of securities in reliance upon this rule or the execution directly with a market maker of such a sale. Neither the filing of such notice nor the failure of the Commission to comment thereon shall be deemed to preclude the Commission from taking any action it deems necessary or appropriate with respect to the sale of the securities referred to in such notice. The requirements of this paragraph, however, shall not apply to securities sold for the account of any person other than an affiliate of the issuer, provided the conditions of paragraph (k) of this rule are satisfied.

(i) *Bona Fide Intention to Sell.* The person filing the notice required by paragraph (h) shall have a bona fide intention to sell the securities referred to therein within a reasonable time after the filing of such notice.

(j) *Non-exclusive rule.* Although this rule provides a means for reselling restricted securities and securities held by affiliates without registration, it is not the exclusive means for reselling such securities in that manner. Therefore, it does not eliminate or otherwise affect the availability of any exemption for resales under the Securities Act that a person or entity may be able to rely upon.

(k) *Termination of certain restrictions on sales of restricted securities by persons other than affiliates.* The requirements of paragraphs (e), (f) and (h) of this rule shall not apply to restricted securities sold for the account of a person who is not an affiliate of the issuer at the time of the sale and has not been an affiliate during the preceding three months, provided the securities have been beneficially owned by the person for a period of at least three years prior to their sale. In computing the period for which securities have been beneficially owned for purposes of this provision, reference should be made to paragraph (d) of this section.

Appendix H

DIRECTORS, OFFICERS, AND PRINCIPAL STOCKHOLDERS

SECTION 16. (a) Every person who is directly or indirectly the beneficial owner of more than 10 per centum of any class of any equity security (other than an exempted security) which is registered pursuant to section 12 of this title, or who is a director or an officer of the issuer of such security, shall file, at the time of the registration of such security on a national securities exchange or by the effective date of a registration statement filed pursuant to section 12(g) of this title, or within ten days after he becomes such beneficial owner, director, or officer, a statement with the Commission (and, if such security is registered on a national securities exchange, also with the exchange) of the amount of all equity securities of such issuer of which he is the beneficial owner, and within ten days after the close of each calendar month thereafter, if there has been a change in such ownership during such month, shall file with the Commission (and if such security is registered on a national securities exchange, shall also file with the exchange), a statement indicating his ownership at the close of the calendar month and such changes in his ownership as have occurred during such calendar month.

(b) For the purpose of preventing the unfair use of information which may have been obtained by such beneficial owner, director, or officer by reason of his relationship to the issuer, any profit realized by him from any purchase and sale, or any sale and purchase, of any equity security of such issuer (other than an exempted security) within any period of less than six months, unless such security was acquired in good faith in connection with a debt previously contracted, shall inure to and be recover-

---

Source: Ticor Print Network/Jeffries Banknote Company *Securities Regulations Handbook,* updated to January 31, 1983

able by the issuer, irrespective of any intention on the part of such beneficial owner, director, or officer in entering into such transaction of holding the security purchased or of not repurchasing the security sold for a period exceeding six months. Suit to recover such profit may be instituted at law or in equity in any court of competent jurisdiction by the issuer, or by the owner of any security of the issuer in the name and in behalf of the issuer if the issuer shall fail or refuse to bring such suit within sixty days after request or shall fail diligently to prosecute the same thereafter; but no such suit shall be brought more than two years after the date such profit was realized. This subsection shall not be construed to cover any transaction where such beneficial owner was not such both at the time of the purchase and sale, or the sale and purchase, of the security involved, or any transaction or transactions which the Commission by rules and regulations may exempt as not comprehended within the purpose of this subsection.

(c) It shall be unlawful for any such beneficial owner, director, or officer, directly or indirectly, to sell any equity security of such issuer (other than an exempted security), if the person selling the security or his principal (1) does not own the security sold, or (2) if owning the security, does not deliver it against such sale within twenty days thereafter, or does not within five days after such sale deposit it in the mails or other usual channels of transportation; but no person shall be deemed to have violated this subsection if he proves that notwithstanding the exercise of good faith he was unable to make such delivery or deposit within such time, or that to do so would cause undue inconvenience or expense.

(d) The provisions of subsection (b) of this section shall not apply to any purchase and sale, or sale and purchase, and the provisions of subsection (c) of this section shall not apply to any sale, of an equity security not then or theretofore held by him in an investment account, by a dealer in the ordinary course of his business and incident to the establishment or maintenance by him of a primary or secondary market (otherwise than on a national securities exchange or an exchange exempted from registration under section 5 of this title) for such security. The Commission may, by such rules and regulations as it deems necessary or appropriate in the public interest, define and prescribe terms and conditions with respect to securities held in an investment account and transactions made in the ordinary course of business and incident to the establishment or maintenance of a primary or secondary market.

(e) The provisions of this section shall not apply to foreign or domestic arbitrage transactions unless made in contravention of such rules and regulations as the Commission may adopt in order to carry out the purposes of this section.

Appendix I

GENERAL RULE 10b-5 OF 1934 SECURITIES EXCHANGE ACT

Rule 10b-5. Employment of Manipulative and Deceptive Devices

It shall be unlawful for any person, directly or indirectly, by the use of any means or instrumentality of interstate commerce, or of the mails, or of any facility of any national securities exchange,

(a) to employ any device, scheme, or artifice to defraud,

(b) to make any untrue statement of a material fact or to omit to state a material fact necessary in order to make the statements made, in the light of the circumstances under which they were made, not misleading, or

(c) to engage in any act, practice, or course of business which operates or would operate as a fraud or deceit upon any person,

in connection with the purchase or sale of any security.

Source: Ticor Print Network/Jeffries Banknote Company *Securities Regulations Handbook*, updated to January 31, 1983

Appendix J

SECTION 13(b)(2) OF THE 1934 SECURITIES EXCHANGE ACT*

(2) Every issuer which has a class of securities registered pursuant to section 12 of this title and every issuer which is required to file reports pursuant to section 15(d) of this title shall—

    (A) make and keep books, records, and accounts, which, in reasonable detail, accurately and fairly reflect the transactions and dispositions of the assets of the issuer; and

    (B) devise and maintain a system of internal accounting controls sufficient to provide reasonable assurances that—

        (i) transactions are executed in accordance with management's general or specific authorization;

        (ii) transactions are recorded as necessary (I) to permit preparation of financial statements in conformity with generally accepted accounting principles or any other criteria applicable to such statements, and (II) to maintain accountability for assets;

        (iii) access to assets is permitted only in accordance with management's general or specific authorization; and

        (iv) the recorded accountability for assets is compared with the existing assets at reasonable intervals and appropriate action is taken with respect to any differences.

*Section 102 of the Foreign Corrupt Practices Act of 1977

Source: Ticor Print Network/Jeffries Banknote Company *Securities Regulations Handbook*, updated to January 31, 1983

BIBLIOGRAPHY

Frederick Lewis Allen. *Only Yesterday*. New York: Harper & Row (Perennial Library Edition), 1964.

American Bar Association. *Corporate Director's Guidebook*. Chicago: American Bar Association, 1978.

American Stock Exchange. *Why list . . . on the American Stock Exchange*. New York: American Stock Exchange, 1983.

Louis Braiotta, Jr. *The Audit Director's Guide*. New York: Wiley, 1981.

Abraham J. Brioloff. *More Debits Than Credits*. New York: Harper & Row, 1976.

Vincent P. Carosso. *More Than a Century of Investment Banking*. New York: McGraw-Hill, 1979.

Robert Chatov. *Corporate Financial Reporting; Public or Private Control*. New York: Free Press, 1975.

Coopers & Lybrand. *Annual Meetings: Questions from Shareholders*. New York: Coopers & Lybrand, 1983.

Coopers & Lybrand. *Audit Committee Guide*, 3rd ed. New York: Coopers & Lybrand, 1982.

Editors of *Fortune*. *The Conglomerate Commotion*. New York: Viking Press, 1970.

Gulf Publishing Company. *The Changing Boardroom*. Houston: Gulf Publishing Company, 1982.

Quinten Johnstone and Dan Hopson, Jr. *Lawyers and Their Work*. Indianapolis: Bobbs Merrill, 1967.

Albert L. Kraus. *Guide to Business and Finance; the American Economy and How It Works*. New York: Harper & Row, 1972.

Royal Little. *How To Lose $100,000,000 and Other Valuable Advice*. Boston: Little, Brown, 1979.

Walter Lord. *The Good Years*. Bantam, 1962.

NASDAQ Chief Executive Conferences. *Part 1, The Stock Market of the Future*. Washington, D.C.: National Association of Securities Dealers, 1982.

NASDAQ Chief Executive Conferences. *Part 2, The Art and Practice of Investor Relations*. Washington D.C.: National Association of Securities Dealers, 1982.

NASD Bylaws. *NASDAQ Issuer Qualification Standards*. Washington, D.C.: National Association of Securities Dealers, 1982.

NASD Report. *The Financial Services Industry of Tomorrow*. Washington, D.C.: National Association of Securities Dealers, 1982.

New York Stock Exchange. *Fact Book 1982*. New York: New York Stock Exchange, 1982.

Technimetrics Investor Relations Programs. *Going Public*. Technimetrics, 1982.

Dana L. Thomas. *The Plungers and the Peacocks—150 Years of Wall Street*. New York: Putnam, 1967.

Ticor Print Network. *A Sample Directors' and Officers' Questionnaire. For Use in Preparing a Proxy Statement and Form 10K*. Los Angeles: Jeffries Banknote Company, 1983.

Ticor Print Network. *Securities Regulations Handbook*. Los Angeles: Jeffries Banknote Company, 1983.

Harold M. Williams. *Corporate Accountability—One Year Later: Appendix K, The Audit Director's Guide*. New York: Wiley, 1981. Pp. 256–259.

Arthur Young. *Financial Reporting and Accounting*. New York: Arthur Young & Co., 1982.

Periodicals

"Adoption of Safe Harbor for Purchases of Certain Equity Securities and Others." *Ticor's SEC Requirements Update*, 19, 1–8 (January 1983).

"Corporate Governance in America." *The American Assembly—Columbia University*, Pamphlet 54, 6 (April 1978).

"Corporate Responsibility, Choices and Challenges for Management." *NASDAQ Company—NASD Consultations*, 1–8 (October 1980).

"Does Listing Enhance Visibility?" *Amex Research Bulletin*, 1–2 (June 1982).

Jack Egan. "On January 6, 1981 Joe Granville Said Sell. . . ." *TWA Ambassador*, 39 (September 1981).

"Experience Growing with Rule 415." *Investors Relations Update*, 6 (April 1983).

Robert J. Flaherty. "The Singular Henry Singleton." *Forbes*, **124**, 1, 45–50 (July 9, 1979).

"How Market Makers Select Their Favorite NASDAQ Securities," *NASDAQ Company—NASD Consultations*, 12–16 (October 1980).

Newspapers

"The Initial Public Offering Market—October 1978-September 1981." *Shearson/American Express Inc.*, 5, 4 (1981).

"Insider Transactions: A Chronicle of Who's Buying Who." *Nelson's Survey of Wall Street Research*, 15, 16–18 (April 1983).

"NASDAQ Market Making at Over 550 Locations." *NASDAQ Glossary Series*, 1, 1–2 (March 1981).

"Marketplace: Institutions, Individuals, or Both?" *Investors Relations Update*, 1–3 (April 1983).

"A Mid-Range Growth Company Is an Economic Marvel." *Annual Report of the American Stock Exchange*, 1–8 (1981).

"The Most Active (Venture Capital) Investors of 1982." *Venture*, 5, 6, 38–44 (June 1983).

"NASDAQ National Market System To Start Up in March." *NASDAQ Notes*, 3, 2, 1 (February 1982).

"New Dimensions in Market Operations." *Annual Report of the New York Stock Exchange*, 6–13 (1981).

"New York Stock Exchange Company Manual." *New York Stock Exchange, Inc.*, March 3, 1983.

"The 1982 All-American Research Team." *Institutional Investor*, 55–89 (October 1982).

"1981 New Listings Reflect Changed Environment at the Amex." *Amex West*, 1 (December 1981).

"Professional Education Course Calendar—May 1983-December 1983." *Arthur Andersen & Co.*, 1983.

"Profile of NYSE New Listings." *New York Stock Exchange Annual Update*, 1982.

"Regulation D of the Securities and Exchange Commission." *Federal Register*, 45, 51, 11250–11252 (March 16, 1982).

"Report of House Subcommittee Recommends That SEC Prescribe Uniform Accounting Principles." *Arthur Andersen's Executive News Briefs*, 4, 20, 1 (December 1976).

John H. W. Rhein. "IPO (Initial Public Offering) Parade." *OTC Review*, 31, 5, 32 (May 1983).

Ardith Rivel. "The Changing Role of the Stockbroker." *Amex Journal*, 1, 12, 1 (December 1982).

"Staff of U.S. Senate Subcommittee Issues Lengthy Study With Respect to the Accounting Profession." *Arthur Andersen's Executive News Briefs*, 5, 2, 1–3 (January 1977).

"29 Recommendations for Improving Shareholder Communications." *NASDAQ News*, 7, 2, 1–4 (August 1982).

Newspapers

Martin Baron. "How To Keep From Being Burned by Hot New Issues." Los Angeles *Times*, V1 (December 27, 1980).

John C. Boland. "Penny Dreadfuls." *Barron's National Business and Financial Weekly*, 10 (August 16, 1982).

Gail Bronson. "Going Public Has Its Rewards, as Liz Claiborne Inc. Discovers." *Wall Street Journal*, 21 (August 10, 1981).

Paul A. Gigot. "Big Fraud Verdict Against Andersen Shakes Up Accounting Profession." *Wall Street Journal*, 31 (February 3, 1982).

Sanford L. Jacobs. "Going Public Provides Money But Changes Lives of Owners." *Wall Street Journal*, 27 (November 15, 1983).

Shirley Hobbs Scheibla. "Speculating With John Shad." *Barron's National Business and Financial Weekly*, 13 (May 30, 1983).

Louis Rukeyser. "Cruel Suggestion: Let's Ignore Granville." St. Louis *Globe-Democrat*. 10C (October 1, 1981).

Private Works

J. Spencer Letts. "On Balance, What I Think. . . ." Personal Communication, March 21, 1983.

Shearson Loeb Rhoades Inc.. "Initial Public Offering Considerations." Presentation to Matrix Science Corporation, New York, 1980.

Index

Accountants, *see* Public accountants
Accounting codes, 45, 50
Accounts payable, 5–6
Accredited investors, 68–69
Ade, George, 89
Affiliate and non-affiliate securities, 159–160, 162–164
Aftermarket securities support, 101–104
Agent's purchase of original stock, 18
American Bar Association guidelines, 156
American Express Inc., 79
American Stock Exchange, 90
Annual audit, 173, 180–181
Annual meeting of shareholders, 176–177
Annual report, 170–173, 180–181
Auction market *vs.* telecommunications, 89–90
Audit committee of the board, 155–158
Auditors, *see* Public accountants

Bache Halsey Stuart Shields, 79
Bailout by company principals, 10, 84–85, 103, 163
Banking Act, 74
Banks, 5–6, 18, 21
 escrowing stocks with, 16
 loans from, *see* Borrowed money
 see also Investment banking firms
Baruch, Bernard, 42
Beneficial ownership of securities:
 definition of, 162, 164–165n
 filing statement of, 175
Berle, A. A., 51
Black Thursday of 1929, 43, 60
Blue Sky laws, 63, 66, 69–70, 126, 148
Board of directors:
 audit committee of, 155–158
 compensation and meetings of, 158
 corporate accountability of, 151–152, 155
 entrepreneur and, 152–153
 independent outside members, 47, 109, 152, 154
 insurance for, 158
 interested outside members, 153–154
 legal risk of members, 157–158
 makeup and role of, 153–154
 management members, 153–154
 oversight committees of, 155–157
 size of, 153
Borrowed money:
 compensatory balances, 31
 costs of, 15, 22–23
 maintenance of financial ratios, 23
 90-day and term notes, 23
 pain factor connected with, 21–22
 prime rate and, 22–24
 requirements for, 5, 21
 unsecured and asset-based, 22–23
 see also Debentures; Banks; Finance companies; SBA loans

Cash demands of a growing business, 5–6, 21

295

Cede & Co., or Depository Trust Co., 177
Certified public accountants, see Public accountants
Chandler Act, 74
Chief executives, see Entrepreneurs; Management
Cohen, Benjamin, 44
"Cold comfort" letter, 134–135
Co-managers in the underwriting, 97
Company counsel:
 affiliate and other restricted stock, 160–161
 decisions on materiality of facts, 109, 119–120
 importance of, 55–59, 121–122
 purchase of original stock by, 18
 reasons for changing, 55–56
 registration statement responsibilities, 121–122
 review of outside reports, 170, 172, 194
 size of law firm, 57–58
 see also Lawyers; Underwriters' counsel
Company forecasts:
 five-year term, 32, 34
 intermediate term, 29–31
Company sale, 27
Company valuation methods, 26, 78
Competitors' review of company reports, 36, 109, 171–172, 189
Conglomerates, 26, 76–77, 79
Consumerism, 46–47, 61, 154
Control person, see Affiliate securities
Coopers & Lybrand, 155
Corcoran, Thomas G., 44
Corporate accountability, 151–154. See also Foreign Corrupt Practices Act; Section 13(b)(2) of Securities Exchange Act
Corporate Democracy Bill in Congress, 46–47, 154
Corporate secretary, 121
CPAs, see Public accountants

Debentures:
 convertible, 18–19, 23–25
 subordinated, 16–17
Debt, see Borrowed money; Debentures
Directors' and Officers' Questionnaires, 110–111
DISC (domestic international sales corporation), 112

Document summation for registration, see Form S-1 document summation
Dow Jones Industrial Index, 9
Due diligence, 118–119, 130–131, 133

Earnings reports, see Outside reports
Entrepreneurs:
 annual report decisions by, 170–171
 associates of, 85, 183–184
 board of directors' relationships with, 152–154
 characteristics of, 3–6, 32, 195
 importance of, 3, 13, 16, 191–192
 mistakes by, 4, 17–18, 24, 77
 replacement of, 17
 sale of acquiring company's stock by, 77
 as selling shareholders in initial offerings, 84–85
 stability of, 191–192
 toast to, 195
 see also Management
Equity:
 difficulty of keeping, 13, 17
 employee buy-back agreement, 18
 struggle to acquire, 13, 16–19, 59
Equity sweeteners, 22–24
Ever Onward Corporation (a composite registration example):
 Blue Sky documents, 148
 closing proceedings, 149–150
 "cold comfort" letter of public accountants, 134–135
 corporate proceedings, 144
 data for NASD, 146
 documents of selling shareholders, 147
 due diligence document request, 118–119, 131
 early registration work, 123–127
 financial statements of, 127
 first registration sessions, 131–133
 going-public functions for, 121–123
 initial public offering, 139–140
 intermediate registration session, 133–134
 key employee attitudes, 130
 managing underwriter for, 120–121
 marketing the proposed issue, 136–138
 press release and "tombstone" announcement, 148–149
 registration windup, 135–136
 SEC review of registration statement,

Index

138–139
SEC registration proceedings, 144–146
size of offering, 118
underwriting documents, 147–148
windup of the offering project, 140–142
Exchange Act, see Securities Exchange Act of 1934

Finance companies, 23
Financial Accounting Standards Board (FASB), 51
Financial architecture, 13, 15–17, 20, 59
Financial game plans, 5, 29–32
Financial printer, 122–123, 132, 134–136, 142. See also Word processor
Financial public relations, 103, 188
Financial services industry, 79–80
Five-year forecast of company:
  form of, 34
  reasons for, 32
Foreign Corrupt Practices Act of 1977, 45–46, 52, 151–152, 155, 157–158. See also Section 13(b)(2) of 1934 Exchange Act
Form S-1 Documents Summation:
  closing proceedings, 149–150
  corporate proceedings, 144
  data for NASD, 146
  documents of selling shareholders, 147
  importance of legal recitals and certifications, 150
  SEC proceedings, 144–146
  underwriting documents, 147–148
Form S-1 registration procedure, see Ever Onward Corporation
Form S-1 registration statement, 6, 105–113, 122
  Business section of, 107, 109
  Business Segment Data, 112–113
  Capitalization of Company section, 107
  Certain Factors section, 107–108
  Certain Transactions section, 107, 110
  Description of Common Stock section, 107
  Dilution section, 107
  Dividend Policy section, 107
  due diligence work for, 118–120, 130–132
  Experts section, 107
  Financial Statements section, 107, 110–113
  item and rule references, 235–240

Legal Opinions section, 107
Management Discussion and Analysis section, 107
Management section, 107
MD&A, see Management Discussion and Analysis
Notes to Financial Statements section, 110–113
outside statements by company management, 100–103
preparatory work for, 123–127
Principal Shareholders section, 107
Prospectus Summary section, 107–108
SEC deficiency letter regarding, 134
SEC filing and review of, 136, 139
Selected Consolidated Financial Data section, 107–108
Selling Shareholders section, 107
task force, see Registration task force
Use of Proceeds section, 107–108
Form S-18 registration statement:
  in general, 105
  item and rule references, 241–257
Form 10K:
  in general, 171–174, 179, 181
  item and rule comments and references, 259–268
Fourth market, 91–92
Frankfurter, Felix, 43, 60

"Go-go" performance funds, 76–77
Going private, 194–195
Going public:
  acceptance of Wall Street criteria, 92
  cachet of company success, 3
  cash settlement after, 9, 150
  company size considerations in, 13
  costs of, 4, 142
  importance of timing in, 3–4, 11, 81–82
  improving equity base and raising capital, 3, 5, 11, 25
  key employees' attitude toward, 130, 132
  stock market perturbation and, 5–10
  time schedule for, 123–127, 132
  unwanted attention by, 189
Going public example, see Ever Onward Corporation
Granville, Joseph, 7–8, 10
Great Depression, 43, 50, 60, 74
Green shoe, see Over-allotment option

Gross spread, 87

Hambrecht & Quist, 97
Harvard Law School, 43, 60
High-leveraged buy outs, 15, 59
High-technology stocks, 4–5

Individual investors, 75, 86, 93, 95–96, 136
Initial public offering:
  buying interest in, 9–10, 99–101
  costs of, 141–142
  countdown to, 139–140
  financial statement requirements, 127
  geographical share distribution, 96
  press release concerning, 148–149
  pricing of, 85–86
  prospective number of shares in, 86–87
  prospective price of, 85–86
  registration under 1934 Exchange Act, 162, 175
  reserved stock in, 96–97, 137
  Rule 415's cost effect on, 79
  sale into "good hands," 9, 101
  selling of, 99–101, 135–138
  selling shareholders, 84–85
  size of, 82–85, 118
  three-year analysis of, 82–84
  windup of, 140–142
Initial public offering example, see Ever Onward Corporation
Inside information, 162–163, 184–186
Insider sale or purchase, 161–162
Institutional investors, 8–9, 75, 78, 80, 93–95, 136
"Interesting" securities, 103–104
International Telephone and Telegraph Corp., 76
Inventory valuation, 112, 131
Investment Advisers Act, 74
Investment banking firms:
  financial services industry and, 79–80
  going public and, 11, 80
  golden years for, 74–76
  public opinion of, 73–74
  retail offices of, 99
  Rule 415's effect upon, 78–79
  unfixing commissions and, 78–79
  see also Regional securities firms
Investment companies, 64

Investors' interest in company, 187–188
IPOs, see Going public; Initial public offerings

Landis, James M., 44, 60
Lawyers, 16, 51
  advice on subordinated debt, 24
  company stock as fee payment, 59–60
  increasing corporate legal costs, 58
  new venture involvement of, 57
  Section 11 of 1933 Act and, 44
  use of special counsel, 132
  see also Company counsel; Underwriters' counsel
Legal risks for board members, 157–158
Legended securities, 160
Letter securities, 160
L. F. Rothschild, Unterberg, Towbin, 97
Liberty Bonds, 42
Litton Industries, 76
Loans, see Borrowed money
Long-term debt, see Debentures

McKinley, William, 41
Mahoney Act, 74
Management, 3, 15–16, 32–39
  annual position paper or brochure, 35–39
  collapse of a game plan, 4–6
  outside presentations of, 29, 32–39
  standards of excellence, 35
  see also Entrepreneurs
Managing underwriter, 7–10, 75, 84–87, 97–99, 126–127, 153
  principal of, 120–121, 189
Market makers, 188
Materiality of facts, 119–120
Mini-conglomerates, 77
Minuteman missile guidance system, 6
Money side, 15–17, 20, 59. See also Investment banking firms; SBA lenders; Venture capital groups
Moody, John, 42–43
Morgan, J. Pierpont, 42
Morgan, J. Pierpont, Jr., 43
Mutual funds, 75–77

NASDAQ:
  Additional List of, 91
  evolution of, 89–91
  market-maker function of, 90

Index

National List of, 90–91
National Market System of, 91
national stock exchanges and, 92
National Association of Securities Dealers (NASD), 79
New Deal of the 1930s, 43–44, 61
Newsweek, 36
New York Stock Exchange, 74, 90
Non-registered securities, *see* Restricted securities

Original stock, 17–18. *See also* Equity
OTC, *see* Over-the-counter *and* NASDAQ
Outside reports of the company:
    annual report, 168, 170–176, 180–181
    company counsel review of, 170, 172, 174
    Form 8-A to SEC, 175, 180
    Form 10K to SEC, 171–174, 176, 179, 181, 259–267
    Form 10Q to SEC, 169, 180–181, 269–275
    proxy statement and card, 175–176, 180–181
    quarterly and year-to-date results, 169, 180–181
Over-allotment option, 10, 86–87, 140
Over-the-counter market, 89. *See also* NASDAQ; National Association of Securities Dealers

Pecora, Ferdinand, 43
P/E multiple or ratio, *see* Price/earnings multiple or ratio
Performance stock, 15, 16
Planning documents:
    five-year term, 32, 34
    intermediate term, 29–32
    position paper or brochure, 35–39
Post-World War II era, 74–77
Preliminary prospectus or "red herring", 99–101
Price/earnings multiples or ratios:
    calculation of, 87–88
    initial public offering pricing, 88
    1978–1981 analysis of, 89
    principal uses of, 76–78, 87, 103
Privately held companies:
    advantages of, 36, 167–168, 194
    alternative ways of raising money, 22–27
    annual position papers of, 35–39
    grass-roots enterprises, 14
    Mom-and-Pop concerns, 14
    sale of interests in, 25–27
    units sold off by large enterprises, 15
Profit Plan Summary:
    comments on, 33
    form of, 31
Prospectus, 99–100, 105–113
    Business section of, 109
    cover format and type of paper, 106
    income statements required for, 108
    Management section of, 109–110
    patent discussion in, 109
    photographs and illustrations, 106–107
    review of other prospectuses, 105–106
    stub period requirements, 108, 127
    table of contents, 107
    Use of Proceeds section of, 108
    see also Form S-1 registration statement; Preliminary prospectus
Prospectus analysis:
    financial footnotes, 110–113
    primary subjects in, 107–110
    review of other prospectuses, 105–106
Proxy solicitation, 177
Proxy statement and card, 175–176
Prudential Insurance Co., 117
Public accountants:
    annual audit by, 173, 180–181
    client's business and, 53
    company inventory valuations and, 53
    final recourse suits against, 49, 52–53
    financial policy review by, 127, 168
    impact of 1933 and 1934 acts upon, 51
    independence of, 53
    1920s' activities of, 50
    quarterly limited review by, 127, 168
    relationships with lawyers, 49, 60
    reserves' and writeoffs' actions by, 112
    Section II of 1933 Act and, 44, 51
    selection of, 53–54
    size of accounting firms, 51–52, 54
    sustained Federal and court pressures on, 49, 155
    unasked-for advice given to, 51
    United States congressional reports on, 51–52
Public attitude toward corporations, 46–47, 60–61, 151–152

Pujo Committee, 42

Quotation service of NASD, see NASDAQ

Reagan administration, 52
Recession, see Business recession
"Red herring" or preliminary prospectus, 99–101. See also Form S-1
Regional securities firms, 75, 78–80
Registrar, see Transfer agent/registrar
Registration statement, see Form S-1; Form S-18
Registration task force:
 constituents of, 131–132
 first sessions of, 131–133
 intermediate sessions of, 133–134
 preparatory work of, 123–127
 windup of, 135–136
 working pressures on, 122
Regulation D under 1934 Exchange Act, 25, 63–69, 84
 accredited investors, 68–69
 brokerage commissions under, 64
 Form D of, 65, 207–213
 importance of, 63–64, 143
 "Restricted Securities" provision of, 65, 69, 98
 Rule 504 of, 64–65, 204–205
 Rule 505 of, 67, 205–206
 Rule 506 of, 67–68, 206
 text of, 197–213
Reserved stock in initial offering, 96–97
Restricted securities, 65–66, 69, 159–160, 163–164
Road shows, 99–101, 137–138
Roosevelt, Franklin D., 43–44, 50, 61
Roosevelt, Theodore, 41
Rosenthal, Benjamin, 46–47
Rule 144 under 1933 Securities Act:
 in general, 159–162
 text of, 277–283
Rule 10b-5 under Securities Exchange Act:
 in general, 162–164, 184–185
 text of, 287

Safe-harbor protection, 64, 184
SBA loans, 23
Seasoned securities, 104, 188, 192–193

SEC, see Securities and Exchange Commission
SEC registration documents (Form S-1) example, see Ever Onward Corporation
Section 13(b)(2) of 1934 Securities Exchange Act:
 in general, 52, 155
 text of, 289
Section 16(b) of Securities Exchange Act:
 in general, 161–163
 text of, 285–286
Securities Act of 1933:
 drafting of, 43–44, 50–51, 60, 74
 major effect of, 60–61
 purpose of, 44, 60, 84
 "stop-order" feature of, 44
Securities analysts, 14, 103, 138, 187–188
Securities community, 10, 32, 73, 75, 187–188. See also Wall Street
Securities Exchange Act of 1934, 45, 60, 74
 regulation 13D and Schedule 13G, 162
 section 13(b)(2) of, 52, 155, 289
 section 16(b) of, 161–162, 285–286
Securities and Exchange Commission (SEC), 45, 63
 audit committee emphasis by, 155
 chairman and staff of, 46
 philosophy of, 44, 51–52, 63, 78, 193
 registration review by, 100
Securities firms, see Investment banking firms
Securities laws and regulation:
 early 1980s' attitudes toward, 193
 genesis of, 41–44, 60
Security Pacific National Bank, 80
Seed money, 15–16, 58–59
Selling concession charge, 87
Selling management shareholders:
 aftermarket sales, 85
 initial public offering, 7, 10, 84
Selling syndicates, 8–9, 97–99
Shad, John, 46, 152
Shareholder relations, 121, 178–179, 189
Shearson Loeb Rhoades, 79
Short position on an offering, 10, 87
Sinclair, Upton, 41
Small Business Administration (SBA), 23
Small Business Investment Incentive Act, 63
Speculation in initial public offerings, 41

Index

State securities laws, *see* Blue Sky laws
Steffens, Lincoln, 41
Stock brokerages firm, *see* Brokerage discount firms; Financial services industry; Investment banking firms
Stock exchanges, 90, 92
Stock market:
  description of, 4–6, 8–10
  1929 collapse of, 43, 60, 74
  people involved in, 4, 80
  unpredictability of, 4–5, 8–11, 81–82, 104
Stock options, 18–19
Stock rights and warrants, 22, 24–25
Stock run ups and downs, 101–102
Stock trading volume, 102–103, 187
"Stop" action of transfer agent, 160
Subordinated debt, 16–19, 23–25
Subscription agreement, 15
Sullivan and Cromwell, 60

Teledyne Inc., 76
Textron Inc., 76
Time, 36
Time schedule for first year, 179–181
Toast to entrepreneurial breed, 195
"Tombstone" announcement, 140–141, 148–149
Transfer agent/registrar, 123, 160, 177–179
Truman, Harry S., 175
Trust Indenture Act, 74

Underwriters' counsel, 8, 118, 132–133, 135–136, 139, 141–142
Underwriting agreement:
  aspects of, 7–9, 133
  draft of, 215–233
  stock sale prohibition under, 102–103
Underwriting costs, 87, 140
Underwriting discounts, 87
Underwriting fee, 87
Underwriting management fee, 87
Underwriting manager, *see* Managing underwriter
United States accounting code proposal, 45, 50–51
United States during the 1920s, 42–43, 50, 74–75
United States Senate committee hearing, 43

Venture capital groups, 5–6, 15, 58–59

Wall Street, 3–4, 8–10, 29, 32, 73–74, 78–80, 85–86, 103
Wall Street Journal:
  company earnings reports in, 168
  "Heard on the Street" column in, 6
Watergate-and-after environment, 51–52, 60–61
Williams, Harold M., 152
Word processor, 122, 124. *See also* Financial printer
World War I, 42, 50
World War II, 43

CREDITS

MSS PAGE

59	"that damned cowboy," Lord, *The Good Years*, p. 38.
59	"on the threshold of business," Vernon Pennington as quoted by Thomas, *The Plungers and the Peacocks*, p. 121.
61	"the prosperity wagon rolled," Allen, *Only Yesterday*, p. 133.
61	"man - in his most vulnerable," Thomas, *Plungers*, p. 142.
61	"The lesson taught," From *Literary Digest* (May 26, 1928), Thomas, *Plungers*, p. 18.
62	"America was essentially a," Chatov, *Corporate Financial Reporting*, p. 24.
65	"placed the agency in a," Ibid., p. 109.
67	"*all* business activities of," From Business Lawyer (1978), Braiotta, *The Audit Director's Guide*, p. 234.
72	"The stock market failure of," Chatov, *Corporate*, p. 53.
73	"controlled, placid practicing," Ibid., p. 68.
73	"to be more modest," Ibid., p. 114.
73	"sometimes forget to ask," Ibid., p. 114.
74	"scandalous episodes of," *Report of House Subcommittee*, p. 1.
74	"the FASB had accomplished," Ibid., p. 1.
75	"*all* business activities of," Braiotta, *Audit*, p. 234.
82	"the lawyer to be a," Johnstone and Hopson, *Lawyers and Their Work*, p. 80.
86	"On balance, what I think," Letter from J. Spencer Letts dated March 21, 1983 to J. S. O'Flaherty.
89	"For him to pick up," Chatov, *Corporate*, p. 114.

93	"set aside a clear and," Regulation D, *Federal Register*, (March 10, 1982) p. 11250.
99	"like its predecessor," Ibid., p. 11252.
100	"Rule 506 requires an," Ibid., p. 11252.
103	"the registration requirements," Ibid., p. 11251.
103	"a basic framework of," Ibid., p. 11252.
115	"securities may be registered," Ticor, *Securities Regulations Handbook*, p. 605.
240	"society's expectations and standards," American Assembly, *Corporate Governance in America*, p. 6.
240	"monitoring the totality," Ibid., p. 6.
240	"should create a management," Ibid., p. 6.
242	"destroys the sense of," *The Changing Boardroom*, p. 34.
246	"incline toward imposing greater," Ibid., p. 49.
248	"When the Commission calls for," SEC General Counsel as quoted in Harold M. Williams' Address (1979), Braiotta, *Audit*, p. 259.
248	"the Coopers & Lybrand study," Ibid., p. 259.
249	"1. To recommend the," American Bar Association, *Corporate Director's Guidebook*, p. 32-33.
250	"1. The internal accounting function," Braiotta, *Audit*, p. 9-10.
250	"in administering the monitoring," Ibid., p. 10.
252	"discharge their responsibilities," Ibid., p. 63.